A History of the

Maratha People

(Volume I)

C. A. Kincaid,

Rao Bahadur D. B. Parasnis

Alpha Editions

This edition published in 2020

ISBN : 9789354035166

Design and Setting By
Alpha Editions
email - alphaedis@gmail.com

A HISTORY OF THE MARATHA PEOPLE

BY

C. A. KINCAID, C.V.O., I.C.S.

Author of 'The Tale of the Tulsi Plant,' 'The Indian
Heroes,' 'Deccan Nursery Tales,' 'Tales from the Indian
Epics,' 'Ishtur Phakde,' etc.

AND

Rao Bahadur D. B. PARASNIS

Author of 'The Rani of Jhansi,' 'Mahabaleshwar ' etc.
Editor, ' Itihas Sangraha.'

VOL. I

FROM THE EARLIEST TIMES
TO THE DEATH OF SHIVAJI

HUMPHREY MILFORD
OXFORD UNIVERSITY PRESS
LONDON, NEW YORK, TORONTO, MELBOURNE
BOMBAY AND MADRAS
1918

TO THE MARATHA PEOPLE
THIS WORK
IS
RESPECTFULLY INSCRIBED

Shivdigvijaya, the *Chitnis*, the *Shedgavkar* and the *Sabhasad Bakhars*, Mr. Rajwade's publications, Ranade's *Rise of the Maratha Power*, Orme's *Fragments* and the vast store of original Maratha papers which Rao Bahadur D. B. Parasnis was able to place at my disposal. I have also studied deeply the poetry of Tukaram, Ramdas, Namdev and Mahipati, and the life of Ramdas by Hanmant Swami.

This first volume ends with the death of Shivaji. The second volume will, if I am spared to continue the work, end with the *coup d'état* of A.D. 1750. The third volume will bring the narrative down to A.D. 1818. It will also contain appendices, giving a short account of the Maratha States between 1818 and the present day.

I have done my utmost to avoid giving offence to my Indian readers. If by inadvertence I have done so, I trust that they will extend me their forgiveness.

C. A. KINCAID.

CONTENTS

ILLUSTRATIONS

MAPS

A HISTORY
OF THE MARATHA PEOPLE

CHAPTER I

INTRODUCTORY

IN the ensuing pages it will be the writer's aim to tell the story
of the country known as Maharashtra. It lies on the western
shore of middle India and is in shape a triangle.* Its base is
the sea from Daman to Karwar. The perpendicular side is
formed by a line running from Daman beyond Nagpur. The
hypotenuse is formed by an irregular line from beyond Nagpur
to Karwar. The area of this tract is over 100,000 square miles
and its population exceeds thirty millions. The race that
inhabits it varies just as Frenchmen of different provinces vary.
But it has distinct characteristics, which differentiate it from
other Indian races. The people of Maharashtra as a rule lack
the regular features of the Northern Indian. Their tempers,
too, are usually less under control than those of the dwellers in
the Gangetic plain. But their courage is at least as high as that
of any other Indian nation, while their exquisitely keen sense of
humour, the lofty intelligence of their educated classes, their
blunt speech and frank bearing rarely fail to win the love and
admiration of those Englishmen whose lot it is to serve among
them the Indian Government.

Maharashtra has three distinct divisions. Of these, the
seaboard below the Sahyadri Mountains is known as the Konkan ;
the tract occupied by the Sahyadris is known as the Mawal ;
while the wide, rolling plains to the east are known as the Desh.
Maharashtra receives from the monsoon a rainfall that varies

---

* Ranade, *Rise of the Maratha Power*, p. 20.

greatly. In many parts of the Konkan 100 inches in a single
year are not unusual. In the Sahyadris as many as 400 inches
have been recorded. In the eastern parts of the Desh a fall of
20 inches is welcomed with the utmost gratitude. The Konkan
is, owing to its low level, hotter than the other two divisions.
It is, however, in parts extremely fertile. The Mawal is cool
and eminently healthy for Europeans, but, except for its rice-
fields, of little value for cultivation. The Desh is barren to the
west, but grows richer to the east, where the deep black soil
needs only rain to produce crops in abundance. The climate of
the Desh, while hotter than that of the Mawal, is still pleasant
and salubrious.

In the earliest period of Indian History on which light has
yet been thrown, we find the Aryan people established only in
eastern Afghanistan and the western Punjab. To this tract
they were long confined either by the forests that grew along
the Ganges River or by the valour of the tribes that dwelt close
to their borders. In course of time, however, they subdued
the forests and the tribes that blocked their path, and by the
8th century B.C. were in complete control of the vast territory
between the Himalayas and the Vindhyas. This immense
tract, watered by the Ganges, the Indus, the Jamna, and a host
of minor rivers and visited by the yearly monsoon rains, should,
it might have seemed, have sufficed for the needs of the conquering race. But the 7th century B.C. saw a great activity among
the nations along the Mediterranean seaboard. The Eternal
City had been founded on the banks of the Tiber, and the
'Wolves of Italy' had begun to peep from their Roman
stronghold at the world, which in the course of eight centuries
they were to subdue from the highlands of Britain to the fast-
nesses of Judea. In Greece the old civilization of Homer had
been followed by another, far more daring and not less picturesque. Dorians and Ionians had planted their colonies from the
Gulf of Tarentum to the south of Sicily. Their triremes and
penteconters fought battles for the trade of the Adriatic.* Their
mercenary soldiers helped Gyges and Ardys of Lydia to check,

* See Bury's *Greece*.

and then to drive back, the Cimmerian hosts to the Crimea. In return they learnt the art of coinage from the Lydians, and letters from the Phœnicians. But it was in the valley of the Nile that civilization made her greatest advance. The conquest of Egypt in 672 B.C. by King Assar-haddon was Assyria's proudest exploit. For twenty-five years the slavery of the Egyptians endured. Then Psammetichus of Sais, of the dark Libyan stock, raised the standard of revolt. To his banner flocked not only natives of Egypt but mail-clad mercenaries from Lydia and Caria. The Assyrian troops were driven from the Nile valley. The old exclusive policy of the ancient Pharaohs disappeared for ever. Greek settlers brought trade and art to the shores of Egypt. A canal cut by Psammetichus' son Necho anticipated the work of De Lesseps by over 2000 years and joined the waters of the Mediterranean to the Gulf of Suez. Not many years afterwards a fleet of Phœnician ships equipped by Necho sailed forth from Suez to circumnavigate Africa. They passed through the Red Sea with a skill which showed long acquaintance with its inhospitable coasts. They waited on the Somali shore until the monsoon storms had passed away. Then doubling the Cape of Good Hope, they returned triumphantly through the Pillars of Hercules and, within two years of their departure, anchored amid the applause of three continents off the mouths of the Nile.

It was hardly possible that such a human ferment should produce no effect in India. Actually the effect was immense. In the 7th century B.C. a great forward movement carried the Aryan race over the Vindhyas, until it died away at the extreme south of the Peninsula. The progress of this movement may be discerned from the two great Sanskrit epics. The first, the Ramayana, tells the story of King Rama of Ayodhya. His father, King Dasharatha, one of a race sprung from the loins of the Sun God, ruled over the country now known as Oudh. When King Dasharatha's eldest son Rama grew to manhood, the king was induced by Rama's stepmother, Queen Kaikeyi, to disinherit him in favour of her own son, Prince Bharata, and to banish Rama for fourteen years into the forest. In obedience

to this sentence the prince, his wife Sita, and his brother Laxman
wandered southwards until they reached the forest of Dandaka,
beyond the Vindhyas. There King Ravana of Ceylon carried
off Sita to his island kingdom. Rama and Laxman followed
to win her back. From this point onwards the Ramayana
becomes a fairy tale. The princes' wanderings brought them
to the abodes of monkeys, apes and bears. And aided by a host
of warlike animals, Prince Rama crossed the Palk Straits and
recovered his bride. It may thus be surmised that when the
Ramayana was written the Aryans had not yet gone farther
south than the Vindhyas. In the Mahabharata we find a different state of things. Its heroes are the race of the Bharatas,
sprung from the loins of the Moon God. Their capital was at
Hastinapura, not far from Delhi. But a quarrel took place
between two families of Bharata princes, the sons of the dead
King Pandu and those of his brother the blind King Dhritarashtra.
The gambling instincts of King Pandu's eldest son, Yudhishthira,
gave for thirteen years the victory to the sons of King Dhritarashtra. But in the end Yudhishthira and his brothers triumphed. Now the youngest of Yudhishthira's brothers, Sahadeva,
is said in the course of his adventures to have subdued the
Pandyas, Keralas, and Andhras, who all lived south of the
Vindhyas. It seems, therefore, certain that when the Mahabharata had reached its present form, the Aryans had explored
the whole sub-continent from the Himalayas to the Palk Straits.

In the epics, Maharashtra bore the name of the Dandakaranya
or Dandaka Forest. That is clear from the mention of the
Godavari, one of the most important rivers in Maharashtra.
Indeed, even to-day, when the Marathi-speaking Brahmans in
the course of sacrifices refer to their country, they call it not
Maharashtra but Dandakaranya. Strangely enough it was one
of the last parts of India conquered by the Aryan invaders.
It was long protected by the peaks and forests of the Vindhyas
and Satpuras. The Aryans overran the Ganges valley from west
to east, and it was not until they reached the eastern shores
of India that they were able to turn the Vindhya Mountains.
They then conquered southern India from east to west. In the

extreme south the Aryans were unable to impose their language on the already highly civilized Cholas, Pandyas and Keralas. But although the Dandakaranya was one of the last of their conquests, the triumph in it of the Aryans was as complete as in northern India. The Rakshasas or aboriginal tribes were soon absorbed or driven from the valleys to the hills. A race sprung from the union of Aryan invaders and captive women took their place, and Marathi, the tongue which the descendants of that race speak to-day, is as closely allied to the ancient Sanskrit as any of her elder sisters in the northern plains.

Another question remains to be solved. How did the Dandakaranya come to be called Maharashtra ? Its inhabitants, proud of their history and of the hundred victories of their forefathers, proclaim that Maharashtra means the great country. The ensuing pages will indeed show how great it became. But it bore the name of Maharashtra when it was still an unknown province. Mr. Molesworth, the well-known Marathi scholar, hinted that the name might mean the country of the Mhars ; but there are numerous grounds for rejecting this surmise. The Mhars are not a people. They are merely a debased section. Nor is their name an ancient one. It is a corruption of the word Mrityuhar or ' remover of the dead.' It must therefore have come into existence, not before the Aryan invasion, but after the Mhars had been reduced to their present miserable condition. From so abject a community no country would take its name. Lastly, the words Mrityuhar Rashtra would not, according to the ordinary laws of linguistic corruption, become Maharashtra. To ascertain the true origin of the name let us revert for a moment to the political history of eastern Europe and northern India.

To the north-west of the Aegean Sea lay the country of Macedonia. Its kings were Hellenic. This circumstance preserved for the Macedonian kings the royal dignities which in Homer's time had been held by kings in every Grecian State. But the strength of the non-Hellenic feudatories and vassals in the western hills rendered the king powerless to meddle in affairs outside his own kingdom. In the Persian War the

Macedonian king Alexander had intrigued with both Greeks and barbarians. In the war between Sparta and Athens, King Perdiccas had followed similar tactics. But in the year 359 B.C. there came to this impotent dominion a man with an idea. He was Philip, the son of Amyntas, and uncle of the infant king. In his boyhood he had been seized as a hostage by the Theban government and had spent his youth in the military school of Bœotia. There he had watched the work of Epaminondas and had seen how a flank attack made by picked infantry, combined with a frontal advance, was irresistible even to the Spartan hoplite. It occurred to Philip that an attack on both flanks by picked cavalry combined with a frontal advance by infantry would be more decisive still. This was his idea and it was destined to change the face of the civilized globe. At the age of twenty-four he returned to his native country and assumed, as regent for his nephew, the Macedonian government. By the aid of the gold mines of Mount Pangæus, he equipped picked cavalry and stimulated their pride by the name of Hetairoi, or companions of the king. The new military tactics obtained successes even greater than those of Epaminondas. The armies of the vassals, of Illyrians, Thebans, Athenians and Spartans, proved alike unable to resist them. In 336 B.C. Philip fell beneath an assassin's knife. To Philip succeeded his son Alexander. But the idea lived on and each year brought it fresh successes. By 335 B.C. all Greece was humbled. The fate of Asia Minor was decided on the Granicus, that of Syria and Egypt on the Issus, that of Persia on the plain of Gaugamela. Yet another victory on the Jhelum placed the Macedonian king in the possession of the western Punjab. To the conqueror's camp there came about this time one Chandragupta Maurya. He was a humble kinsman of the Nanda king who ruled at Magadha. For political reasons he had fled his country and he now tried to tempt Alexander to the conquest of Magadha. The revolt of his troops forced the king to turn a deaf ear to Chandragupta. But if the exile had failed in his chief aim, his visit to Alexander's camp had not been fruitless. His natural abilities had been improved by travel and by contact with a western people. He had learnt the value of discipline and a new system of tactics. When the Macedonian king left India, Chandragupta, thrown on his own resources, organised a revolt, attacked the Macedonian garrisons, drove them out, and fixing his capital at Pataliputra or Patna, founded a dynasty which was to last for 137 years. On Chandragupta's death his son, Bindusara, succeeded him, and he in turn was followed by the great Buddhist emperor, Asoka. Instead of armies, Asoka sent forth in every direction ministers of religion to preach the teachings of Buddha. These missions he recorded in inscriptions carved in rocks all over northern India. On no less than four of those which still survive, Asoka inscribed that he had sent missionaries to the Rastikas. These Rastikas or Rashtrikas were the dwellers in the Dandaka Forest. Proud of their independence, or for some kindred reason, they came in later years to call themselves Maharashtrikas, and so the country which they occupied came to be known as Maharashtra and its people as Marathas.*

---

* Bhandarkar, *Deccan*, p. 9. But see the article on the Ancient Geography and Civilization of Maharashtra by Mr. Kane. He interprets Maharashtra to mean 'the great country,' *i.e.*, the great forest country south of the Vindhyas. *Per contra* see Mr. Rajwade's *Maharashtracha Vasahat Kal* (The Colonization of Maharashtra), wherein he lays down that Maharashtra comes from Rashtrikas, *i.e.*, the leading men of the *rashtra*, or country Maharashtrikas meant chiefs among the leading men.

CHAPTER II

THE SATAVAHANA OR ANDHRA KINGS

CIRCA 185 B.C. TO A.D. 250

THE empire founded by Chandragupta began to crumble away after the death of Asoka. It terminated in 185 B.C. by the assassination of the last Maurya king, Brihadratha, by his chief general, Pushpamitra, the founder of the Sunga line. Like most Indian usurpers Pushpamitra was a man of talents and vigour. He soon extended the boundaries of the shrunken empire, until in the south they reached the Narbáda River and in the west the frontiers of the Punjab. The Sunga dynasty endured for 112 years, but of Pushpamitra's successors little is known. His grandson Sumitra was assassinated on the boards of the royal theatre, to which he was inordinately attached. The last Sunga king, Devabhuti or Devabhumi, lost his life while engaged in a licentious intrigue. The murderer was the dissolute king's prime minister. His name was Vasudeva Kanva and he and his descendants ruled for 45 years, till they in turn were swept away by the rise of the Andhras.

Hitherto the paramount rulers of India had been northern kings. But the new dynasty, as powerful as any that preceded it, came from the south. On the shores of the Bay of Bengal, between the mouths of the Krishna and Godavari Rivers, dwelt the Andhra people. Of the Dravidian race, they spoke the musical Telegu. Their wealth and power had been renowned from ancient times. Megasthenes, a Greek envoy at the court of Chandragupta, wrote with admiration of their thirty walled cities, their countless villages, their 100,000 foot soldiers, their 2000 horsemen and their 1000 war elephants.* They appear in edicts, dated 206 B.C., as tributaries of Asoka.

---

* See Vincent Smith, *Early History of India*, p. 206.

But when the strong hand of the great Buddhist emperor was removed by death, the Andhras speedily recovered their independence. From being vassals they became rivals and in the end destroyed the Kanva kings and overran Maharashtra. The Andhra dynasty lasted for about 300 years.* But for a time its rule over Maharashtra was interrupted by a foreign tribe named the Sakas. The discovery of this fact forms one of the romances of epigraphy.

In a small cave at Nasik was found an inscription which recorded that it had been scooped out by a lieutenant of King Krishna of the Satavahana race. In a cave close to Nanaghat, the precipitous pass which near Junnar leads from the Mawal to the Konkan seaboard, is a similar inscription. Close by are human figures. One bears the name of King Simuka Satavahana, another that of King Shri Satakarni. There is a second set of inscriptions in caves at Nasik, Karli and Junnar. Four of them speak of the generosity and charities of a certain Ushvadata, the son-in-law of King Nahapana, the great Kshatrapa. Lastly there is a third set of inscriptions at Nasik, which praise the feats of arms of King Gautamiputra Satakarni, who restored the glories of the Satavahana race. One of these records that the cave was constructed in the 19th year of the reign of King Pulumayi and describes Gautamiputra as having ' destroyed the Sakas, the Yavanas and Pallavas, left no trace or remnant of the race of Khagarata and re-established the glory of the Satavahana family'. The names in the first and third sets of inscriptions, Krishna, Simuka, Shri Satakarni, Gautamiputra are all to be found in certain ancient documents called the Puranas as the names of the Andhra kings. This led Sir R. Bhandarkar to the now universally accepted conclusion that the Andhra and the Satavahana kings were identical. The second set of inscriptions led him to a still more important discovery. The name of King Nahapana, the great Kshatrapa, was a strange one for an Indian king. But if he was not an Indian king, what was he ? Now King Gautamiputra is said in the third set of inscriptions to have destroyed Sakas, Yavanas and Pallavas. Now Pallavas

* Bhandarkar, *Deccan*, p. 29.

were Indians, Yavanas were Greeks, but **Nahapana** is not a Greek name. It is, as I have said, not an Indian one. Nahapana, therefore, was probably a Saka.

About 170 B.C. certain Chinese hordes known as the Yueh-chi driven from China by the Hiungnu, a tribe of nomads, came into contact with another horde called the Sakas and drove them southwards. The fugitive Sakas forced their way into India and made themselves masters of Mathura and Taxila, Kathiawar and Ujjain. But in earlier times the Sakas had acknowledged the Parthian kings as overlords and had themselves borne the title, not of king, but of satrap. To this latter title they clung long after they had become independent. Thus Nahapana the great Kshatrapa was a descendant of some Saka chief who had forced his way into Maharashtra. Once satisfied that Nahapana was a Saka, Dr. Bhandarkar made another surmise. The resemblance between the word Saka and the Saké or Shaké* era which prevails south of the Narmada could hardly be fortuitous. Now if the Shaké era was founded by the Sakas, they did it in all probability to celebrate some great achievement. Thus the Sakas probably conquered the Deccan when the Shaké era began, that is to say in A.D. 78.

The dominion, however, of these foreign kings did not long vex Maharashtra. About A.D. 150 an Alexandrian Greek, called Ptolemy, wrote a book on geography. Therein he has recorded that a certain Polemios ruled at Baithan. Now Baithan is clearly Paithan on the Godavari, then the capital of the Andhra viceroyalty of Maharashtra. Sirios Polemios can be identified with King Pulumayi in the third set of inscriptions. Therefore before A.D. 150 Saka rule in Maharashtra had vanished. It is easy now to reconstruct the story. In A.D. 78 the Saka chief forced his way either through the Vindhyas or along the Konkan seaboard. For some fifty years he and his descendants occupied Maharashtra. The Andhras fell back on their other provinces. Then led by a capable and active prince, King Gautamiputra, they drove out the Sakas. The third inscription, however, mentions Pulumayi as king. But the

---

* The Shaké era is commonly known as the Shalivahan era.

Puranas show that Pulumayi was the son of King Gautamiputra.
It seems therefore probable that after the re-conquest of Maharashtra, Gautamiputra made his son Pulumayi either viceroy or
joint king. Nor was this the only victory of Gautamiputra.
In the inscription quoted above he is said to have left no trace
of the race of Khagarata. Dr. Bhandarkar has conjectured
that the Saka king of Ujjain, whose ancestor was Khagarata
or Kshaharata, indignant at the fate of his southern brethren,
tried to help them. He shared their defeat and lost his life.
This conjecture finds support in a charming legend still current
in Poona. It is as follows. In Paithan on the banks of the
Godavari there dwelt in the house of a potter a Brahman girl
who had two brothers. One day the Brahman girl went to
bathe in the Godavari. But as she bathed, her beauty won
the heart of no less a lover than Shesha, the great serpent king,
upon whose coils the god Vishnu takes his rest in the centre
of the milky ocean. To refuse such a wooer was impossible.
The serpent king changed himself into a man and became the
lover of the Brahman girl. The child born of this romance was
brought up by its mother in the house of her landlord, the
potter. At this time there reigned in Ujjain a mighty king called
Vikramaditya, or the Sun of Valour. To him one day the sage
Narada foretold that death would come to him from the hands
of a boy aged two, whose mother was still unwed. It was now
a matter of life and death to Vikramaditya to discover the boy
and to destroy him. The royal messengers and spies searched
in vain for the king's foe. At last Vikramaditya called to his
aid Vetal, the great ghost king.* On Vetal's arrival, Vikramaditya told him of Narada's prophecy and begged him to find
out where the murderous infant lived. Away on the search
went Vetal and his troopers until at last the ghost king saw
playing at Paithan a boy of two, near whom stood an unmarried
girl who seemed to be his mother. Vetal guessed that this was
the infant for whom he sought, and told Vikramaditya. The
latter led out his whole army to destroy the two-year-old boy.

* Rings of white stones representing Vetal, the ghost king, and his troopers
are often to be seen outside Deccan villages.

But even so Narada's prophecy came true. The tiny child had learnt in the potter's house to make clay images of men, elephants and horses. His father, the serpent king, taught him a charm by which to make them live ; and vast though Vikramaditya's army was, it was soon overwhelmed by the still greater host that sprang from the clay to meet it. The child afterwards became king and ruled with such good fortune that he founded the Shalivahan era to commemorate his glory. Now Shalivahan is merely another way of pronouncing Satavahan. Therefore, the king of the legend, who defeated the lord of Ujjain, was no doubt the great Satavahana king, Gautamiputra. But the era which he is said to have founded was the Shaké era, which he inherited from the conquered Sakas.

The Andhras did not long retain their conquests north of the Vindhyas. A capable Saka leader, named Rudradaman, arose in Kathiawar and drove the Andhras out of the country. King Pulumayi, Gautamiputra's son, took his daughter in marriage ; but the alliance did not stay the arms of Rudradaman. About A.D. 150 * Rudradaman had recovered all the provinces in northern India which Gautamiputra had taken from the Sakas. Pulumayi died, according to Dr. Bhandarkar, in A.D. 150 or according to Mr. Vincent Smith in A.D. 163. His immediate successor was his brother Sivasri. But the only notable Andhra king after the death of Pulumayi was Gautamiputra Yajnasri. He appears partially to have avenged the defeats of Pulumayi. The dynasty finally passed away in the early part of the 3rd century A. D.†

Nevertheless, in spite of our ignorance of the personal achieve ments of most of the Andhra rulers, there are many indications that the dynasty synchronized with a time of great prosperity in Maharashtra. The hills of the Deccan and the Konkan abound with caves excavated about this time by rich merchants, goldsmiths, carpenters, corn-dealers and even by druggists. The fortune of a single banker enabled him to make the great central cave at Karli. Interest, as one of Ushvadata's inscrip-

---

* Vincent Smith, *Early History of India*, pp. 210-11.

† A. D. 218, according to Dr. Bhandarkar.

tions show, varied form 5 to 7½ per cent., rates which compare
favourably with those of modern times. Nor is this a cause for
wonder. The treatment of Egypt by her Roman conquerors
had been peculiarly favourable to the Hellenic genius. Macedonia and Syria were crushed and plundered until they came
to resemble other provinces of the empire. But the danger
which Rome had incurred from Antony's infatuation for
Cleopatra had led Augustus to treat Egypt in a different way.
His court poet Virgil wrote twelve books of immortal verse to
warn his countrymen against the dangerous beauties who haun-
ted the northern shores of Africa. The emperor made the
administration his own peculiar care and forbade Italians of
senatorial rank to visit Egypt without his special leave. Protected from internal disturbance and foreign attack, yet not
interfered with by the Roman administrators, the talented
Greeks of Alexandria obtained a full scope for their develop-
ment. Systems of philosophy founded in Attica reached per-
fection in Egypt. Astronomy and mathematics made amazing
progress. But it was in geography that human knowledge
made its greatest advances. Seamanship was peculiarly the
gift of the Hellene. From every village on the Erythrean coast,
Greek sailors fitted out ships to explore the eastern seas. The
Gulf of Oman, the Persian Gulf, the Arabian Sea, the western
shores of India, became intimately known to them. They
ventured as far as the Malay Peninsula and brought back such
stores of precious metal that it acquired the name of the Golden
Chersonese. Other Greek fleets, more audacious still, disdained
the confines of the Indian Seas. Heading resolutely east,
they emerged into the Pacific and sold the products of Europe
in the emporiums of China.* Nor was this all. In A.D. 116
Trajan pushed the Roman frontier to the Persian Gulf. The
caravan routes of Arabia were guarded by Roman fortresses and
Roman legions. Thus the mighty empire of Europe was at
several points along its frontier linked by sea to the vast peninsula of India. Year by year ships from Egypt brought to India
the commodities of the West. In exchange they took back

* See article on Ptolemy's geography in the Encyclopædia Britannica.

her onyx, cotton and muslins. The coast line of Maharashtra,
then as now, offered the most convenient anchorages to foreign
ships. And it requires no great flight of fancy to imagine how,
to the great profit of the Maratha people, the trade of southern
India passed through the Western Ghats to be shipped to Meso-
potamia, Arabia and Egypt, just as to-day it roars through the
Bhor and Nasik Ghats on its way to Basra and Genoa, to Mar-
seilles, Liverpool and London.

A legend exists which shows that the Andhra period was one
not only of military and mercantile, but also of literary, activity.
A certain ghost known as Kanabhuti brought to one Gunadhya,
a minister of King Shalivahan, seven volumes of stories, all
written in blood. Gunadhya accepted them and offered them as
a gift to his royal master. Disgusted with the strange language
and the stranger script, King Shalivahan returned the books to
Gunadhya. The latter, furious at the failure of his present, burnt
six of the seven volumes. The remaining volume fell into the
hands of Gunadhya's pupils or clerks. They were acquainted
with the ghost language and pronounced the book charming.
Their verdict came to King Shalivahan's ear and he made a
further effort to read Kanabhuti's stories; and once he had
mastered the difficulties of Kanabhuti's literary medium, he
was as charmed with the tales as Gunadhya's pupils. Now the
ghost language of Kanabhuti was no doubt the Maharashtri
dialect, born of the attempts of the Rashtrikas to speak Sanskrit;
and the reign of Shalivahan, that is to say the years when
the Andhra kings held sway,first saw the use for literary purposes
of that vigorous, supple, graceful and copious tongue, Marathi.

CHAPTER III

THE efforts of Oriental scholars to peep into the history of
Maharashtra between the death of the last Andhra king,
Pulumayi IV, about A.D. 218[*] and the rise of the Chalukyas
has not hitherto been crowned with any great success. It seems
however that for about seventy years a dynasty of Abhiras or
cowherds were in power and that they were driven out by
a branch of the Rashtrikas, the people to whom Maharashtra
owed its name. A *kula* or family of the Rashtrikas made
themselves masters of the Deccan and are known in history
as Rashtrakutas.[†] In the sixth century they were driven from
power by a new dynasty, that of the Chalukyas. Several
graceful legends have been woven round the origin of these
vigorous princes. One tells how on a certain morning the god
Brahmadeva was engaged in his devotions. The god Indra
approached him and bewailed the sinfulness of the earth. No
living man, so said Indra, ever performed sacrifices or offered
libations to the gods. Brahmadeva looked angrily at his hand,
which was then hollowed, that it might hold the water needed
in his ceremonial. Instantly there sprang from the great god's
hand two heroes by name Harita and Manavya. They founded
a family destined to achieve great glory, and because they
were sprung from Brahmadeva's hollow hand or Chaluka, they
became known as Chalukyas. Another tale[‡] relates that Harita
and Manavya were the sons of the sage Manu.[§] One day Harita
was pouring out a libation to the gods, when from the spray

[*] Bhandarkar, *Deccan*, p. 29. Mr. Vincent Smith gives the date as A.D. 225.
[†] Bhandarkar, *Deccan*, p. 36.
[‡] Fleet, *Deccan*, p. 17.
[§] Manu was the son of the god Brahmadeva.

of his waterpot sprang the founder of the new dynasty. All the legends agree that the Chalukya kings first ruled at Ayodhya, the capital of the divine Ramchandra. The god Vishnu gave them a banner on which was displayed a wild boar. This denoted not only the impetuous valour of the Chalukya armies but indicated that they were under the god Vishnu's special protection.* Nor was the god Vishnu the only divine friend of the Chalukyas. The god Kartikeya or Kartikswami, born to Shiva by the daughters of the Fire-god, Agni, himself led to battle the hero-kings of Ayodhya. And with his and Vishnu's help, they forced their triumphant way to the southern shores of India.

The first prince whose name survives in the inscriptions is one Jayasinha, which being interpreted means 'the lion of victory.' It seems probable that he was a military adventurer from the north, who conquered Maharashtra from its native princes, the Rashtrakutas. His grandson Pulakesi I made Vatapipura, the modern Badami, his capital, and assumed the titles of Prithvi Vallabha or 'Husband of the Earth' and Satya-sraya or the 'Support of Truth.' Kirtivarman, the son and successor of Pulakesi I, was also a capable prince. He added to his father's kingdom the northern Konkan and northern Canara. An inscription in a cave temple at Badami has enabled Sir R. Bhandarkar† to fix the date of his accession in A.D. 566 or 567. After a reign of twenty-four years Kirtivarman died leaving three young sons and a brother Mangalisa. It was the continuous aim of Mangalisa to secure for himself and his son the throne of Vatapipura. But the talents and vigour of Kirti-varman's eldest son Pulakesi II rendered Mangalisa's efforts vain. In A.D. 611 Pulakesi II defeated decisively his uncle Mangalisa, who with his son fell on the field of battle. These civil troubles led the Rashtrakutas under a chief called Govinda to attempt the recovery of their former power. A rebellion, too, broke out in the provinces subdued by Pulakesi's father. But no diffi-

---

* Vishnu in his third incarnation took the form of a boar to raise the earth from the bottom of the sea whither a demon called Hiranyaksha had dragged t.

† Bhandarkar, *Deccan*, p. 38

culties proved too great for the new sovereign. The rebels, defeated in the field, soon abandoned the Rashtrakutas. The latter surrendered to Pulakesi and, graciously treated, became his faithful allies. But of all Pulakesi's victories none brought him more honour than his repulse of King Harsha Siladitya. This powerful monarch was the son of a chief named Prabhakar, who rose to power in the Punjab by a succession of victories over the White Huns. After a short reign Prabhakar's elder son Rajyavardhan was assassinated and in A.D. 606 Harsha mounted the throne that he was to fill gloriously for fifty years.* A Persian saying has it that while there is room for seven beggars under one blanket, there is no room for more than one king in seven climes. And Harsha, having made himself master of the greater part of Hindustan, found it intolerable that south of the Vindhyas Pulakesi should still retain his independence. In A.D. 620 he collected together troops from every country which owned his authority. Harsha's successes had been largely due to his twenty thousand cavalry and the mobile character of his infantry. But in the Vindhya forests the cavalry proved useless and, mobile as Harsha's foot soldiers were, they were slow compared with the fleet-footed Maratha hillmen in the service of Pulakesi II. Harsha repeatedly attacked and was as often defeated. At last, weary of a campaign in which his army had all but perished, he made peace and accepted the Narbada River as his southern frontier.

A contemporary account of Pulakesi and his people has in a strange manner survived to modern times. In the sixth century B.C. about fifty miles south of the Himalayas and a hundred miles north of Benares city, there stood upon the banks of the Kohana River a town called Kapilavastu, the capital of a petty tribe called the Sakyas. The king's name was Suddhoddana and his chief troubles were the frequent droughts and the absence of a royal heir. At last, when he was forty-five years old and his hopes had almost died, his chief queen Mahamaya bore her husband a son. To the child was given the name of Siddhartha.

---

* Vincent Smith, *Early History of India*, p. 338.

He grew to manhood and, when nineteen years old, was married
to his cousin Yasodhara. He at first gave himself wholly to
a life of pleasure. But in his twenty-ninth year such a life
began to pall. As he one day drove through his pleasure ground,
the sight of a broken down old man turned his mind to serious
thoughts. These thoughts became graver still when he saw one
day a leper and another day a dead body. One night, as the well-
known story tells us, he left his wife and child and went out into
the wilderness a penniless wanderer. He sought at first, so we
are told, to learn wisdom from the Brahman sages, but they did
not satisfy him. At last prolonged meditation under the Bodhi
tree led him to found a faith known as Buddhism. In most
essentials, it differed little from Hinduism. But it denied the
existence of the gods and the existence of caste. The new
doctrines made at first slow progress, but the conversion of
Asoka spread them all over India. From India they extended
in the reign of the Kushan king Kanishka to China.
The Hun invasion broke off intercourse between China and
India and certain religious difficulties induced in A.D. 400
one Fa Hien and five companions to visit India. Two
centuries later another pilgrim named Hiuen Tsang made
the arduous pilgrimage. He travelled widely through India
and made admirable notes on what he heard and saw in
his travels. And no part of his book is so interesting
as that in which he has related his visit to the Maharashtra
country and the court of Pulakesi II. I quote the following
passage :—

"The kingdom of Moholatcha (Maharashtra) has a circumference of 6000 li. To the west of the capital runs a
big river; the circumference of the town is thirty li. The
soil is rich and fertile and yields a great harvest of corn.
The climate is hot. The manners of the people are simple
and honest. They are tall and proud and distant. Whoever
does them a kindness can count on their gratitude. But
he who does them an injury never escapes their vengeance.
If anyone insults them, they risk their life to wash out the
affront. If anyone in distress begs their help, they forget

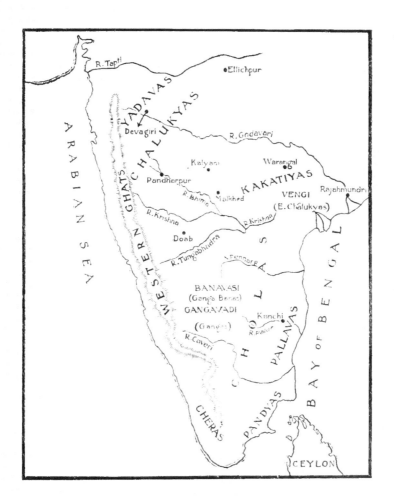

SKETCH MAP TO ILLUSTRATE THE EARLY PERIOD.

their own safety in their efforts to help him. When they
have an insult to avenge, they never fail to warn their
enemy beforehand. This done, they don their armour
and fight lance in hand. In battle they pursue the fugitives
but never kill those who surrender. When a general has
lost a battle they do not inflict on him corporal punishment.
They make him dress in women's clothes and thus force
him to commit suicide. The state keeps a body of several
hundred fearless champions. Every time they get ready
for a fight, they get drunk, and once drunk, a single champion lance in hand will challenge ten thousand foes. If he
kills anyone as he goes to battle, the law does not punish
him. Every time the army sets out on a campaign, this
chosen body leads the way with drums beating. Besides
these picked troops, there are hundreds of fierce war elephants. When the battle is about to open, the elephants
are given strong liquor to drink. They then rush forward
and trample everything underfoot. The king, proud of his
soldiers and his war elephants, despises and insults the
neighbouring kingdoms. He is of Tsatili (Kshatriya)
stock; his name is Poulokiche (Pulakesi). His views are
broad and profound and he dispenses as far as the most
distant spots his kindliness and his favours. His subjects
serve him with absolute devotion. To-day the great king
Siladitya (Harsha) bears from the east to the west his
victorious arms; he conquers distant races and makes the
nations near him tremble. But those of his (Pulakesi's)
kingdom are the only men who have never yielded to him.
Although several times he has put himself at the head of
all the forces of the five Indies, although he has called to his
aid the bravest generals of all countries, although he has
himself marched to punish the men of Maharashtra, he has
not yet overcome their resistance. From this fact alone
it is possible to judge their warlike habits and customs.
The men love study and practise at the same time heresy
and truth. There are a hundred monasteries, which contain
about five thousand monks. There are a hundred temples

to the gods. The heretics of the different sects are very numerous."*

The fame of Pulakesi was not confined to India. It reached the ears of Chosroes II, king of Persia. In A.D. 625 he not only received but returned a complimentary embassy from the Chalukya king. And a large fresco painting at Ajanta still portrays for the benefit of the learned the reception of the Persian envoys by the great Pulakesi.

Unhappily the Chalukya king outlived his good fortune. To understand how disaster overtook him, we must turn to the early history of southern India. When the Aryans penetrated the extreme south, they found there three highly civilized Dravidian nations, the Cheras (or Keralas), the Cholas and the Pandyas. Of these the Cheras lived on the south-west coast from Cannanore to Trivendram. The Cholas occupied the Madras districts to the south of the Mysore State. The Pandyas dwelt in the extreme south from Travancore to Ramnad. The governments of these nations, the Aryans humbled but did not destroy. They imposed on them their religion but not their language nor their script. Thus the Cheras, the Cholas and the Pandyas recovered from the Aryan invasion and in course of time began to prosper. During the Andhra domination they actively helped that warlike people to substitute a southern for a northern overlordship. From time to time also they fought among themselves. When history begins the Cholas are the most powerful of the three nations. About the end of the second century A.D., the Cheras are the strongest. During the darkness which fell over India after the fall of the Andhras they allowed a fourth power to dominate them. This power was that of the Pallavas. They lived at first between the Caveri and the South Pennar Rivers on the south-east coast. They extended their possessions northwards across the South Pennar and made Kanchi, the modern Kanjeveram, their capital. A further movement carried them across the North Pennar River to the southern banks of the Krishna. This brought them into collision

---

* I have translated this from M. Julien's French translation of Hiuen Tsang's travels.

with the Chalukyas. A long and indecisive warfare followed. But at last King Narsinhavarman, the greatest of the Pallava monarchs, mounted the throne. He drove the Chalukya forces back along the Krishna. Finally he stormed the Chalukya capital Badami and in this overwhelming calamity Pulakesi perished. *

For thirteen years after Pulakesi's death the Chalukya power remained broken. His eldest son Chandraditya fell back on Vengi, the ancient home of the Andhras, between the Krishna and the Godavari. Nevertheless Pulakesi's second son, Vikramaditya I, succeeded after a long struggle in restoring the greatness of the Chalukya empire (A.D. 653).

The Chalukya dynasty endured for about seventy years after the death of Vikramaditya I, when it was overthrown by two successive kings of the indigenous Rashtrakuta stock, Dantidurga and Krishnaraja (circa A.D. 753).

As I have already mentioned, the Rashtrakutas were a powerful family of Rashtrikas, who, before the coming of the Chalukyas from the north, ruled over Maharashtra. During the early troubles of the reign of Pulakesi II, they sought vainly to recover their independence. The vast abilities of that monarch rendered the effort vain. But what was impossible in the seventh century A.D. became possible in the eighth. The new Rashtrakuta dynasty began with King Dantidurga. He was the great-grandson of Govinda, the Rashtrakuta chief who had rebelled against Pulakesi II. Beaten and pardoned, he became one of the great king's trusted allies. His son Karka and his grandson Indra inherited in turn Govinda's fief. But although vassals, their power was continually on the increase, and from time to time the Chalukyas deigned to give to the Rashtrakutas their own daughters in wedlock. Indra received the hand of a Chalukya princess, who was herself descended from a previous union between the two families. From this union sprang Dantidurga. He rebelled against Kirtivarman II, the last Chalukya king of the early dynasty. Somewhere in southern India, Dantidurga defeated the Chalukya army of

---

* See Aiyangar, *Ancient India*, Chapter I.

occupation. Swiftly following up his success, Dantidurga attacked and took Badami. He died childless and was succeeded about A.D. 753 by his paternal uncle Krishnaraja. This prince completed the work of Dantidurga and utterly destroyed the Chalukya power. To use the picturesque language of the inscriptions, " He churned the Ocean of the Chalukya race and drew from it the Laxmi of paramount sovereignty." Having thus rid himself of his former overlord, he caused to be made a thank-offering to the god Shiva. He had carved out of the solid rock a temple so beautiful that the gods, so it is affirmed, could hardly believe it to be the product of human hands. And even the architect who designed it asked himself how he had been able to do it. For more than a thousand years this work has attracted pilgrims from all parts of India and to-day English and American tourists, to whom the very name of Rashtrakuta is unknown, gape at it every winter with awed wonder. For the work of Krishnaraja is none other than the matchless temple of Kailas at Ellora. Krishnaraja reigned some time between A.D. 753 and 775. His eldest son Govinda II succeeded him but his throne was soon usurped by his younger brother. This warlike prince bore the name of Dhruva, that of the legendary child who worshipped the god Krishna with such fervour that he at last won an immortal throne in heaven, whence he still looks down as the pole star on the earth. But the new monarch's admiring subjects called him Nirupama, or the Incomparable One.

The rise of the Rashtrakutas had been almost as fatal to the Pallavas as to the Chalukyas. The Pallava empire was now divided into three parts. One branch, known as the Gangas,* ruled over the western portion. Another branch, known as the Ganga Banas, ruled the centre. The kingdom of the main branch of the Pallavas was reduced to the districts on the eastern coast. Upon this disorganised dominion Dhruva fell. He led into captivity the Ganga prince and capturing Kanchi from the Pallavas forced them to pay a yearly tribute of elephants.

---

* The Gangas' country was called Gangavasi or Gangavadi. The country of the Ganga Banas was known as Banavasi.

The reign of Dhruva's tenth successor Krishna III was note-worthy from his successful struggle against the Cholas. Forced by the rise of the Pallavas to become their vassals, the Cholas and the Pandyas upon their overlords' decline began once again to struggle for the overlordship of the extreme south. A series of able kings extended the Chola frontier until it marched with that of the Rashtrakutas. In A.D. 947 the Chola king Rajaditya invaded the Ganga kingdom to drive out the Chalukya prince Perumanadi, who had established himself there. To the latter's relief marched Krishna III. A bloody battle was fought at Takkolam, in which Rajaditya was defeated and slain. Krishna III took full advantage of his victory. The Rashtrakuta army occupied Kanchi, now a Chola town, and besieged Tanjore. But Rajaditya's brother Gandaradittan succeeded in saving the Chola country from complete annexation.

The last Rashtrakuta king was Kakkala, the great-nephew of Krishna III. Brave though he was, he was unfortunate. Harsha and Munja, the Parmara kings of Malwa, invaded Maharashtra and carried their arms up to Malkhed, the Rashtra-kuta capital, now in the dominions of H. E. H. the Nizam. Weakened by this attack, Kakkala was overthrown by a Chalukya hero named Tailapa. The latter, sprung from an insignificant collateral branch, ousted the Rashtrakutas in A.D. 973 after they had ruled Maharashtra for over two hundred years.

The fame of these powerful princes has long perished in India. But it has in a curious way been preserved by Arabian writers. Early in the eighth century the Arabs had established themselves firmly in Sind. Their nearest neighbours and therefore their enemies were the Gurjara kings of North Guzarat and Rajputana. The latter were also the enemies of the Rashtrakutas. A common interest united the Arab and the Rashtrakuta rulers; and a friendly commerce developed between Arabia and Mahara-shtra. Musulman merchants visited the court of a certain Balhara of Mankir and described him in their books of travel as the greatest sovereign in India. The learning of Dr. Bhandarkar discovered that they thereby meant the Rashtrakuta sovereigns. Mankir was a corruption of Malkhed or Manyakheta their capital. Balhara was a corruption of Vallabharai, or the well-beloved sovereign, a title which they had borrowed from the early Chalukyas.

THE first duty of Tailapa after his overthrow of the Rashtrakutas
was to secure his northern frontier from the Parmara danger.
He conciliated his new subjects by marrying Jakkaba, the
daughter of Kakkala, and then set forth to attack Malwa. For
a number of years the honours of war were fairly divided. Indeed
King Munja's inscriptions claim for him victory in no less than
six campaigns. But in A.D. 995 fortune at last inclined decisively in favour of Tailapa. King Munja crossed the Godavari,
hoping no doubt to repeat his successful invasion in the reign
of the last Rashtrakuta. But Tailapa attacked the Parmaras
with their backs to the great river. Unable to recross it they
were all but exterminated. King Munja was taken prisoner.
At first Tailapa treated with consideration his royal captive.
But Munja returned Tailapa's courtesy by an attempt to escape.
It failed, and Munja felt the full weight of the Chalukya's dis-
pleasure. He was put in prison and taken out daily to beg
the food denied him by his jailor. At last, probably to his relief,
he was beheaded.

In A.D. 997 Tailapa's eldest son Satyasraya succeeded his
father. The northern frontier had been pacified by the vigorous
action of Tailapa. But a danger no less great now threatened
Maharashtra from the south. As I have mentioned, Gandaradittan, the brother of Rajaditya, saved after his brother's defeat
and death the Chola country. During the decline of the Rashtrakutas the Cholas recovered their power, and after conquering
the extreme south resolved to carry through Rajaditya's plan
and drive from the Ganga country the family of Perumanadi.
Satyasraya marched south to meet them, but was completely

defeated by the great Chola king Rajraja I, the great-nephew
of Gandaradittan. The Cholas then overran Maharashtra,
pillaged it, and spared neither women, children nor Brahmans *
(A.D. 1000).

In A.D. 1008 Satyasraya died and left his shattered kingdom
to his nephew Vikramaditya I. The latter enjoyed power for
only a few months, when King Munja's nephew, King Bhoja,
the legendary hero of Central India, avenged his uncle's death
by defeating and killing Vikramaditya I (A.D. 1019). The
latter's brother, Jayasinha, in turn avenged Vikramaditya's
death. For to use the picturesque words of an inscription,
" he was the moon† of the lotus which was King Bhoja,"or in
other words humbled him. Jayasinha was less successful against
the Cholas, then in the zenith of their power. Rajraja the
Great, after overrunning Maharashtra annexed Gangavadi
or the Ganga country and established his frontier along the
Tungabhadra and the Krishna. All India south of those rivers
was his. Between the Krishna and the Godavari, the Eastern
Chalukyas still ruled in Vengi. But by conquest and the
marriage of his daughter Kundavvaiyar to the Eastern Chalukya
king, Vimaladitya, ‡ he had bullied and bribed the latter to be
his subordinate vassal. To the north of Vengi, as far as the
Mahanadi River, Rajraja had conquered all Kalingam. And he
was master also of the Maldives and the Laccadives. In A.D.
1012 Rajendra, Rajraja's capable son, succeeded his father.
He made an expedition into Orissa and brought back as captives
the king and his younger brother. While Rajendra was absent,
Jayasinha thought the time favourable for an attack on his
line of communication. He was, however, severely defeated,
and Rajendra carried his victorious armies as far as the Ganges ;
and his inscriptions relate that he made his subject kings carry
its sacred waters back with their own hands to Kanchi.§

In A.D. 1040 Jayasinha died and his son Someshwara I succeeded him. The new king, better known perhaps by his title

---

* Vincent Smith, *Early History of India*, p. 431.
† This is Dr. Bhandarkar's surmise (*Deccan*, p. 61).
‡ Aiyangar, *Ancient India*, p. 114.
§ To commemorate this feat he assumed the title of Gangai Konda.

Ahavamala, or the great in war, spent his reign in a ceaseless struggle against Chola aggression. The Chola empire now extended in a half circle round the Chalukya kingdom. Ahavamala therefore moved his capital from Yatagiri (30 miles south of Malkhed) to Kalyan, the modern Kalyani in the Nizam's dominions. Kalyan was a more central spot and the change on the whole was justified by success. In A.D. 1052 he fought against Rajendra's son and successor, Rajadhiraja, the great battle of Koppam. Both sides claimed the victory. But Rajadhiraja fell in the battle. And as we find later Ahavamala's sons viceroys of Banavasi (the country of the Ganga Banas) and of Gangavadi * (the country of the Gangas), it is only fair to assume that the fruits of the battle were the conquest of these two provinces from the Cholas. The close of Ahavamala's reign was not so fortunate.

In A.D. 1052, on the death of Rajadhiraja, his brother Rajendra II was crowned king of the Cholas. Ten years later he died and was succeeded by a third brother Virarajendra. The chronic hostilities between the Cholas and Chalukyas became once more acute on account of a disputed succession in Vengi. The son of Vimaladitya, the Eastern Chalukya, and of Rajraja the Great's daughter, Kundavvaiyar, took in marriage Ammanga Devi, the daughter of Rajendra I, Rajraja's son. The offspring of this marriage was Prince Kullottunga.† He claimed to succeed his father on the Eastern Chalukya throne. It suited his overlord, the Chola king, to set aside Kullottunga's claims in favour of the latter's uncle Vijayaditya. The boy appealed to Ahavamala, who went to his help, but was defeated first at Bejwada and afterwards at Kudal Sangam, the junction of the Krishna and the Tungabhadra. Ahavamala would not accept either defeat as final. In A.D. 1069 he sent an autograph letter to the Chola king inviting him to meet him again at Kudal Sangam and try once more the fortune of battle. In the true spirit of

---

* *Ancient India*, p. 113.

† *Ancient India*, p. 115. The Prince's real name was also Rajendra, but I shall throughout call him by his title Kullottunga, by which he is remembered.

chivalry, Virarajendra accepted the challenge. He gathered
his army on the southern banks of the Tungabhadra and Krishna
and waited. But Ahavamala never came to make good his
challenge. He had been attacked by a malignant fever and
in despair resolved to drown himself. He caused himself to be
carried on a throne to the banks of the Tungabhadra at some
distance from the spot where he had meant to meet King Virarajendra. There in the presence of a vast multitude he bathed
in the river's sacred waters. He distributed, although faint
with age and sickness, a large sum of money in charity. His
life-work now done, he walked back into the water until it
reached his lips. The royal bands then crashed out a farewell
salute. Ere the music had ended, the Chalukya king had sunk
beneath the waves.

On Ahavamala's death, his eldest son Someshwara II succeeded. The story of the prince's reign and of his deposition
by his younger brother Vikramaditya II has been told by a
Kashmirian court poet named Bilhana. This story has been
accepted by both Dr. Bhandarkar and Mr. Fleet. It requires,
however, to be modified in the light of the later information
collected by Mr. Aiyangar. Bilhana has said nothing but
good of Vikramaditya. But he really was by no means the
model prince portrayed by his biographer. During Ahavamala's
lifetime, Vikramaditya's courage and capacity had all but induced
the king to nominate him, and not Someshwara. He, however,
forbore from doing so. On his death a bitter rivalry broke out
between the two brothers, and Vikramaditya repaired to Virarajendra's camp at Kudal Sangam and obtained his promise
of help against Someshwara. To seal the promise Virarajendra
gave Vikramaditya his daughter in marriage. At the same
time he invaded the Chalukya country and burnt Kampili.
But before he could achieve any decisive success, Virarajendra
fell ill and died. Prince Vikramaditya, having lost his father-
in-law, counted on the support of Virarajendra's son Adhiraja,
his own brother-in-law. But there now appeared as the latter's
rival Prince Kullottunga. He had, as I have said, been forced
by Virarajendra to give up his throne to his uncle Vijayaditya.

But the hour of his revenge had now struck and he pretended to the Chola throne as the grandson of Rajraja the Great. He had behind him an army with which he had recently harried Malwa. With its help, and in spite of Vikramaditya, Kullottunga deposed his cousin Adhiraja. At the same time he deposed Vijayaditya, and at one time became king both of the Cholas and of the Eastern Chalukyas. Vikramaditya was now in dire peril. He extricated himself with skill. He affected to be reconciled to his brother Someshwara II and for some time he lived with him on the best of terms. But Someshwara's incapacity alienated the governors of several of his provinces, and these Vikramaditya won over to his side. Among them were Seuna Chandra Yadava, the governor of north-west Maharashtra, Achugi II, the Sinda chief of Yelburga, and Ereyanga Hoysala, the viceroy of Gangavadi.

In A.D. 1076 Kullottunga invaded the Chalukya kingdom. When Someshwara II marched to meet him, the Chalukya army revolted to Vikramaditya. The latter then deposed his elder brother, and as Vikramaditya II became king in his stead. He proved a most capable monarch and at once took steps to repulse Kullottunga's invasion. The war lasted for four years without any decisive result. In A.D. 1080, the two kings made peace, but some years later the successful treason of Vikramaditya II tempted his younger brother Jayasinha to rebel in his turn. Jayasinha was at the time viceroy of Banavasi and received support from the Chola king. But Vikramaditya II attacked and defeated Jayasinha on the banks of the Krishna. Jayasinha fled but was afterwards caught skulking in a forest. He was brought to Vikramaditya II, who spared his life but no doubt imprisoned him. Vikramaditya II had thereafter a long and prosperous reign, which in all lasted fifty years. At his court lived the renowned Vidnyaneshwara, the author of the *Mitakshara*, still the chief authority on Hindu law in Maharashtra. When he had completed his work he sang in several stanzas the splendour of the town where he had worked, the glory of the king whose bounty had fed him and above all his own transcendent merits. I quote the following stanza as a sample :—

> " On the surface of the Earth there was not, there is not and there never will be a town like Kalyana ; never was a monarch like the prosperous Vikramarka (Vikramaditya) seen or heard of and what more ? Vidnyaneshwara, the Pandit, does not bear comparison with any other. May this triad which is like a celestial creeper exist to the end of this Kalpa."

Kullottunga died in A.D. 1118. It is probable that his end was hastened by the severe defeat of his army by the Chalukya viceroy of Gangavadi, Bitti Deva Hoysala. During the early troubles of Vikramaditya's reign, the Cholas had gained a firm footing in Gangavadi. But in A.D. 1116, Bitti Deva Hoysala attacked them and drove them to the east of the Kaveri. Vikramaditya II survived his great rival more than eight years, dying in A.D. 1127. He was succeeded by his son Someshwara III, who assumed the title of Bhulokamala, or Lord of the dwellers upon the earth. He reigned only eleven years, but in that time he won a reputation for learning not wholly undeserved. A work of the royal author, *Abhilashitartha Chintamani*, has survived to the present day. In five parts are described the tasks and duties of kingship. The first part instructs the pretender how to acquire a kingdom. The second part teaches him how to keep it. The third, fourth and fifth parts indicate the pleasures in which a king may indulge without detriment to himself or his kingdom. Under cover of these themes the learned author touched on astronomy, astrology, rhetoric, poetry, music, painting, architecture and medicine. And his wondering subjects gave him yet another title, that of Sarvadnya Bhupa, or the king who knows everything.

Someshwara III died in A.D. 1138. His son Jagadekamala succeeded him and reigned for twelve years. He was followed on the throne by his brother Tailapa II. In the reign of this king the power of the later Chalukyas fell to pieces. The cause of the decay can be traced to the treason of Vikramaditya II. Having made the viceroys of Someshwara II his fellow conspirators, he suffered them to become all but independent chiefs. After Vikramaditya's death they paid merely a nominal homage to his successors. But even that was now denied by one Vijjala, the viceroy of Banavasi. Profiting by a success gained against a frontier tribe, the Kakatiyas of Warangal, Vijjala made himself war-minister and commander-in-chief. He next imprisoned his master. Tailapa II escaped and took shelter with the chief of the Sindas (A.D. 1150).*

Vijjala then proclaimed himself king of the Chalukya dominions. But his rule was not destined to endure. It fell to a religious revolution. A certain Brahman called Basava Madhiraja attracted Vijjala's notice through the beauty of his sister Padmavati. Vijjala appointed him his first minister. But Basava gave offence to his master, who was a Jain, by founding the Lingayat religion. Eventually Vijjala dismissed his minister ; but the latter took up arms and supported by his followers defeated Vijjala and put him to death. Vijjala's son Sovideva avenged his father : having routed Basava, he pursued him to a place called Ulavi on the Malabar coast. There Basava committed suicide. His nephew Chenna Basava came to terms with Sovideva, but the revolt gave an opportunity to Someshwara IV, the son of Tailapa II, to restore the Chalukya power.

Someshwara IV striking northwards with the aid of a skilful general named Bomma recovered the southern part of his father's kingdom. Over this he ruled until A.D. 1189, when a fresh revolution drove him to take shelter somewhere on the south-western frontier of his father's dominions. Thereafter he disappeared. A general scramble for the Chalukya empire ensued. From this confusion merged the two great viceregal families, the Yadavas and the Hoysalas. To the Kakatiyas of Warangal fell also a certain share of the spoils.

---

* *Ancient India*, p. 248.

CHAPTER V

THE YADAVAS OF DEVAGIRI

A.D. 1189 TO 1294

BOTH Yadavas and Hoysalas claimed most ancient pedigrees. The Yadavas asserted their descent from no less an ancestor than Vishnu's eighth incarnation, King Krishna of Dwarka. The Hoysalas maintained that the founder of their line was one Sala, who saved a Jain saint from a tiger. The Jain was sitting in a village temple, when a tiger rushed at him. In despair the saint called to Sala, who was standing by, " Poy, Sala " (Strike, Sala). Sala ran to his help, and killing the monster with a single blow of his walking-stick, assumed the name of Poysala to commemorate the event. In course of time Poysala was corrupted into Hoysala.* The historian, however, will be content to trace both families to the two great viceroys who assisted Vikramaditya II to usurp the Chalukya throne. At that time the governor of the districts between the upper reaches of the Krishna and the lower course of the Tapti was Seuna Chandra Yadava. The governor of Gangavadi, taken by Ahavamala from the Cholas, was Ereyanga Hoysala. Their defection ensured Vikramaditya's success. During the long reign of Vikramaditya II, the Hoysalas rose rapidly to power and Ereyanga's grandson Bitti Deva† actually rebelled against Vikramaditya II. He suffered defeat but found compensation in the victorious campaign against Kullottunga already mentioned. By A.D. 1130 he had made himself master of all modern Mysore and of Hangal and Lakshmeshwar in the Dharwar district. In A.D. 1138 upon the death of Someshwara III, he again rebelled, but was foiled by the loyalty of the other great viceroys. In A.D. 1141 Bitti Deva died and was succeeded

---

* *Ancient India*, p. 228.
† He is also known as Vishnu Vardan : *Ancient India*, p. 235.

by his son Narsinha, who held his own against the usurper Vijjala. Narsinha died in A.D. 1173 and was followed by his son Vira Ballala. This vigorous prince ruled until A.D. 1220. He was at first defeated by Bomma when that general in A.D. 1183 restored Someshwara IV to the Chalukya throne. But when the revolution of A.D. 1189 broke out, Vira Ballala had his revenge. He defeated Bomma and drove his army across the Krishna.

While the power of the Hoysalas was growing in the south, that of the Yadavas was rising with equal rapidity in the north. Seuna Chandra Yadava was the life-long and trusted friend of Vikramaditya II and left to his son Parammadeva an hereditary viceroyalty. Parammadeva and his successors remained loyal to the Chalukya kings until the usurpation of Vijjala (A.D. 1187). They then began to regard themselves as independent, and when Someshwara IV tried to recover the Chalukya kingdom Billama Yadava, the then chief of the Yadavas, successfully opposed him. When Vira Ballala finally defeated the Chalukya general Bomma, Billama Yadava seized the whole country north of the Krishna and had himself formally crowned king in his capital town Devagiri (A.D. 1191).

The frontiers of the rival viceroys now met, and a struggle between them was inevitable. At first the Hoysalas were successful. In A.D. 1192 Vira Ballala won a decisive victory at Lakhundi in Dharwar. Billama was succeeded by his son, Jaitrapala, who won some petty campaigns against the Kakatiyas of Warangal. But it was Singhana, Jaitrapala's* son and successor, who raised the Yadava dynasty to its greatest power (A.D. 1210). He successfully invaded Malwa and Guzarat and conquered all the lower Konkan and the South Maratha country from the Hoysala chiefs ; and European officials will read with interest that he was one of the first patrons of their health resort Mahableshwar. Singhana's† long and successful reign

---

* Mukandraj, the first Marathi poet, lived in the reign of Jaitrapala I.

† Singhana founded Shingnapur, the famous shrine of Mahadeva, a family god of the Bhosles. In his reign, Sarangdhar wrote the Sanskrit work on music *Sangitratnakar*. The country of the Yadavas was known as Seuna Desh, from the founder of the dynasty, Seuna Chandra.

lasted until A.D. 1247, when he was followed by his grandson
Krishna II. The inscriptions claim for him that he defeated
the Hoysalas, the Gurjaras and the king of Malwa. He died in
A.D. 1260, leaving the throne to his brother Mahadeva. The
latter's greatest success was his reduction of the northern
Konkan, where a chief named Someshwara had made himself
independent. Mahadeva invaded his country with a large
force of elephants. His tactics were successful, and Someshwaia,
driven from the land sought refuge in his fleet. But Mahadeva's
navy pursued him and destroyed his ships. In this disastrous
naval action Someshwara was drowned.

In A.D. 1271, there ascended to the Yadava throne Rama-
dev, the son of Krishna, and the nephew of Mahadeva. A melancholy interest attaches to his name as the last great chief of the
Yadava dynasty. His early years were prosperous enough.
His armies invaded both Malwa and Mysore and he was un-
questionably the greatest king in Peninsular India. A hectic
splendour, too, illuminated his reign. In it flourished the
minister Hemadri or Hemadpant. In it also appeared Dnyandev, the first of the great Maratha poets of the Pandharpur
school. The former of these is the hero of many stories still
current among the Marathas. One legend relates that Bibhishan,
a demon subject of King Ravana of Ceylon, the ravisher of Sita,
had flown over to India. In order to rest himself, he took off
his turban and placed it by his side. Soon afterwards Hemadpant chanced to pass by. He saw the demon's gigantic turban
and thinking it a couch flung himself upon it and was soon
asleep also. The demon rose first and without noticing the
slumbering Hemadpant replaced the turban on his own head.
Then soaring in the air, he flew back to Ceylon to report his
observations to his royal master. When the unhappy Hemadpant awoke, he found himself travelling through the air at a
prodigious speed. He wisely held his tongue and tightened
his grip on the turban. When the demon reached the shore
of the great southern island he again removed his turban to cool
himself after his long flight. As he laid it down he noticed the
cowering Hemadpant. The demon asked his unwilling prisoner

how he had come there. Hemadpant explained and prayed for mercy. The demon granted Hemadpant his life. Hemadpant, growing bolder, asked for a parting present. The demon gave him a seed of jowari or Indian corn. From this one seed were to spring the mighty jowari harvests that are gathered by millions of peasants every Indian winter. Hemadpant, however, did not appreciate its value and asked for further gifts. The demon gave him two more. The first was a bug, the progenitor of the countless myriads that have ever since been the plague of Indian beds. The second was the Modi alphabet. From this legend we can, I think, surmise that Hemadpant encouraged to the utmost of his powers Deccan agriculture. He may possibly have cleared tracts of forest land to widen its area. We may also perhaps guess that about this time Modi writing began to be used in Marathi correspondence. Hemadpant's fame does not rest on this single voyage. He is supposed to have invented the style of architecture known as the Hemadpanti; and many a ruined temple in country villages is said to have been built under the great minister's superintendence. Architect, traveller and counsellor of King Ramadeva,* Hemadpant still found time to reduce to writing the ancient religious practices and ceremonials that had been handed down by countless generations and the principles of medicine as then understood. The *Chaturvarga-chintamani* and the *Ayurveda-rasayana* survive to-day to prove how the busiest of men occupied his leisure.†

For twenty-three years Ramadeva had ruled prosperously. The valour of his armies guarded his far-flung frontier. The wisdom of Hemadpant secured the prosperity of his subjects and filled the treasury of the monarch. The poet Dnyandev wrote of King Ramadeva as the 'dispenser of justice' and the ' abode of all arts.' But the time was at hand when he and his people were to drink to the dregs the cup of defeat and humiliation.

* In A. D. 1271 Ramadeva gave 3 villages to 71 Brahmans. The conditions of the gift were that the Brahmans must live in the villages, must not mortgage them, must not entertain concubines, nor gamble, nor carry arms. They should spend their whole time in religious duties.

† **Hemadri** also wrote the *Rajaprashashti*, a history of the Yadava family: Sardesai, *Marathi Riyasat.*

In the year A.D. 1294 amid a profound peace a mob of terrified peasants brought word to the king, as he sat·in his doomed city, that an Afghan army was advancing towards it by forced marches.   At its head rode Ala-ud-din, the nephew of Jalal-ud-din Firoz Khilji, emperor of Delhi.

CHAPTER VI

THE AFGHAN CONQUEST OF THE DECCAN

ACCORDING to Ferishta, the Khilji Afghans were descended from Kalij Khan, the son-in-law of Jenghiz Khan, the Moghul conqueror. The author of the *Seljuknama* traces their descent from one Khulich, the son of Turk, the grandson of Japhet and the great-grandson of Noah. Whatever his descent, Jalal-ud-din Firoz was early in the Emperor Kaikobad's reign made governor of Samana. Summoned by Kaikobad to help him overthrow his minister, Jalal-ud-din by a succession of skilful villainies made himself supreme ; he had Kaikobad removed and in A.D. 1288 mounted in his master's stead the throne of Delhi. The new emperor had two sons and two nephews. All were able, daring men. But the ablest and the most daring was the emperor's elder nephew Ala-ud-din. And Jalal-ud-din regarded this resolute prince as the main support of the new monarchy. He bestowed on Ala-ud-din the hand of his daughter and the governments of Bengal and of Oudh. But if Ala-ud-din won the favour of his uncle, he failed completely to win the love of his wife. The quarrels of the princess with her husband were artfully fomented by the Empress Malika Jehan, who had guessed the treacherous and ambitious aims of her nephew. At last Ala-ud-din resolved to rid himself by one stroke of all his enemies. He asked for and obtained leave to attack Chanderi, a Rajput fortress to the west of Central India, and about 100 miles north of the Vindhya Mountains. His real design was to attack Ramadeva Yadava. In the course of a Central Indian campaign, Ala-ud-din had heard stories of the great wealth accumulated at Devagiri. If he could but seize it, he could return to Delhi as a pretender to his uncle's throne. With

8000 horse Ala-ud-din at first marched west towards Chanderi.
When he had nearly reached it, he suddenly changed his direction
and marched southwards through the Vindhyas and the Satpuras
until he reached Ellichpur, the largest northern town in the
Yadava dominion. There he lulled all suspicions by declaring
that he had quarrelled with his uncle and meant to offer his
sword to the Raja of Rajamandri, that is to say to the Eastern
Chalukya prince, who still ruled at Vengi as a vassal of the
Yadava kings. The credulous Hindus believed Ala-ud-din and
let him rest his troops close to their city. After a few days
Ala-ud-din struck his tents and pressed on by forced marches
towards Devagiri.

It was the news of this advance that the terrified
peasants announced to Ramadeva. The Yadava king
was taken completely by surprise. Ramadeva's ·eldest son
Shankardeva was with his mother on a pilgrimage. The king,
however, did not despair. He gathered together 3000 or 4000
men and occupied a position four miles in front of the capital.
Here he was defeated and driven with his troops into the citadel
inside the town. Ala-ud-din now entered Devagiri. Delighted
with the success of his first stratagem, he tried a second one. He
had only 8000 men, he said, but close behind him was following
the main army of Jalal-ud-din. It was 20,000 strong and
would overwhelm the whole country. The Marathas were again
deceived. The king's vassals, instead of obeying Ramadeva's
summons for help, fled to fortify their own strongholds against
Jalal-ud-din's arrival. Ramadeva in despair offered Ala-ud-din
fifty maunds of gold and a quantity of pearls and jewels if he
would return to Delhi. The prince, aware that his communications were long and perilous, agreed to the ransom and prepared to retrace his steps. But the king's son Shankardeva,
anxious to help his father, added to his misfortunes. He collected a large Maratha force and led it to Devagiri. A battle
took place a few miles from the city. The Hindus outnumbered
the Afghans by three to one, but Ala-ud-din's stratagem won him
the day. He had left 1000 troops under one Malik Nasrat
to attack Ramadeva if he sallied from Devagiri. At a critical

moment Malik Nasrat left his post and advanced to Ala-ud-din's
help. With great presence of mind, Ala-ud-din ordered his
men to call out that the Delhi army had arrived. The dust
hid the smallness of Malik Nasrat's force. A panic seized the
Maratha army. It fled in every direction, leaving the unhappy
king to defend as best he could his invested stronghold. At
first Ramadeva hoped to hold it until help came from his
southern feudatories and allies. His garrison, when retreating,
had taken with them a vast quantity of bags and stored them
in the citadel. Some Konkan traders had brought them into
Devagiri and the garrison believed them to contain grain.
Ramadeva relying on this great store of provisions sent messengers to all parts of southern India asking for help. After they
had left, Ramadeva opened the bags to make an inventory
of their contents. Then for the first time he learnt that they
were filled with salt. The situation was now hopeless and
Ramadeva reopened negotiations with Ala-ud-din. The prince
was shrewd enough to guess that the garrison were hard pressed
and put every obstacle in the way of a settlement. At last,
when the garrison were almost starved to death, he demanded
as his peace terms the cession of Ellichpur and its dependencies
and a ransom of 600 maunds of gold, 2 maunds of diamonds,
rubies, pearls, emeralds and sapphires, 1000 maunds of silver,
and 4000 pieces of silk. The king had no alternative but to
comply; and on the twenty-fifth day after Ala-ud-din's arrival
at Devagiri, he started homewards, taking with him the accumulated treasures of the Yadavas.

With incomparable skill, the prince retreated through
Central India to Bengal. He had been absent from his
government for six months and had ceased to correspond
with the Delhi secretariat. At first Jalal-ud-din suspected
treason. But when news reached him from private sources
that his nephew had seized at Devagiri a fabulous treasure,
the emperor passed from suspicion to transports of delight. He regarded the spoils of the campaign as already his.
Ala-ud-din, however, had now in his hands the weapon which he
had set forth to seek. With all speed he made himself secure

in his provinces of Oudh and Bengal. Next he sent his younger
brother, Almas Beg, to remove, if he could, all doubts from his
uncle's mind. Almas Beg had talents but little inferior to
those of Ala-ud-din. He depicted his brother as torn by remorse.
He had been guilty of disobedience. Without the emperor's
leave he had raided Devagiri. And nothing less than the sight
of his uncle's face and the sound of his beloved voice conferring
pardon would save Ala-ud-din from the crime of self-destruc-
tion. The emperor bade Almas Beg invite Ala-ud-din to court
with every assurance of his forgiveness. Almas Beg pleaded
that his brother dared not go to Delhi. His enemies at court
had his uncle's ear and his arrival would be followed at once
by his execution. Let the emperor come himself to Karra,
the capital of the Oudh province, and there comfort and forgive
his unworthy nephew. The emperor's household warned him
against the folly of such a course. But the ready wit and the
silver speech of Almas Beg baffled the friends of Jalal-ud-din.
The credulous old man went with Almas Beg to the Oudh
frontier. There he was induced to go unarmed and unescorted
to meet Ala-ud-din. The uncle embraced his nephew and
freely pardoned him. A moment later Jalal-ud-din was stabbed
and his head struck off. Malika Jehan, on the news of her
husband's death, tried to oppose the accession of his murderer.
But Ala-ud-din distributed a share of his treasures among
his soldiers and slung gold balls among the villagers, as he
advanced on Delhi. A few weeks later Ala-ud-din was emperor
and with the exception of Almas Beg the whole household of
Jalal-ud-din Khilji had been confined or assassinated (A.D.1296).

Upon the retreat of Ala-ud-din, Ramadeva set himself to
restore, as best he could, prosperity to his ruined capital. It was
not, however, likely that the new emperor would forget the adventure of the prince. In A.D. 1306, ten years after his accession,
he determined to reduce Devagiri to vassalage. The ostensible
motive of the expedition was the failure of Ramadeva to pay
tribute. But to it was added another and a more romantic
one. At the beginning of Ala-ud-din's reign there ruled in
Guzarat a Waghela Rajput called Karan, but nicknamed Ghelo,

or the Rash.* He had a prime minister called Madhava, whose talents, indeed, had raised Karan to the throne. Unhappily for both king and people Madhava had a beautiful wife, Rup-sundari. Karan fell in love with her, and taking advantage of Madhava's momentary absence from Anhilwad Patan, the capital, sent an armed force to seize her.† A fight ensued and in it the minister's brother fell. His widow thereupon resolved to die a *sati*. Before she entered the flames she called down a fearful curse on the king and on the city. The king, so prophesied the *sati*, would be driven from his kingdom by the barbarian. His wife and his daughter would be torn from him and he himself would die a homeless wanderer. When Madhava came back to Anhilwad Patan he found his home ruined. Hearing of the *sati's* curse he fled to Delhi, that he might secure its fulfilment. He obtained an interview with Ala-ud-din and told his tale. The emperor, delighted with the pretext, sent his brother Almas Beg, now exalted by the title of Alaf Khan, to subdue Guzarat. The duty was well performed. Karan Ghelo was defeated. Anhilwad Patan fell. The chief queen, Kamaladevi, was taken and was sent to Delhi to be the concubine of Ala-ud-din. Karan Ghelo fled with his daughter to the court of Ramadeva Yadava, who gave him for his resi-dence Baglan, a fort in the Nasik district. The beauty and birth of Kamaladevi won her the favour of Ala-ud-din and in course of time she grew reconciled to her lot. One thing, however, was needed to make her happiness complete and that was the company of her daughter. She told this to the emperor, who had also learnt with indignation that Ramadeva had sheltered Karan Ghelo. He equipped an army of 100,000 men, over which he placed a favourite eunuch named Malik Kafir. At the same time he issued orders to Alaf Khan to advance on Devagiri from Guzarat. On the way he was to take Baglan and to secure if possible Karan Ghelo's daughter. The latter, Devaldevi by name, was four years old at the time of her father's

---

* The literal meaning of Ghelo is mad. But Karan was rash rather than mad.

† The full story is admirably told in the famous Guzarati novel *Karan Ghelo* by the late Mr. Nanda Shankar.

flight and had now grown into a beautiful maid of fourteen. Ramadeva had asked Karan Ghelo to give her in marriage to Shankardeva his son. But the Rajput king, although in exile, had yet deemed his lineage too high to give his daughter to a Yadava of Devagiri. An envoy sent by Alaf Khan, who demanded the surrender of Devaldevi for Ala-ud-din's harem, caused Karan to change his mind. And he resolved to marry her to a Maratha prince, rather than prostitute her to a barbarian emperor. He refused Alaf Khan's demand and held Baglan as long as he could against the Afghan army. For two months his resistance was successful. Famine at last forced him to leave his stronghold. He fell back with his troops on Devagiri, followed by Alaf Khan. As he retreated, Karan sent a body of horse by a separate route to convey Devaldevi to the arms of the young Maratha. The plan would have succeeded but for unforeseen ill fortune. Alaf Khan pursued Karan's troops to a day's march from Devagiri, when in despair at Devaldevi's escape he called a two days' halt. During the halt three hundred Afghans, unknown to Alaf Khan, slipped out of camp to visit the Ellora caves. As they started homewards, they saw some Hindu cavalry across their way. The Afghans, flushed with success, attacked and soon dispersed them. As the conquerors fought over the women whom the fugitives had left behind, they learnt that one was no other than the beautiful Devaldevi. Overjoyed they took her to Alaf Khan, who at once took her to Delhi. A few weeks after her arrival, the emperor's son Khizr Khan, won by her beauty, obtained her in marriage, and the devotion of her husband and the triumph of her own charms led her to forget the absence of her father and the miseries of her country.

Malik Kafir with the main Afghan army drove back the Maratha forces until he reached Devagiri. Ramadeva saw that further resistance was hopeless. He beat a parley, and presenting himself at Malik Kafir's camp, offered to pay full arrears of tribute and an ample indemnity. The offer was accepted and Ramadeva not long afterwards visited Ala-ud-din at Delhi. There the new vassal was received with great honour. The

title of Ray-i-Rayan or Hindu King of Kings was conferred on
him, and in return for his homage, he was permitted not only
to retain Devagiri but to govern Navasari, a district on the
seacoast of Guzarat (A.D. 1308).   The following year Malik
Kafir passed by Devagiri to plunder the Kakatiyas of Warangal.
Ala-ud-din had already tried to reduce them from a base in
Bengal.   But the expedition had failed, and to Malik Kafir was
committed the task of retrieving the glory of the Delhi arms.
Ramadeva received and obeyed the command to aid Malik
Kafir as a subordinate ally.   Attacked both by the Musulman
general and the Yadava king, the Raja of Warangal yet made a
stout defence.   It was only after a siege of several months that
he opened negotiations.   Malik Kafir was not unwilling to
accept terms.   His losses had been severe ; Ramadeva's loyalty
hung on events ; and accepting 300 elephants, 7000 horses and
a large store of money and jewels Malik Kafir returned in
triumph to Delhi.

The year A.D. 1310 saw the downfall of the Hoysalas.   They
had been pressed southwards by the later Yadava kings but
they still ruled the larger portion of the present Mysore State,
and their capital was Dwara Samudra.*   Legends of their
wealth were current in Delhi and Ala-ud-din bade Malik Kafir
plunder them as he had plundered the Yadavas.   On the way
from Delhi Malik Kafir again halted at Devagiri.   But in the
course of the preceding year (A.D. 1309) Ramadeva had died
and his son Shankardeva sat on the throne of the Yadavas.   The
memory of Devaldevi made him less pliant than his father.
He refused either help or supplies.   Nevertheless he did not
openly attack Malik Kafir.   The latter, leaving a force to watch
Devagiri, attacked with his main army the Hoysalas.   They
offered a poor resistance, and with a vast store of fresh booty
Malik Kafir returned northwards.   The news however of
Shankardeva's conduct kindled resentment in Ala-ud-din,
which was heightened by his subsequent behaviour.   After the
Delhi army had retired, Shankardeva withheld his tribute.
Malik Kafir once more invaded the Deccan, stormed Devagiri

---

* The modern Halebid.

and beheaded Shankardeva (A.D. 1312). Then laying waste
Maharashtra he swept through the whole of southern India.
All the old southern thrones, those of the Pallavas, Cholas,
Pandyas and Cheras toppled over one after the other until at
last the triumphant general rested to erect a mosque at Rameshwaram. With the booty of the conquered peoples Malik Kafir
was returning to Delhi, when he received an urgent summons
from Ala-ud-din. Drink and lust, war and intrigue had worn
out the iron constitution of the great emperor. Khizr Khan,
on whom he had bestowed Devaldevi, neglected his father. In
the loneliness of age and ill-health, Ala-ud-din summoned Malik
Kafir to his side. He was the one person whom the emperor
trusted and he betrayed the trust with the basest ingratitude.
On reaching Delhi, he at once began to plot the extermination
of the whole Khilji house. Alaf Khan, the brother who had
helped Ala-ud-din to the throne, was long dead ; and the arts
of Malik Kafir led Ala-ud-din to believe that his sons, Khizr
Khan and Shadi Khan, were concerned with the queen's relatives in a treasonable scheme. At the same time news came that
Guzarat, Rajputana and the Deccan had revolted. Malik Kafir
laid the blame on the conspirators. The queen and her sons
were arrested. Her kinsmen were beheaded and the emperor,
isolated from his kinsmen, soon died of a poisoned meal prepared
for him by Malik Kafir (A.D. 1316). On the emperor's death
Malik Kafir put out the eyes of Khizr Khan and Shadi Khan,
arrested Ala-ud-din's fourth son Mubarak Khan, and placing
Ala-ud-din's youngest son Umar Khan, then aged seven, on the
throne, began to govern in his name. It now seemed that the
new Sejanus, more fortunate than his Roman prototype, had
brought his schemes to a happy issue. But at the very moment
of success, his good fortune left him. One night he sent a band
of assassins to kill Mubarak Khan. The latter happened to
wear round his neck a string of jewels. With it he ransomed
his life. The assassins, fearing punishment for their neglect
of duty, sought out Malik Mashir, the captain of the guards and
a devoted servant of the dead emperor. Prompt in action,
Malik Mashir rushed with his men into Malik Kafir's room, and

killing him together with a number of other eunuchs privy to his schemes, placed Mubarak Khan on the throne of Delhi.

The new emperor, who was not without ability, at once planned the subjugation of the revolted provinces. In A.D. 1317 Mubarak's general Ain-ul-Mulk reduced Rajputana and Guzarat. In A.D. 1318 Mubarak himself undertook the recovery of the Deccan. Upon Malik Kafir's departure, Harpaldeva, a Yadava noble, who had married Ramadeva's daughter, led on her behalf a rebellion. With the aid of the neighbouring chiefs, he overcame most of the Musulman garrisons and for over a year ruled Maharashtra. But on Mubarak's advance Harpaldeva's allies deserted him. He himself fled, panic-stricken towards the western hills. Before he could reach them, a body of Musulman horse overtook him and brought him into Mubarak's presence. He ordered Harpaldeva to be flayed alive. After death his head was cut off and fixed over the main gate of Devagiri. The rebellion once crushed, the emperor took steps to prevent its recurrence. He built a chain of forts from the Vindhya Mountains to Dwara Samudra. And for more than three hundred years the Maratha people dwelt beneath the rule of Musulman kings.

CHAPTER VII

THE DECCAN UNDER DELHI AND THE RISE OF VIJAYANAGAR

A.D. 1316 TO 1351

THE history of Maharashtra from the time of its conquest to that of the Bahmani revolution is the history of the Delhi empire of which it formed a part. The Emperor Mubarak, after he had reduced the Deccan, believed that his duties were over and that he might pass the rest of his life in vice and pleasure. His natural ability was soon extinguished, and misgovernment produced rebellion. His cousin Malik Asad Uddin was the first to plot against the throne. The plot was discovered and Asad Uddin executed. With him perished the emperor's blind brothers, Khizr Khan and Shadi Khan, as well as Umar Khan, the unhappy child on whose head Malik Kafir's treason had for a moment placed a crown. The beautiful Devaldevi was torn from Khizr Khan and carried to Mubarak's harem. Disgusted with the treachery of his relatives, Mubarak gave his entire confidence to one Hasan, a converted sweeper, on whom he bestowed the title of Malik Khusru. The new favourite repeated the tactics of Malik Kafir and penetrating to the extreme south brought back 120 elephants and a great store of jewels and gold. His success led Malik Khusru to plan a rebellion in the Deccan. Failing to win over the other imperial officers, he tried to destroy them. The scheme failed and Malik Khusru was sent in chains to Delhi. But such was the dexterity of the low-born adventurer, that he turned the tables on his accusers and induced the emperor to believe that they and not he were guilty. The imperial officers were disgraced and their estates confiscated. The graceless low-caste now persuaded Mubarak that the sweeper caste was the only one in which trust could be placed. With the emperor's leave he summoned twenty thousand of them to Delhi. With their aid Malik Khusru plotted his master's destruction. It was in vain that Mubarak's tutor Zia-ud-din warned his former pupil. Mubarak's ears were deaf to all remonstrances. The same night both tutor and emperor were assassinated by Malik Khusru and for the first and last time in history the crown of Delhi was worn by a sweeper. The new sovereign distributed the ladies of Mubarak's harem among his fellow caste-men, reserving Devaldevi for himself. The mere touch of such a wretch was worse than death to a high-born Rajput lady. And in Malik Khusru's embraces the unhappy princess more than expiated her father's crime and fulfilled to the uttermost the curse of the *sati*.

The rule of the new emperor, detested as a traitor by Musulmans and as a low-caste by Hindus, was not destined to endure. On the marches of Afghanistan lived a veteran named Ghazi Beg Tughlak. His father was a Turkish slave of the Emperor Ghyas-ud-din Balban. His mother was a Jat woman of Lahore. From early youth to mature manhood the life of Ghazi Beg Tughlak had been spent in the camp and on the battlefield. His courage and talents had raised him from the rank of sepoy to that of warden of the marches. In this high office he fought and won twenty-nine pitched battles against the Tartar hordes, who looked longingly towards the rich plains of India. And with a just pride he raised at Multan a mosque on which he inscribed the tale of his triumphs. When the news of Mubarak's death reached Ghazi Beg, he struck his camp and set out at once for Delhi. Malik Khusru and his caste-men defended the approaches of the capital with the courage of despair. But the skill of Ghazi Beg and the valour of his veterans overcame their resistance. Malik Khusru fled the field only to be taken and slaughtered; and Ghazi Beg entered Delhi in triumph. When he reached the gate he asked, with feigned humility, whether any yet lived of the house of Ala-ud-din. If any such still survived, let him be brought forward and placed on the throne. The crowd shouted that all had perished. Even yet the conqueror feigned aversion from the crown. "Then, O people of Delhi," he cried, "choose ye among the nobles of the empire the most

4

worthy to succeed and I swear that I shall abide by your choice."
The mob thundered in answer the name of Ghazi Beg Tughlak,
and lifting him in their arms, they hailed him as Shah Jehan,
or sovereign of the universe. Ghazi Beg accepted the crown
but refused the title. Custom, however, required some change
of name. In memory possibly of his father's master, Ghyas-ud-
din Balban, he called himself Ghyas-ud-din Tughlak. And on
August 23, A.D. 1321 he became emperor of Delhi.

The new monarch's vigour soon restored order in Hindustan.
Near Kabul he built a chain of forts which during his reign
closed firmly the northern passes. He sent his eldest son Alaf
Khan to subdue the Raja of Warangal, who in the recent
tumults had withheld his tribute. Alaf Khan attacked Warangal
from Devagiri. But the campaign failed. The Kakatiya Raja,
Pratap Rudradeva II, defended his town with spirit. The hot
winds destroyed the health of the besiegers. At last a report
spread that the emperor was dead and that a revolution had
broken out at the capital. Believing the report true, several
officers deserted with their commands. The prince took alarm
and retreated with all haste. But so severe were the losses
in the attack and retreat that of the whole army only 3000
returned to Devagiri. There Alaf Khan found the report to be
false and enquired into the conduct of his faithless officers.
Two alone survived. The rest had been killed or taken by the
Hindus ; and the two survivors had soon reason to envy the fate
of their comrades. The prince sent them to Delhi. There
Ghyas-ud-din had them buried alive, observing with grim wit
that as they had buried him alive in jest he would bury them
alive in earnest. The emperor placed Alaf Khan in command
of a fresh army. This time the prince took great pains to secure
his communications. Crossing the Godavari at Rakshasabhuvan,
he advanced south-south-east to Bedar. Taking it by storm,
he made it his base and then marched due east on Warangal.
After a prolonged defence Pratap Rudradeva surrendered. He
and his family were sent as prisoners to the emperor and the
Kakatiya country was added to the provinces of Delhi. Ghyas-
ud-din Tughlak now marched in person to subdue Bengal.

There Kana Khan, the nominal viceroy but actual ruler, hastened to submit, and after a short campaign in Tirhut to the south of Nepal, Ghyas-ud-din turned his face homewards. As he neared the capital he met Alaf Khan, who, surrounded by a brilliant array of nobles, waited to congratulate his father. In a handsome wooden structure specially erected by the prince, Ghyas-ud-din held a reception and received the felicitations of his courtiers. When the ceremony was over, the emperor sent for his carriage. The prince and the nobles hastened to leave the building, for it was their duty to guard on horseback Ghyas-ud-din as he entered his vehicle. At last only Ghyas-ud-din Tughlak, his infant son, and five attendants remained inside the temporary palace. The roof suddenly collapsed, destroying in its fall every one beneath it. The emperor died as became the former warden of the marches. His body was found arched across his son's body, whose life he had vainly tried to save. The vulgar invented many causes for the calamity. Elephants, so some said, had pushed down the building from without. Others asserted that the lightning had struck it. Others more ingenious still maintained that Alaf Khan had erected the building by magic and that when he left it, the magic that had supported it left also, and thus it collapsed. But all, save a very few, believed that whatever the immediate cause, the mishap had been contrived by the treachery of Alaf Khan. At one stroke he thus removed the occupant of the throne and his favourite son. And as Mahomed Tughlak, the prince, in A.D. 1325, became emperor of Delhi.

Upon the new sovereign nature had showered with both hands her choicest gifts. In the course of a long reign he met no equal as a captain in the field. But generalship was but one of the varied talents of Mahomed Tughlak. He was deeply versed in Greek logic and Greek philosophy. He had studied profoundly astronomy and mathematics. He knew intimately the Arabic and Persian languages. His speeches and letters were for centuries the wonder and the model of the Delhi secretariat. His Persian verses have been preserved and are still read with pleasure by Persian scholars. Anticipating by 500 years the

British Government, he built hospitals for the sick and alms-houses for widows and orphans. When he mounted the throne the highest hopes were formed of this most eloquent and accomplished prince. But when he died, he had fully earned the name of the most blood-thirsty despot in Indian history.

In the second year of Mahomed Tughlak's reign, he was threatened by a Moghul invasion. But buying it off, he devoted his attention to the subjugation of southern India. And to use Ferishta's phrase, he so subdued Tailangana (another name for Warangal), the southern Konkan and Dwara Samudra, or Mysore, that they might have been villages near Delhi. After this campaign, the emperor subdued eastern Bengal to its farthest frontiers and Oudh to the foot-hills of the Himalayas. But the cost of these wars and the lavish gifts which Mahomed Tughlak bestowed on the learned men of his time exhausted his treasury, already depleted by the ransom paid to the Moghul invaders. The fertile mind of the emperor then conceived a scheme as ingenious and disastrous as any projected by Law or Patterson. He had heard that the Chinese government had from early times issued paper money. He resolved, instead of bank-notes to issue copper coins with the nominal value of gold pieces. But he failed to grasp that the Chinese bank-notes were issued only by the emperor and were really but promissory notes signed by him. Mahomed Tughlak allowed, or at any rate failed to prevent, the bankers of all India from issuing copper tokens as fast as the Delhi mint. The result may easily be imagined. Every tax-payer hastened to pay taxes in the new coinage. Foreign merchants paid their debts with tokens but demanded their dues in gold. At last, when the country was exhausted by this absurd scheme, the emperor conceived another hardly less so. China was a rich country. Its over-flowing treasuries would soon refill his. He must, therefore, conquer it. To realize this wild project 100,000 horse under Khusru Malik, the emperor's nephew, advanced into Nepal. The hardy Nepalese resisted their progress step by step. Never-theless after desperate fighting Khusru Malik reached the fron-tiers of China. There a mighty Chinese force awaited the

attack of his attenuated squadrons.   The general in despair
ordered his troops to retreat.   But neither in attack nor in
flight was there any safety.   The rainy season began.   The
mountain paths became torrents and swept away the Indians'
supplies and baggage trains.   The Chinese harried their rear-
guards.   The mountaineers renewed their attacks and, at last,
of all that host but a few stragglers from the lines of communication returned to tell Mahomed Tughlak the fate of his army.
He at once ordered their execution.

Disgusted with Delhi as the scene of his failures, Mahomed
Tughlak resolved to move the capital thence to Devagiri. From
this new metropolis he hoped to subdue India as far as Cape
Comorin and with the spoils of his foes to restore his own bankrupt finances.   The migration of the court and of the public
offices did not content him.   He ordered the whole Delhi
population to move to Devagiri.   Nor was one single person
permitted to evade the command.   According to the graphic
story of Ibn Batuta, the Imperial police found, on searching Delhi,
but two solitary recusants.   The one was blind and the other
bedridden.   Mahomed Tughlak directed that the former should
be shot to Devagiri by a catapult and that the bedridden man
should be dragged thither by the leg.   A few pieces of the blind
man's flesh and one leg of the bedridden man eventually reached
the new capital. The emperor built a road from Delhi to Devagiri
and endeavoured to distribute food to the travellers on the
way.   Yet even so, half the population died on the road and many
more died on reaching Devagiri.   Nor did the Marathas gain
what the inhabitants of Delhi lost.   The tyrant resolved to make
Devagiri worthy of an emperor's residence ; and as he had no
funds with which to pay workmen he achieved his aim by
forced labour.   By the weary arms of suffering Marathas he built
the fort of Daulatabad on a mass of rock not far from the city.
The perimeter of the fort was 5000 yards.   Galleries ran inside
the stronghold.   It was abundantly supplied with water.   And
the engineers of the time declared it impregnable.   The new
capital completed, Mahomed Tughlak set out to enslave what
still remained free in southern India.   Before he could do so he

had to occupy the great fortress of Kondana, twelve miles from
Poona, of which a romantic tale will be told hereafter. It was
defended for eight months by a Koli chief named Nagnak, who
repulsed all the assaults of the imperial troops. When famine
overcame his resistance, he skilfully evacuated the stronghold.
The emperor returned to Devagiri to recruit his war-worn army.
While they rested he received news that Malik Bairam, viceroy
of the Punjab, had rebelled. The emperor had come to see
that while Devagiri was a good base for the conquest of southern
India, it was dangerously far from his northern possessions.
He therefore bade all his chief officers send as hostages their
families to Devagiri. Malik Bairam hesitated. The imperial
messenger charged him with treason. The indignant viceroy
struck off his accuser's head and then sought safety in the crime
which he had so hotly repudiated. The emperor hastened
to the Punjab and soon defeated and slew his turbulent servant.
He now tried fresh means to replenish his coffers. He increased
so largely the taxes on the fertile tract between the Ganges and
the Jamna that the ruined population burnt their houses and
fled into the woods. Enraged at yet another financial failure,
Mahomed Tughlak organized a hunting party. Surrounding
the woods, he and his guests shot down in hundreds the wretched
tax-payers, as his beaters drove them out of the coverts. Universal terror now led to universal rebellion. The viceroys of
eastern Bengal and the southern Konkan revolted. The
emperor returned to Devagiri and imposed so large a levy on the
surrounding provinces that it also rebelled. His army, however, soon reduced Devagiri to its former slavery and he set out
to restore order in the southern Konkan. On the road a pesti-
lence attacked his troops. Numbers perished and the emperor
himself almost died. On his recovery he gave up the expedition,
and on returning to Delhi he authorised the city's former inhabitants to return there also. A great migration from Devagiri
ensued. But very few of the emigrants reached the land of
their desire. A famine broke out in Central India and as they
passed through the stricken province, they also suffered and fell
by the way-side.

Mahomed Tughlak's mind now conceived a strange explanation of the continual troubles of his reign. They were not, as one or two presumptuous advisers had insinuated, due to his financial schemes or to his cruelties. The real cause was the wrath of God. Although assiduous in his prayers and the builder of many mosques, Mahomed Tughlak had not had his accession confirmed by the Arabian Caliph. A stately embassy, laden with presents, made its way to Arabia and begged that the Caliph would condescend to forgive the past and now proclaim the emperor's accession as lawful and proper. The Caliph graciously consented and sent an envoy with a letter conferring on the emperor what he already possessed. Mahomed Tughlak met the envoy on foot twelve miles from Delhi, placed the Caliph's letter on his head and had it opened and read with the greatest solemnity. He ordered his mosques publicly to degrade all previous emperors (including his own father) who had not received the confirmation of the Caliph. Then he awaited with confidence the dawn of happier times. His hopes were vain and his calamities grew more numerous than ever. About this time Krishnadeva, a relative of Pratap Rudradeva II, the imprisoned Raja of Warangal, escaped captivity and plotted rebellion. To his plot he won over the Raja of Vijayanagar.

The rise of this kingdom is the most interesting and important event of the fourteenth century. To the north of the Tunga-bhadra River stood the fort of Anegundi. Its rulers were the petty chiefs of Kampila, or Kampili, eight miles to the east, who were vassals first of the Chalukyas and then of the Yadavas. In A.D. 1336 Mahomed Tughlak's nephew Bahauddin rebelled, and being defeated, fled from the terrible emperor to the court of Kampila. The Hindu chief received the high-born fugitive with chivalrous courtesy. He entertained him hospitably and refused to surrender him. This brought on the chief the Delhi army. Undaunted, the chief sent Bahauddin under an escort to a neighbouring kingdom and took refuge in his stronghold at Anegundi. Surrounded and famine-stricken, the Raja resolved to die like a Rajput king. He caused a huge fire to be lit. In it his wives and those of his garrison threw themselves. Their honour safe, the Raja and his nobles opened wide the gates and rushing on the besiegers died fighting. The emperor placed as viceroy over Anegundi a Musulman noble named Malik.

But although the prince and his kinsmen had perished, their spirit had survived. Two brothers named Harihar and Bukka, who had served Pratap Rudradeva II, fled when Warangal fell in A.D. 1323 and entered the Kampila service. Their talents attracted the notice of the prince and they respectively rose to be his minister and his treasurer. They survived the sack of Anegundi and afterwards fomented the opposition to Malik's rule, while artfully pretending to be his friends. Through their ingenuity Malik was degraded from the viceregal throne and in his stead Mahomed Tughlak raised Harihar* to be Raja of Kampila. Wisely he withdrew his capital to the southern bank of the Tungabhadra and founded a new city, to which he gave the inspiring name of Vijayanagar, or the city of victory. To it flocked all the brave or broken men of the Deccan, rajas who had lost their kingdoms, barons who had lost their fiefs, devout men who fled from the pollution of the foreigner, fighting men who wished to cross swords once again with the hated invader. The ancient kingdoms of the Cholas and the Pandyas, of the Cheras and of the Pallavas, acknowledged the new king as their suzerain and soon became absorbed in his dominion. Within its frontiers the Hindu races of southern India stood for two and a half centuries heroically at bay. In A.D. 1342 Harihar died. His reign had been peaceful. But his brother and successor Bukka, henceforth known as Bukka Raya, was of a more warlike mould. He seized the chance of using the resources of Vijayanagar on behalf of a kinsman of his former master. He entrusted a force to Krishnadeva, who retook Warangal. Upon this success, the rebellion spread through the entire Deccan ; and in a few months the emperor's sole possession south of the Vindhyas was Devagiri, overawed by the great stronghold of Daulatabad. He sent Kutlugh Khan, his one-time tutor, to recover the Deccan.

---

* See Sewell, *A Forgotten Empire*, Chap. II.

Kutlugh Khan had partially succeeded, when he was recalled to
make way for Ain-ul-mulk, the governor of Oudh. The latter
was a smooth-tongued courtier and a great favourite of the
emperor. He had hoped to secure a high office at Delhi, and
furious at his banishment to a distant province, he rebelled.
A great battle took place on the banks of the Ganges in which
Mahomed Tughlak's valour won the day. Nevertheless he
persisted in his resolve to recall Kutlugh Khan. The latter
dutifully obeyed the order. But directly he had left the Deccan,
rebellion broke out afresh and the emperor's southern dominion
was once more limited to a single city.

He now conceived a new financial scheme. The miseries and
above all the poverty of India were, according to his latest
theory, due to the small area of her cultivation. If this were
extended, the emperor would soon possess a brimming treasury
and rule over a prosperous and obedient people. He, therefore,
chose 100 officers and entrusted to each 60 square miles of
country and bade them cover it with intensive cultivation. He
made large advances to enable them to carry through the plan.
The officers, many of whom knew nothing of farming, failed
completely, and most fled with what remained of their advances.
Their conduct led the emperor to assign another cause to his
troubles. It was not the wrath of God which pursued him.
Misfortunes came because he elevated nobles to high commands.
Born amid wealth and honour, they appreciated but little the
emperor's favours. In future he would bestow the great offices
of state on the low-born only and supported by their gratitude
he would end his days in peace and comfort. In pursuance
of this new plan he appointed Aziz, a liquor seller, to govern
Malwa. The latter began the tenure of his office by treacherously assassinating seventy Musulman nobles at a dinner party.
This act so pleased the emperor that he distributed his governments between Lacchena, a singer, two gardeners named Peru
and Munga, Balu, a weaver and Makhil, a slave. They saw that
Aziz had won his master's approval by assassinating the nobles
in his province. They followed his example ; the result was that
those nobles who escaped summoned their kinsmen, who every-

where revolted. The first to rise were those of Guzarat, where Makhil the slave had been appointed viceroy. Aziz went to Makhil's help, but was defeated and slain. The emperor hastened to Guzarat and, as usual, his talents and vigour crushed the rebellion. He now resolved to assassinate all the leading Musulmans in Devagiri. Makhil the slave was sent to seize them. He did so. On the way northwards they guessed the fate that awaited them and overpowered their guards. Returning to Devagiri they renounced their fealty to Delhi. The emperor marched as was his wont to the storm centre. He defeated the nobles and besieged them in Daulatabad. But in the absence of Mahomed Tughlak, the Guzarat nobles once more took up arms. Almost insane with rage, he raised the siege of Daulatabad and returned to Guzarat. As he did so the peasantry and hillmen harassed severely his retreat. Nothing, however, daunted the courage of the furious emperor. He forced his way into Guzarat, defeated the nobles and drove them into Sind. He followed them across the Indus, determined to extirpate their whole race even if his absence from India cost him his empire. On the way a heavy meal of Indus fish brought on an attack of fever. But even fever failed to stay Mahomed Tughlak. He still pressed on in pursuit of his enemies. But the very violence of his pursuit proved their salvation. The fever, which careful treatment might have cured, rose with neglect. And on March 20, A.D. 1351, Mahomed Tughlak died some 30 miles from Thatta in Sind.

On the emperor's retirement from the Deccan the rebellion of the nobles spread until its repression would have taxed the entire strength of the Delhi empire. Joined by the forces of Warangal and Vijayanagar, they defeated at Bedar the imperial troops marching under Imad-ul-mulk, his son-in-law, to restore order. Imad-ul-mulk perished on the field. The imperial authority gone and the emperor's army destroyed, it only remained for the Deccan nobles to choose a king to reign over them. Their first leader was one Ismail Afghan, who mounted the throne under the title of Nasaruddin. But in the defeat of Imad-ul-mulk a certain Hasan had greatly distinguished

himself. Seeing that his courtiers turned to Hasan rather than
to himself Nasaruddin prudently abdicated in his favour. The
new king had begun life as the servant of one Gangadhar or
Gangu, a Brahman by caste and an astrologer by profession.
The story runs that when Hasan was one day ploughing a piece
of land, lent to him as a reward for good service by his master,
he unearthed a copper vessel containing some gold coins. He
took them to Gangadhar, who, delighted with his servant's
honesty, brought it to the notice of Mahomed Tughlak, then
still Prince Alaf Khan. The latter told his father, who summoned
Hasan to his presence and gave him the command of 100 horse.
Gangadhar then drew Hasan's horoscope and learning from it
his future rise to greatness, made him promise that if ever he
became a king, he would assume the name of Gangu and employ
his former master as his minister of finance. When Mahomed
Tughlak sent Kutlugh Khan to be viceroy of the Deccan, the
latter took Hasan as an officer of his suite. At Devagiri he won
the viceroy's confidence and was one of the leading Deccan nobles
when they renounced their loyalty to Delhi. When Imad-ul-
mulk tried to recover the Deccan, Nasaruddin appointed
Hasan to command the rebel forces. They won the day but
the victory of his commander proved Nasaruddin's ruin. On
his abdication Hasan mounted the vacant throne. In the hour
of his prosperity he remembered his promise to Gangadhar.
He sent for him and gave him the keys of his treasury, and he
had himself crowned under the title of Ala-ud-din Hasan Gangu
Bahmani, thus founding what is known in history as the
Bahmani empire.

CHAPTER VIII

THE BAHMANI KINGDOM

A.D. 1347 to 1526

THE new king of the Deccan was as able a monarch as he had been a subject. His vigorous rule soon restored Musulman authority in the country round Devagiri. Then, finding Devagiri not sufficiently central, he removed his capital to Gulbarga, a town some 20 miles north of the Bhima ; and from that base he reduced the whole country from the Bhima River in the north to the Tungabhadra in the south, and from the fort of Choul in the west to the town of Bedar in the east. Gangadhar, the former master of the new king, proved as capable a treasurer as Hasan proved a sovereign and at no previous time was the Musulman yoke more firmly fastened on Maharashtra than during the reign of this fortunate slave. The latter, however, did not live long to enjoy the fruits of his skill and prudence. In August, 1357, he received an invitation from Prem Rai, a descendant of Karan Ghelo to help him conquer Guzarat. Hasan accepted the invitation. He sent ahead the vanguard of his army under his eldest son, Prince Mahomed. The prince advanced with expedition until he reached the beautiful wooded valley through which winds the Tapti River. An ardent sportsman, he soon forgot in the pursuit of tiger the object of his campaign. He sent such glowing accounts of his trophies that the king pressed forward to join him in the chase. But its fatigues proved too great for a frame exhausted by war, intrigue and government. He contracted malaria and returned to Gulbarga, where he lingered for six months. At last on the point of death he sent for his youngest son Mahmud and asked him to read a passage from the book before him. It was the Bostan, and without

design the boy read from it the words written by Sadi of the
Persian King, Jamshed:

> "I conquered the world by valour and independence, but
> was unable to subdue the power of the grave."

The dying king recognized in the words of the dead poet his
own approaching end. He nominated his eldest son as his
successor, bade his children farewell and a few minutes later
died. He left behind him the name of a loyal friend and a
generous enemy, and the long endurance of Musulman rule in
southern India was due to the care with which Hasan Gangu
laid its foundations (A.D. 1358).

To Hasan succeeded his eldest son Mahomed, who assumed
the title of Mahomed Shah Bahmani I. The beginning of the
new king's reign was troubled by the threats of the Rajas of
Warangal and Vijayanagar, Krishnadeva and Bukka Raya.
They demanded upon pain of war the restitution of all lands
taken from them by Hasan Gangu. Mahomed Shah acted with
prudence. For eighteen months he amused the Hindu ambassadors with promises and negotiations and secretly prepared
his army. When it was ready, he dismissed the envoys, attacked
the allies, and defeating them, forced Bukka Raya to fall back
within his frontiers and Krishnadeva to pay a large ransom
in gold and jewels. A peace ensued which lasted for twelve
years, when it was again disturbed by the Hindus. Vinayakdeva, the son of Krishnadeva, seized some horses destined for
the Bahmani king. The latter with 4000 cavalry hastened
towards Vailam Pillam,* the scene of the offence. He sent on a
few of his troopers disguised as traders, who declared that they
had been pillaged by robbers. The town guards gathered
round them and became so absorbed in the tale, that they did
not observe until too late the advance of the rest of the army.
They then in vain tried to shut the gates. They were cut down,
and in the ensuing confusion the Bahmani troopers took the
town. Vinayakdeva retreated into the citadel. The same
night he fled, but was overtaken and brought before Mahomed
Shah. The king, pleased with his success, had no wish to kill

---

* Haig, *Historical Landmarks of the Deccan*, p. 7.

the prince. But the latter abused his captor with such obscenity that Mahomed Shah's good humour vanished. He had Vinayakdeva's tongue cut out and had him shot from a catapult into a vast bonfire, wherein he was instantly consumed.

For two years Krishnadeva continued the war. Then, unable further to resist, he made a humiliating peace. He ceded Golconda, and a number of elephants and horses, and paid a ransom of 33 lakhs of rupees. When the treaty was signed, the Hindu ambassadors informed the conqueror that if he would bind himself and his successors to respect for ever the frontiers of Warangal, the Raja could make Mahomed Shah a present worthy not only of a king but of an emperor. Mahomed Shah, devoured with curiosity, agreed to a perpetual peace and received his reward. Pratap Rudradeva II had prepared for Mahomed Tughlak a beautiful throne known as the Takhti Firoz, or the throne of azure. It was of solid gold studded with precious gems. Pratap Rudradeva had died before its completion. His kinsman Krishnadeva, a rebel against the emperor, had retained it. He now presented it with all humility to the new suzerain of the south.

The king's next campaign was against Vijayanagar. One evening he sat in his pleasure gardens, listening to a band of musicians as they sang the couplets of Amir Khusru. Pleased with the song and intoxicated with forbidden liquor, he ordered his minister to prepare for the singers a draft on the Vijayanagar treasury. The minister, thinking the order but a drunken man's whim, wrote the draft but did not send it. Next morning, however, the king compelled him to do so. The Raja of Vijayanagar seated the messenger who brought the draft on an ass and sent him home. Knowing that war was now imminent, Bukka Raya made a surprise attack on the fortress of Mudkal in the Doab, the land between the Krishna and Tungabhadra Rivers, and put the garrison to the sword. The Bahmani king, on hearing the news, vowed that he would avenge the disaster by killing 100,000 Hindus. Nor did he fail to keep his vow. The Raja fell back on Adoni, a fortress south of the Tungabhadra. Near that stronghold a battle took place in

which the Hindus were completely defeated. The Musulmans
ravaged the country-side, killing its entire population. Bukka
Raya retreated to Vijayanagar. Mahomed Shah laid siege
to it. But the main Hindu army so harassed his force and
its communications that he had recourse to a stratagem. He
feigned a serious illness and struck his camp. Bukka Raya,
overjoyed, followed him, harassed his retreat and fell into the
Bahmani king's trap. The latter recrossed the Tungabhadra
and halted in a spacious plain. The same night he made a
daring attack on Bukka Raya's camp and killed 10,000 of the
Raja's troops. The latter then sued for peace. It was granted,
but by one of the articles the Raja had to honour the king's
draft and pay the musicians. Except for the revolt of a certain
Bairam Khan which Mahomed Shah suppressed without difficulty, the rest of the king's reign passed in peace. He died in
A.D. 1375 and left behind him the name of a valiant soldier
and a vigorous administrator. But to the Musulman historian[*]
his chief glory lay in his having killed within 17 years no less
than 500,000 Hindus.

Mahomed Shah's son, Mujahid Shah, followed his father on
the throne of Gulbarga. The new king had all the qualities of
a great prince, except the power to control his temper. His
mind was vigorous and highly cultivated. His person was
majestic. And such was his strength that when but fourteen
years old he overcame the greatest wrestlers in his father's
dominions. At his accession he was only nineteen years old
and not unnaturally looked to win glory at the expense of his
neighbours. The Doab served as a pretext. The bulk of it
had been annexed by Mahomed Shah Bahmani. But a few
towns here and there remained in the joint possession of Hindus
and Musulmans. Mujahid Shah sent an envoy to Vijayanagar
with a haughty message. "Joint possession," said the Musulman envoy, "is the fruitful cause of dispute. Let the Raja
of Vijayanagar withdraw his troops to the south of the Tungabhadra, and the two powers will in future live together in amity."
"The whole Doab," replied the indignant chief, "is the country

[*] Ferishta.

of my ancestors. If the barbarian wants peace let him withdraw
his pretensions to all lands south of the Krishna." The envoy
returned to Gulbarga and war ensued. Bukka Raya camped
on the southern bank of the Tungabhadra, intending to await
there the attack of Mujahid Shah. Suddenly a panic spread
among the Hindus. They learnt that Mujahid Shah had in a
recent hunt slain single-handed a tiger. Bukka Raya withdrew
his army into the woods for six months. Mujahid Shah pursued
him and guerilla warfare raged through the Western Ghats and
Kanara jungles. At last Bukka Raya's health suffered so much
that he fell back on Vijayanagar. A battle took place near the
city. Mujahid Shah was victorious but his losses had been so
heavy that he resolved to retreat. He then learnt that his
uncle Daud Shah, whom he had posted on a narrow neck to
guard his rear, had left his post to join in the battle. The safety
of the Musulman army was now gravely imperilled. Nevertheless the discipline of the Bahmani troops and the courage and the
endurance of Mujahid Shah enabled him to withdraw without
disaster. He vented, however, so vehemently his wrath on Daud
Shah that the latter, brooding over the reprimand, plotted the
king's murder. A year later chance favoured him. The king
had been fishing and had gone to rest with only a single slave to
guard him. While the king slept Daud Shah and three assassins
entered his room. The glare on the water had hurt the king's
eyes, so that he could not see his enemies. Daud Shah stabbed
his nephew through the body. His companions killed the slave
and then cut in pieces the dying monarch.

Daud Shah, his revenge gratified, aspired to mount the throne
of his murdered nephew. But his aims were baffled by the
courage of Ruh Parva Agha, the dead king's sister. One month
and five days after Mujahid Shah's death, an assassin procured
by her stabbed Daud Shah, as he prayed in the great mosque
at Gulbarga. Daud Shah removed, the princess proclaimed
that none of the traitor's stock should profit by his villainy.
Blinding his son, Mahomed Sangam, she placed on the throne
Mahmud Shah the youngest son of Hasan Gangu, the boy who
had read the lines of Sadi to his dying father (A.D. 1378). In

the disorders that followed the murder of Mujahid Shah, Bukka
Raya of Vijayanagar overran the Doab. But upon the accession
of Hasan Gangu's son, he withdrew his armies, offered his con-
gratulations and promised tribute. The new king, who had
never expected the good fortune of a throne, had passed his
youth and manhood in the study of Persian and Arabic. His
private munificence had supported a number of poets and
writers. And he wished his court to be adorned by the greatest
Persian poet of the time, the renowned Khwaja Hafiz of Shiraz.
He sent a brother poet Mir Faiz Ulla with an ode and a sum of
money to invite Hafiz to Gulbarga. The great poet, flattered
by the king's condescension, embarked at Ormuz. His ship
had hardly weighed anchor, when a great storm forced it back
to port. Hafiz had suffered so terribly from sea-sickness that
he insisted on landing and gave up the voyage. And instead
of his company, Mahmud Shah was forced to be content with
six stanzas in which the poet extolled the beauties of Shiraz,
as an excuse for not leaving it.

Mahmud Shah reigned for nineteen years in perfect peace
with his Hindu neighbours. No wars added to his dominions
nor emptied his treasury. But when famine broke out, his
husbanded resources enabled him to feed his people with grain
brought at his expense from Malwa and Guzarat. Ala-ud-din
Khilji, to boast of his victories, gave himself the name of the
second Alexander. Mahmud Shah's subjects, proud of his
learning and moderation, conferred on him the nobler title of
the second Aristotle. On April 25, A.D. 1397, the wise and just
king died of fever, leaving to succeed him his eldest son Ghyas-ud-
din. This unhappy prince was only seventeen at his accession
and at once plunged into the wildest excesses. Among his
Turkish slaves was one Lalchin, who had a beautiful and accomplished daughter. The prince demanded her for his harem.
The hot blood of Turkestan boiled at the insult. Luring
Ghyas-ud-din to his house by a promise to gratify his desire,
the slave flung his master on his back and blinded him with a
dagger. Lalchin then assassinated the twenty-four principal
nobles of the court and placing Shamsuddin, Ghyas-ud-din's

5

brother, on the throne, hoped to govern the Deccan in his name. The daughters, however, of Mahmud Shah were married to Firoz Khan and Ahmad Khan, the two younger sons of Daud Shah; and they instigated their husbands to avenge their brother. Lalchin tried to seize them but they fled to Sagar. There they gathered round them a considerable force and risked a battle with the royal army. Defeated, they disguised their aims by treachery. They affected submission, prayed for, and obtained pardon. A fortnight later they skilfully seized the persons of Lalchin and Shamsuddin. Lalchin they handed over to the vengeance of Ghyas-ud-din, who although blind cut him to pieces with a sabre. Shamsuddin's eyes were put out and he passed from a throne to a dungeon. And Firoz Khan, under the title of Firoz Shah Bahmani, assumed the crown which his father Daud Shah had vainly sought to wear (November 15, 1397).

The talents of the new king distinguished him even among the gifted princes of the Bahmani line. He was a consummate linguist. He had studied deeply such varied sciences as botany, geometry, and logic. He conducted twenty-four campaigns against the Hindus and extended the frontiers of the Bahmani empire further than any previous king. But his most extraordinary quality was his love of female beauty. In this he equalled, if he did not surpass, King Augustus I of Poland and Saxony. At first he felt some doubts whether Islam permitted more than four wives. But convinced by the Shia doctors that the Prophet had approved temporary unions, he on a single day received 300 women into his zanana. From that day onwards his agents continually brought to his seraglio the fairest faces of Greece and Italy, Russia and Tibet, Afghanistan and India. Within its walls the polyglot king conversed with every inmate in her own language; and according to Ferishta, he bestowed on each of his mistresses such attention that she thought herself the sole object of the royal affections. There seems, however, no doubt that in the end his excesses weakened his mind and led to his downfall.

Of Firoz Shah's twenty-four campaigns, two deserve special mention. In A.D. 1379 Bukka Raya of Vijayanagar had passed away, leaving to his son a mighty kingdom defended by a large and well-disciplined army. His son, Harihar II, was as peaceful as his Musulman contemporary, Mahmud Shah. In A.D. 1398 he was advanced in years, and his son, afterwards Bukka II, had already usurped most of his father's powers. With or without the king's leave, the prince set in motion the armies of Vijayanagar and overran the Doab. He reached the southern banks of the Krishna before the Bahmani forces had time to mobilize. The Krishna was in high flood and Firoz Shah saw no way to cross it. At this moment one Kazi Shiraz offered his services to the king. He would assassinate Prince Bukka or his son, and in the alarm thereby caused, Firoz Shah could cross the Krishna and destroy the enemy. Firoz Shah agreed and collected a number of rafts for his army. Kazi Shiraz, with seven friends, went disguised as beggars to the harlots' quarters of the Hindu camp. There the Kozi affected to fall in love with a pretty courtezan, who accepted his attentions. One evening, however, his mistress told him that she was engaged to dance and sing before the prince's son. The Kazi, like a distracted lover, begged her to take him with her. The girl objected that the prince would only admit musicians. "But I too am a musician," pleaded the Kazi, and taking from his mistress her rebek, he played and sang and, calling his companions, danced with such skill that she gladly took with her the whole party. After the dancing-girl had displayed her art and charms, she begged the prince to let the Kazi and his companions dance also. Leave was given and the Kazi and his friends began a dagger dance. So brilliant was their execution that the prince let them draw closer and closer. Suddenly they plunged their daggers into the hearts of the prince and his courtiers. The assassins then ran out, and cut the ropes of the tent, so that it fell upon the party inside. Mingling with the crowd they spread every kind of alarming report. In the ensuing confusion 4000 Musulmans crossed the river and slaughtered the Vijayanagar troops like sheep. Prince Bukka, distracted by the loss of his son and the defeat of his army, fell back on his father's capital, where the aged

Raja, who had all his life loved peace, gladly paid Firoz Shah £ 400,000 in order again to obtain it.

Another of Firoz Shah's campaigns contained an equally romantic episode. In Mudkal, one of two great strongholds in the Doab, dwelt a beautiful girl named Nihal. Her family were *sonars* or goldsmiths and her parents wished to wed her to a boy of her own caste. But she pleaded so earnestly for a respite that the marriage was postponed. An old Brahman who happened to visit her parents was so struck with her beauty that he spent eighteen months in teaching her to dance and sing. The teacher was an expert but so apt was the pupil that she at length surpassed her master. The delighted Brahman went to Vijayanagar. There Harihar II had died the year after the loss of his grandson. His son Bukka II had succeeded and had died early in A.D. 1406. In his place there now reigned his younger brother Deva Raya I. To him the Brahman sang so fervently the praises of the maid Nihal, that at last the king felt that life would be worthless unless he possessed her. He sent back by the Brahman rich presents for the girl's parents and promised to make her his queen. But again Nihal begged that her parents would not part her from them. The Brahman returned to Vijayanagar and told the Raja the failure of his mission. Deva Raya I, furious with disappointment, sent 5000 cavalry to take her. But ignorant of their object the parents and their daughter fled. At the same time Firoz Shah, indignant at the unprovoked invasion, attacked the cavalry, routed it and in turn invaded Vijayanagar. The Raja's troops were everywhere defeated. His great fortress of Bankapur fell and in the end he was forced to give his own daughter in marriage to Firoz Shah with the town of Bankapur as her wedding dowry. It then transpired that the goldsmith's daughter had from the first believed that her fated husband was a Musulman prince. For this reason she had rejected a marriage with a sonar boy and the embraces of a Hindu sovereign. On learning this, Firoz Shah had her brought to court, and finding that her beauty exceeded all description, he gave her in marriage to his eldest son Hasan Khan.

In **A.D.** 1417 Firoz Shah, in spite of Mahomed Shah's treaty of perpetual peace with Warangal, tried to seize Pangal, a stronghold to the north of the Krishna and within the frontiers of the Warangal Raja. Now for the first time good fortune left him. The garrison defended the fortress so resolutely that after two years their defence was unshaken, while the besieger's army had dwindled to almost nothing. Changes too had occurred at Vijayanagar. Deva Raya I had died in A.D. 1412. His grandson Deva Raya II was now on the throne. The new king was in the flower of his age. Vigorous in body, ambitious of glory, surrounded by the fiery chivalry of the south, he led his army northwards to help his Hindu brother. Firoz Shah should have raised the siege and fallen back on Gulbarga. His pride forbade him. He faced the enemy and lost his entire army. He himself escaped with the greatest difficulty from the battlefield. Deva Raya II overran the Doab, but he was eventually driven out by the vigour of Firoz Shah's brother, Ahmad Khan. His brother's victory was more fatal to the king than his own defeat. The king's son Hasan Khan, naturally a weak prince, had become so enamoured of the lovely Nihal that, abandoning all business, he had given up his entire time to his wife. The disgusted nobles turned their eyes to Ahmad Khan. Civil war broke out. The royal forces were overthrown and the king was besieged in Bedar. In despair he opened the gate of the town and abdicated in his brother's favour. Ten days later Firoz Shah died and his brother, under the title of Ahmad Shah Bahmani, reigned in his stead (March 1422).

The new king's abilities were equal to those of Firoz Shah and he had not dissipated his vigour in the royal zanana. He treated Prince Hasan with great kindness and gave him a beautiful palace in which to enjoy the company and the charms of the goldsmith's daughter. He also took steps to meet the attacks of the Rajas of Warangal and Vijayanagar, who had gained confidence during the civil strife. The hostile forces neared each other until they were only divided by the Tungabhadra. Alarmed by the sight of the Musulman army, the Raja of Warangal deserted his ally. Nevertheless Deva Raya held his ground and defied Ahmad Shah to cross the river. Under cover of a dark night Ahmad Shah did so, and one of his patrols surprised Deva Raya as he lay asleep in a sugar-cane plantation. He was clad in scanty attire and the Musulman soldiers took the half-naked man to be a common villager. They made him carry for them a bundle of sugar-cane. As the fight developed, the patrol left Deva Raya to join their comrades, and unwounded, the Raja returned safely to his army. His narrow escape, however, affected his nerves, and with all haste he broke off the action and retreated to Vijayanagar. Ahmad Shah now overran the country round the capital, slaughtered the wretched villagers with their women and children and defiled their most sacred temples. Exasperated at the king's inhumanity, five thousand Hindus swore to kill him. Closely their spies watched his movements. One day they brought word that the king, accompanied by only two hundred guardsmen, was hunting twelve miles from his camp. The five thousand Hindus galloped with all haste to the spot. Fortunately for the king a body of archers joined him at this moment and by sacrificing themselves enabled their master to reach a mud fort not far away. There the arrival of a large body of troops drove off the Hindus. The king now blockaded Vijayanagar so closely that Deva Raya was glad to offer peace. The king, sobered by his recent danger, was glad to accept it. The Raja paid a large sum as tribute and the king marched northwards to punish the Raja of Warangal. That unlucky prince paid to the full the penalty of his faithlessness. His army was destroyed. His capital was stormed. He lost at once his country and his life. Henceforth Warangal, under the name of Telingana or Tailangana, became a province of the Bahmani kingdom.

In 1429 Ahmad Shah after a successful campaign in Malwa suffered a severe reverse at the hands of the Musulman monarch of Guzarat. Ahmad Shah had sent his general Malik-ul-Tujar, a Persian adventurer, to reduce the lower Konkan. When this feat had been accomplished, the general in an excess of zeal took the island of Bombay, now the capital of the English, then the property of the king of Guzarat. The latter protested,

but Ahmad Shah endorsed his general's act. A battle followed
in which the Deccan army suffered a complete defeat. And
Bombay Island was again occupied by the troops of Guzarat.
After a reign of 12 years and 11 months Ahmad Shah died. His
reign was on the whole successful. He left his kingdom larger
than he had found it. But a deep stain of cruelty rests upon
his fame. Yet in spite of it he is the only Musulman king of
India on whom his people conferred the title of " Wali " or
saint. And if the tale be true, it must be conceded that he
fully earned it. For once, after a two years' famine, he obtained
by his prayers and intercessions a bountiful monsoon (February
24, 1435).

The early reign of the new king Ala-ud-din Shah, the son of
Ahmad Shah, was troubled by domestic disturbances. In spite
of his kindness to his younger brother, Mahomed Khan, the
latter attempted with the aid of Vijayanagar to usurp the throne.
After a fiercely contested action near Bedar the royal troops
won the day and Mahomed Khan fled. The generous king,
however, forgave his brother, and recalling him to the capital
made him governor of Raichur. His next trouble came from
his wife. He had been married in youth to Malika Jehan,
daughter of Nassir Khan, King of Khandesh. She had retained
her husband's affection until his general, Dilavar Khan, brought
him from a western campaign the lovely daughter of a Konkan
baron. Skilled in music, witty, amiable and beautiful, she
at once effaced from the king's heart the picture of Malika
Jehan. The neglected wife appealed to her father. He raised
a large army and allied himself to the King of Guzarat, and a
number of Deccan nobles invaded Berar. Ala-ud-din Shah,
fearing treason, dared neither leave his capital nor entrust
his army to any of his nobles. At last he thought of Malik-ul-
Tujar, whose capture of Bombay had led to his severe defeat.
Malik-ul-Tujar accepted the command of his army but dismissed
all the Deccan officers, alleging that his former disaster had been
due to their treachery. Success justified his act. With a
force only 7000 strong he defeated Nassir Khan, ravaged
Khandesh and effectually crushed both the rebels within and the

invaders without. Returning in triumph to Bedar, now the
capital of the Bahmanis, Malik-ul-Tujar was received outside the city by the king's eldest son. Honours were now
showered on him by his grateful master, who went so far as to
give to all Persian* and foreign officers precedence over all
Deccanis and Abyssinians. This unfortunate act created an
enmity between the two classes of officials, which in the end
destroyed the Musulman power in the Deccan.

About this time Deva Raya II of Vijayanagar, depressed
by continual defeat, called upon his priests and nobles to explain
the frequent successes of the Bahmani kings. "Their territory,"
said Deva Raya, "is smaller than my own; their courage is no
greater than ours and their religion is barbarous." The
Brahmans replied that heaven had ordained that for 30,000 years
the Musulmans should oppress the Hindus. The nobles gave
a more manly answer. "The Musulmans," they replied,
"are better mounted and more skilled as archers. Let the Raja
keep a large force of trained bowmen and victory will once
more return to his banners." Deva Raya accepted the advice
of his nobles and enlisted not only Hindu archers but also several
thousand Musulman mercenaries. After training the new
levies, Deva Raya set forth to conquer the Bahmani kingdom.
He at first met with some success. He surprised Mudkal and
advanced to the southern bank of the Krishna. There, however,
he met the fate which awaits mere imitators. In a series of
actions the copy proved unequal to the original. The Raja's
troops were defeated. The Raja himself was invested in
Mudkal. Now convinced that to overthrow the Bahmani
kingdom was beyond his power, he, for the rest of his life,
acknowledged the Bahmani king as his overlord and paid him
tribute.

After the defeat of Vijayanagar, Ala-ud-din Shah resolved
to seize and garrison all the Konkan fortresses. The Konkan
plains had long been in the hands of the Bahmanis. But the
giant strongholds of the Western Ghats were still the refuge
of robber barons. They paid or withheld tribute as it suited

---

* Malik-ul-Tujar was a Persian.

themselves and preyed continually upon the merchants and
cultivators who owed allegiance to the Bahmani power. The
mightiest of these mountain forts was the great hill of Khelna,
now known as Vishalgad. Surrounded on the east, north
and south by dense forests, it drops on the western side a sheer
2000 feet. To reduce Khelna was the king's ambition. He
again gave the command to Malik-ul-Tujar. The royal army
descended into the Konkan from Junnar, and the general took
several small hill forts as he advanced south. Among the
chiefs whom he overthrew was a Maratha baron named Shirke,
whom Malik-ul-Tujar forced under pain of death to turn
Mahomedan. Shirke plotted a signal revenge. He affected
to become a loyal subject and a true believer and offered to
guide Malik-ul-Tujar's army through the Khelna forests. The
few Deccani officers whom the general had still with him
distrusted Shirke and deserted. But Malik-ul-Tujar trusted
blindly his mortal enemy and let him guide the army to the
spot where the undergrowth was thickest. There Shirke
escaped and made his way to Shankar Rai, the baron of Khelna.
The two returned with a large Maratha force, surprised the weary
Musulmans, and slew 7000 of them, including their general.
The few foreign officers who survived wished to report at head-
quarters the treachery of the Deccanis. But the latter were
beforehand with the king and induced him by their arts to
order the massacre of their traducers. The unfortunate foreigners fled to Chakan, where the Deccanis treacherously took
and killed a large number. A handful however escaped to
Bedar and told Ala-ud-din Shah the truth. The latter, doubly
enraged at his defeat and his foolishness, restored the foreign
officers to favour and executed the deserters.

The last three years of Ala-ud-din's reign were darkened
by illness and rebellion. An eruption on his foot confined
him to his room and gave rise to the report of his death. The
report induced his nephew Sikandar Khan to rebel. He obtained
the support of the kings of Malwa and Khandesh. But in the
hour of peril rose the high spirit of Ala-ud-din Shah, and he
took the field at the head of his army. The invaders retreated ;

Sikandar Khan submitted ; and Ala-ud-din Shah returned to Bedar, where he died happy in his final triumph (April 3, 1458).

To the wise and capable Ala-ud-din Shah succeeded. his son, Prince Humayun, to whom his subjects rightly gave the name of Zalim or the Tyrant. His accession was followed by a fresh revolt of Sikandar Khan, who now, as the king's cousin, claimed a share in the kingdom. At the same time the king's younger brother Hassan Khan tried to usurp the throne. Resolutely Humayun met both dangers. He crushed the palace conspiracy and blinded Hassan. He defeated and slew Sikandar Khan in a hard-fought battle. But while Humayun was absent from his capital he received news of a fresh disturbance. Hassan Khan's friends managed by a forged order to enter his prison and to release him and a number of those imprisoned with him. The blind prince then raised an army and at first defeated the royal troops. But when Humayun returned with his main forces he gained a complete victory. Hassan Khan fled, but was seized by the governor of Bijapur and handed over to the royal mercy. But the anxieties which he had undergone had unsettled the king's mind. From the date of his victory to the end of his reign his conduct was that of a raving madman. He prepared an arena in Bedar. And there in the presence of the whole city, he gave a free rein to his cruel temper. First Hassan Khan was thrown to and devoured by a man-eating tiger. His companions were beheaded one after the other, and then the unhappy women of their households were publicly violated by the lowest scum from the Bedar prisons. The spectacle ended with the torture and massacre of 7000 persons, most of whom had little or no concern with the prince's rebellion. Nor did this revenge satisfy the king. Thenceforward he acted towards his loyal subjects as he had acted towards the rebels. To gratify a passing whim he would execute or torture them or violate their women. At last after a reign of three and a half years a just fate overtook him. His servants fell upon him when drunk and tore him to pieces (September 4, 1461).

The tyrant left a son, Nizam Shah, but nine years old, to succeed him; but the king's infancy gave ample scope to the abilities of the queen mother. They were at once fully tested. The Hindu chief of Orissa, descended from the ancient house of Warangal, marched southwards to place a kinsman on its throne. The invasion was checked and the Hindu army retreated. A second attempt in the following year was even more disastrous. The Orissa chief's whole army perished and he himself barely escaped with his life. To celebrate the victory the queen mother resolved to marry her son and chose for his bride one of her own relatives. Unhappily the excitement of the ceremonial proved too much for the boy king. His head suddenly sank forward on his breast. His body fell to one side; and when the courtiers rushed to support him he was already dead of heart failure (July 30, 1463).

To the dead king succeeded his still younger brother Mahomed Shah Bahmani II. The twenty years during which the prince reigned saw the Bahmani power reach its greatest height and then crumble almost to pieces. Its rise and its collapse had a common cause in Khwaja Mahmud Gawan, the king's minister. This loyal and gifted man was connected with the royal house of Persia. His ancestors had for several generations been hereditary Vazirs to the Persian princes of Jhilan. The enmity of Shah Tamasp forced the young Mahmud to leave his country. He became a merchant and in the course of his travels came to Bedar, intending to journey thence to Delhi. Ala-ud-din met him, was attracted by his qualities and made him a noble of his court. In the reign of Humayun Shah he rose to be first minister. This office he filled with great distinction during the minorities of Nizam Shah and Mahomed Shah II: and after the latter came of age, he yet remained in favour. So long as his master hand guided the Bahmani affairs, the state prospered. He first dictated peace to the king of Malwa and then marched against Shankar Rai of Khelna. After two campaigns he captured the great Maratha stronghold and ravaged all Shankar Rai's lands, thus avenging the defeat of Malik-ul-Tujar. He then made a surprise attack both by land

and sea on the Vijayanagar fortress of Goa. The Hindu kingdom had recently passed through troubled times. Deva Raya had died of wounds inflicted by his own brother. To him succeeded his son Deva Raya III, and then his grandson Virupaksha I. Ever since the reign of Deva Raya II, the Vijayanagar cavalry had been mounted on imported horses. The importers were the Musulman traders of Bhatkal. In A.D. 1469, either on religious or commercial grounds, they began to sell their animals to the Bahmani monarch. Virupaksha I, furious with the merchants, ordered their massacre. Ten thousand Musulmans perished. The rest fled to Goa, where they founded a city, which now yielded gladly to the arms of Mahmud Gawan. Two years later Virupaksha I tried to retake it. He was aided by Vikrama Rai, the chief of Belgaum. But the Bahmani king forestalled their offensive by storming Belgaum. And soon all Vikrama Rai's lands were added to the Bahmani dominion.

In A.D. 1475 a great famine devastated the Deccan. This tempted the Raja of Orissa once again to invade Telingana. But a good monsoon restored Mahomed Shah's prosperity and his minister equipped so efficient an army that not only was the Raja driven from Telingana but he soon had lost Orissa also. Forced to sue for peace he obtained it by surrendering his elephants and abandoning all claims to Telingana. Several, however, of the Hindu barons had revolted to aid the Raja. The leader of these was one Bhim Raja, the feudal lord of Kondapalli, a large town some 20 miles from the mouth of the Krishna. On the defeat of the Orissa forces, the unfortunate chief was cut off from all hope of success. After six months' siege he prayed for and obtained pardon. But although the king forgave the noble, he vented his anger on the priests. And to win the title of Ghazi, or holy one, he destroyed the largest temple in the town and with his own hand slaughtered the attendants. The sacrilege alienated his Hindu subjects and must have disgusted the broader-minded among his Musulman followers. Both remembered that through a Brahman's kindness Hasan Gangu had risen to a throne and in the calamities that followed both saw divine retribution for the cruel deed.

Nevertheless so long as Mahmud Gawan remained the king's minister, no evil befell his master. Shortly after the fall of Kondapalli, Mahmud Gawan reduced Masulipatam, held for Vijayanagar by the Raja's relative Narsinha Raya, who some years later was to usurp the southern throne. But the continual successes of Mahmud Gawan excited the envy of his fellow nobles. They forged a letter purporting to be written by the great minister to the Raja of Orissa offering to share with him the Bahmani kingdom. They next induced a drunken slave to seal this paper with Mahmud's seal. Then they showed it to the king. The latter, intoxicated at the time, would hear no explanation nor hold any inquiry. An Abyssinian slave cut off Mahmud Gawan's head in his master's presence and the same blow severed the sinews of the Bahmani empire.

One Yusuf Adil Khan had been adopted as a son by Mahmud Gawan. The romance of his career might have been a tale told by Shaharazadi. He was the younger brother of Mahomed II, the sultan who stormed Constantinople. While Yusuf was still a child the sultan had ordered his execution. His mother substituted for her son a Georgian slave and sent Yusuf to Alexandria. When he was sixteen years old his nurse divulged his secret. To escape his brother's vengeance, he fled to Shiraz. There he dreamt that a divine form bade him go to India, where a throne awaited him. He reached India in 1459, was entrapped by a merchant and sold at Bedar as a Georgian slave. The purchaser was Mahmud Gawan. The slave of the great minister soon rose to power. On the murder of his patron, he and two other high officers, Imad-ul-mulk and Khudavand Khan, revolted and extorted from the king the government of Bijapur for Yusuf Adil Khan and the two viceroyalties of Berar for his two confederates. The Bahmani king then enquired into the charge against Mahmud Gawan, and finding that he had been duped did his utmost to repair the wrong. But the rebel nobles had gone too far to retrace their steps. They refused to appear at court and became independent in all but name. Their conduct so preyed on the king's mind that he became a slave to drink. At last on March 26, 1482, he died in a fit of delirium tremens, exclaiming that the ghost of Mahmud Gawan was tearing out his entrails.

After the murder of Mahmud Gawan, the dead king had appointed one Nizam-ul-Mulk as his minister. He was by birth a Brahman and the son of one Bahiru of the Kulkarni family of Pathri in Berar. Captured in infancy by some troopers of Nizam Shah Bahmani, he was brought up as a Musulman and made the companion of the youthful Mahomed Shah. His keen Brahman brain soon mastered Persian and Arabic, and winning the favour of Mahmud Gawan he became viceroy of Telingana. As a converted Hindu his inclination led him to join the Deccan party, who hated Mahmud Gawan as a Persian and a foreigner. With his own hand he forged the letter which caused the minister's ruin. When Mahomed Shah's twelve-year-old son Mahmud Shah succeeded his father, Nizam-ul-Mulk continued to be his minister. He at first sought to destroy Yusuf Adil Khan ; he induced him to enter Bedar with a small escort and then fell upon him with the royal forces. But the gallant Turk defended himself long enough for his own troops and those of his ally Imad-ul-Mulk to break open the gates and enter the city. A street fight ensued in which 8000 men lost their lives. At last Yusuf Adil Khan and Imad-ul-Mulk extricated themselves and retreated, the former to Bijapur, the latter to Berar. Nizam-ul-Mulk now foresaw the break-up of the empire and bestowed all the western provinces in fief to his son Malik Ahmad. The king retaliated by plotting his assassination. The minister fled and sought to seize the royal treasure. The attempt failed and Nizam-ul-Mulk perished. But on his death, the Bahmani empire, shattered by Mahmud Gawan's murder, fell to pieces. Malik Ahmad declared himself independent as Ahmad Nizam Shah, king of Ahmadnagar. Subduing the whole country from Bid to the sea-coast and from the Khandesh frontier to the south of Poona, he established what is known in history as the Nizam Shahi dynasty. About the same time Yusuf Adil Khan had himself crowned in Bijapur as Yusuf Adil Shah, thus founding the Adil Shahi dynasty. His action was copied by Imad-ul-Mulk, one of the two viceroys of Berar. Making himself master of the whole province and renouncing his allegiance, he founded the dynasty known as Imad Shahi. To the Bahmani king there now remained merely the territory round Bedar and the province of Telingana. Soon one of the remaining pieces fell away. The governor of Telingana, Kutb-ul-Mulk, a Persian adventurer, usurped his trust and founded the Kutb Shahi line of Golconda. Only Bedar now remained. But even at the capital the king's weakness enabled his minister Kasim Barid to become all-powerful and to bequeath his power to his son Amir Barid. The latter imprisoned his unfortunate master, who died on December 26, 1518, after an inglorious reign of 37 years. Ahmad Shah, Mahmud Shah's son, died of want two years after his nominal accession. His cousin, Ala-ud-din II, was assassinated in A.D. 1521 by Amir Barid, who shortly afterwards poisoned Ala-ud-din the Second's successor, Wali Ulla. Ahmad Shah's son, Kalim Ulla, was now the sole survivor of the Bahmani house. He mounted the pageant throne in A.D. 1526, the year in which the Emperor Babar won the field of Panipat. He in vain begged the conqueror to pity his fate. But Babar's task was already great enough for his strength. Kalim Ulla then fled from Bedar to Bijapur. But finding that he had exchanged but one state prison for another, he fled to Ahmadnagar. There the Nizam Shahi king treated him with the respect due to fallen greatness. And in some measure of dignity and comfort the last Bahmani king passed the remainder of his life. His death left the throne of Bedar vacant. Amir Barid's son, Ali Barid, ascended it and founded the Barid Shahi dynasty of Bedar (A.D. 1539).

CHAPTER IX

MOGHULS AND PORTUGUESE

IN the preceding chapter a reference has been made to the Emperor Babar. We must, therefore, return for a moment to the history of northern India. After the death of Mahomed Tughlak in A.D. 1351 the Delhi empire fell slowly to pieces. In 1354 one Haji Elias founded what is known as the Purbhia dynasty of eastern Bengal. In 1387* Dilavar Khan, the imperial viceroy, made himself king of Malwa. In 1388 Malik Raja, once a trooper, declared himself king of Khandesh. In 1390 a menial of the imperial household named Muzaffar Khan founded the kingdom of Guzarat. Four years later a fifth province fell away and became the prey of a eunuch called Malik Survur. At last Delhi became the scene of disorders as violent as any that had raged in its dependencies. While the streets of the capital ran with the blood of contending partisans, the news spread that the Amir Timur with 100,000 men had crossed the Indus and was advancing by forced marches through upper India.

Although Timur claimed to be the descendant of Jenghiz Khan, he was actually a Berlas Turk. He had, however, after years of hard fighting subdued the inheritance of Jagatai,† one of Jenghiz Khan's sons, and in 1369 he had himself crowned in Samarkand as sole king of the Jagatai Moghuls. The next 30 years he spent in reducing the Moghuls of the Caspian and the vast lands between the Ural and the Volga. To the south he conquered Persia from Khorasan to Kerbela. And in 1398, when in his sixtieth year, the troubles at Delhi drew his restless

---

* This is the date given by Ferishta. The *Imperial Gazetteer* gives the date as 1401.

† The word is sometimes spelt Chagatai and the Marathas corrupted it into *Chakatyachi badshahi*.

spirit to conquer Hindustan. As Timur advanced through northern India, the grass, so his troops boasted, ceased to grow and behind them no eye remained open to weep for the dead. After a feeble resistance the Delhi government was overthrown, Delhi fell and its entire population was butchered. Its vast wealth was either plundered or destroyed. Having thus undone in a few days the labour of centuries. Timur and his barbarians retired to Samarkand, leaving Delhi to anarchy and famine. The anarchy endured for over 100 years. At last Ibrahim Lodi made himself undisputed master of what remained of the Delhi empire, only to learn that Babar, king of Ferghana, had entered India to claim the inheritance of Timur (A.D. 1526).

It was written of Lauzun that his life resembled the dreams of ordinary persons. With even more truth, the same can be said of the Emperor Babar. He is the darling of India's historians. But in a book where the history of northern India is sketched merely to make that of the Deccan intelligible, it is impossible to give to this valiant adventurer the place which he deserves. His father Umar Sheikh Mirza was the great-great-grandson of Timur, and his share of the conqueror's empire was the beautiful country of Ferghana now known as Kokan, on the upper reaches of the Syr Daria. When Sheikh Mirza died in A.D. 1499 Babar was only 12 years old and his infancy tempted his uncles to despoil him of his rights. Thirty years the heroic youth spent in losing and in retaking Ferghana. In the course of these wars he became king of Kabul and from Kabul he set forth for the last time to win back his own. Defeated by the Uzbeg Turks, he at length gave up the hopeless quest and turned to one more arduous still, the conquest of India. With only 12,000 men he entered it by way of Lahore and met Ibrahim Lodi on the field of Panipat. The imperial forces outnumbered Babar's by ten to one; nevertheless Babar stretched out his lines until they outflanked those of Ibrahim. He then harassed the enemy's flanks with bodies of mounted archers. The emperor tried to force Babar's centre but was repulsed by salvoes of massed artillery. The imperial army then fell into disorder. Babar led a counter-attack and completed the rout.

6

Ibrahim Lodi was slain and Babar proclaimed himself Emperor of India. His next great battle was with the Rana Sanga of Chitor, whom he decisively defeated at Sikri. But nothing in Babar's life became him like the leaving of it. His eldest son Humayun was stricken with a violent fever. The court doctors had pronounced his case hopeless, when Babar resolved to offer his life to the Most High instead of that of his child. Three times the emperor walked round the prostrate prince, his lips moving in silent prayer. Then staggering backwards he cried in a loud firm voice, "I have borne it away." Instantly the fever left Humayun and struck down Babar in his place. Faith had made the one whole and had killed the other. The war-worn founder of the Moghul empire died on December 26, 1530, and his body was borne far away to the north and buried amid the flowers and the cool running streams of Kabul.

He was followed on the throne by the son whose life he had saved. Twenty years afterwards Humayun fell, as he walked down the stairs of his library, and died a few hours later. His son Akbar, the greatest prince but one who ever occupied an Indian throne, succeeded him. In the course of his reign he reunited to the Delhi empire most of the kingdoms which had come into being after the death of Mahomed Tughlak. In 1564 he annexed Malwa. In 1572 he conquered Guzarat. In 1599 he reduced Khandesh. The sovereignties of Jaunpur and Bengal had already vanished. In them Akbar firmly established the imperial authority. And now, master of all northern India, Akbar began to meditate the conquest of the Deccan.

At this point the history of Maharashtra from the fall of the Bahmani kingdom demands our attention. But before returning to it I wish to sketch shortly an event of the first importance, the arrival of the Portuguese. For not only did they conquer a portion of Maharashtra but they showed the way round the Cape to other European peoples. And to-day the sovereign of one of them bears the proud title not only of King of England but of Emperor of India.

The founder of the Portuguese kingdom was a Frenchman. In A.D. 1086, Alfonso, the Spanish king of Leon, suffered a

complete reverse in the battle of Zalaca and lost all Spain
to the south of the Ebro. In despair King Alfonso summoned
to his aid the chivalry of northern Europe. Among the gallant
knights who flocked to his banners was one Henry, Count of
Burgundy. To him King Alfonso gave in marriage his illegitimate daughter Theresa, with the counties of Coimbra and
Oporto and the title of Count of Portugal. Their son was the
famous Alfonso Enriquez, the founder of Portuguese independence. His greatness, so the legend runs, displayed itself from
infancy. Fire played round his cradle without hurting the god-
like child. Attacked when a boy by a pack of mountain wolves,
he slew them all single-handed and returned home without a
scratch. He passed his manhood in fights against the Moors
and the Spaniards. The former he routed on the field of Ourique
and by the walls of Santarem. The latter he overcame in the
famous Tourney of Valdevez, and thus secured the independence
of Portugal. Ninth in descent from Alfonso Enriquez was King
John the Great, renowned both as soldier and administrator,
but greater still as the father of Prince Henry the Navigator.
This pre-eminent prince is the common glory of Portugal and
England. He was the third son of King John and of Queen
Philippa, daughter of John of Gaunt, the founder of the House
of Lancaster. At the siege of Ceuta his bravery had been con-
spicuous even among the gallant nobles of Portugal. At the
disaster of Tangier his fortitude was proof against the darkest
frowns of fortune. But his mind turned rather to study than to
war. In Herodotus he read that Necho's fleet had circumnavi-
gated Africa. He too, he thought, would circumnavigate it, and
bringing back from India boundless wealth, would make Portugal
first among the nations. Prince Henry settled at Sagre near
Cape St. Vincent and thence sent forth every year Portuguese
captains to explore the north-west shores of Africa. Year by
year the daring seamen crept further and further along the coast
of the great continent. As they went they found the Azores,
St. Michael, Madeira, the Canaries and the Cape Verde Islands
The prince, however, never let his thoughts wander from the
Indian route. One by one Cape Bojador, Cape Blanco, Cape

Verde, and the Rio de Oro yielded their secrets to the bold explorers. Prince Henry died in 1460, thirty-six years before the final triumph. But his spirit never ceased to fire his countrymen. In 1471, Fernando Bom crossed the equator and discovered Cape Catherine. Next Diego Cam discovered the Congo, and in 1486, Bartholomew Diaz doubled the southern point of Africa. To it he gave the name of Cabo Tormentoso, or the Cape of Storms. But King John I, more far-seeing than his captain, saw in the discovery the dawn of success. He therefore named it the Cape of Good Hope. Three years later the dreams of Prince Henry became realities. In the household of King Emmanuel was a gentleman called Vasco Da Gama, who was the son of an experienced sailor named Estavao Da Gama and had himself served at sea with distinction. Him King Emmanuel chose for the final effort. His brother Paul Da Gama and one Nicholas Coelho, both tried captains, volunteered to go with him, and on the July 3, 1497, a fleet of four ships weighed anchor on the most memorable enterprise that the world had seen. Of these one was a store ship and the total equipage of the fleet numbered but 160. The voyage has been described by Camoens in an epic poem based on the *Æneid* and equal, if not superior, to its model. According to the author of the *Lusiad*, the old gods fought for and against Da Gama. Bacchus, jealous of his ancient renown as the conqueror of India, did his best to thwart the heroes who would eclipse his fame. Venus, who saw in them the qualities that had made the sons of her darling Æneas masters of the world, worked for them and at last brought them safe to their goal.

At first, fair weather smiled on the Portuguese. They passed with a favouring wind the Canary and Cape Verde Islands. Then they encountered heavy storms and were driven as far west as St. Helena. At last able to head once more for Africa, they touched at St. Helena's Bay on the western coast of Cape Colony. They landed, but, unable to converse with the negroes, they again weighed anchor and headed for the Cape. A storm now overtook them, which was to try to the utmost Da Gama's resolution. The sailors mutinied and demanded the return of

the fleet. Da Gama and his brother Paul put them in irons and
stood by the helm night and day. At last after many days of
little food and less sleep, they guided the fleet safely to Table
Bay. With danger passed away the mutinous spirit of the
crews ; and in delightful weather they coasted along the southern and then the eastern shores of Africa. But their trials
were by no means over. A violent current carried them southwards from Cape Corrientes, which thereby earned its name.
But the tempests again caught them and drove them out of the
current. On January 10, 1498, they neared the shore and
finding the natives friendly they christened the country Terra di
Natal. On March 1, they saw four islands off the coast of
Mozambique. Shortly afterwards seven ships sailed out to
meet them. At first all went well. The strange squadron was
that of the viceroy of the Arab king of Quilon. The captains
hailed Da Gama in Arabic, to which the interpreter, taken by
him on board before he left the Tagus, replied. Fancying the
strangers to be Musulmans from Morocco, the Mozambique
ships supplied all their wants. But the viceroy soon learnt
that Da Gama and his men were Christians and he plotted their
destruction. Their superior artillery saved them, and still
heading northwards they reached Mombasa. It also belonged
to the king of Quilon, and here a treacherous pilot tried to run
them aground. But with Venus' help and their own adroitness
they once more escaped, and a day or two later reached Melinda
in the modern province of British East Africa. Here the king
was as kind as the Arabs of Mozambique and Mombasa had been
inhospitable. On April 22, with a trusty pilot and a favouring
wind, the Portuguese sailed north until they crossed the line
and with a passion of joy saw Orion and the Great Bear shine
on them, as they had seen them shine in their far off homes in
Portugal.

The fleet headed now eastwards and three weeks later
the sailors saw on the eastern sky the mountains above
Calicut. Two leagues from shore the Portuguese squadron
anchored and was soon surrounded by a great number of boats.
In one of them Da Gama sent a messenger ashore. A vast

crowd welcomed him in the most friendly way. But, unable to talk to them, the messenger was at a loss what to do. At last a voice greeted him in excellent Spanish. By an incredible chance a Tunis Moor, who had often undertaken contracts for the Portuguese government, happened to be at Calicut and he gladly offered himself as interpreter. The ruler of Calicut was a Hindu prince called the Samuri, and his chief revenues were derived from the Mopla or Arab traders established on his coasts. Acting on their counsel he induced Da Gama to land, imprisoned him and then tried to destroy his fleet. But the bearing of Da Gama and the vigilance of his officers defeated the Arab intrigue. The Samuri, struck with Da Gama's courage, ordered his release. He returned to his ships, but the Arabs, furious at his escape, attacked his little squadron with twenty barges filled with armed men. The Portuguese cannon and a fortunate storm dispersed his assailants, and Vasco Da Gama headed once more for the Tagus. But further troubles and dangers awaited him. Arabs and pirates attacked him. One of his ships grounded on a sand bank. His heroic brother Paul Da Gama died on the homeward journey. Nevertheless the dauntless courage of the Admiral bore him through every trial and at last amid the frantic enthusiasm of the Portuguese nation Vasco Da Gama landed at Lisbon. He had brought home neither gold nor spices, neither cargoes nor plunder. Of his 160 men only 55 lived to return. But he had discovered a secret by which the Portuguese were to reach the height of glory. After Da Gama, went out Cabral, and after Cabral, Da Gama again, the Almeidas and the Albuquerques; but they went no longer as curious explorers or peaceful traders. Their warships darkened the seas; their transports carried battalions across half a world. They built fortresses in Cochin and Cannanore, Quilon and Div. At last in 1510 Alfonso Da Albuquerque took, lost and retook Goa from the king of Bijapur and made it the capital of the eastern empire of the Portuguese. Thus again after 1800 years Europe forced open one of the gates of India.

CHAPTER X

THE AHMADNAGAR KINGDOM

A.D. 1490 to 1600

In my eighth chapter, I sketched the history of the Bahmani empire until the death in A.D. 1549 of Kalim Ulla. That empire had in reality ceased to exist since A.D. 1490 when Ahmad Nizam Shah first declared his independence. Of the five principalities formed from the Bahmani empire that of Golconda was the ancient Warangal peopled by Telegus. The kingdom of Bijapur was in the main peopled by Canarese ; Berar and Bedar were peopled partly by Marathi and partly by Hindi speaking races. On the other hand Ahmadnagar state was, apart from the Musulmans, peopled entirely by Marathas. Within its frontier the great Maratha revolution had its birth. At Junnar, one of its fortresses, Shivaji was born. At Poona, one of its towns, Shivaji passed his boyhood. His grandfather Maloji and his father Shahaji were nobles in the Ahmadnagar king's employment. I shall therefore continue at this stage the history of the Marathas, by relating the rise and the fall of the Ahmadnagar kingdom.

The first king of Ahmadnagar, Ahmad Nizam Shah, was the son of the minister Nizam-ul-Mulk, whose death has been described towards the close of Chapter VIII. Nizam-ul-Mulk, to prepare for himself either a secure retreat or an independent kingdom, bestowed the country from the fort of Shivner to Daulatabad as a fief on his son. The latter was one of the first soldiers of the age. Under cover of his father's authority, he subdued not only the fief bestowed on him, but the whole line of the Sahyadris from Shivner to Purandar. Thence he descended into the Konkan and was engaged in reducing it, when he heard of his father's assassination. He at once returned to Shivner,

renounced his allegiance to the Bahmani kingdom, and prepared
to resist to the utmost the attacks of the royal troops. Such
was the rebel's repute as a soldier, that Mahmud Shah Bahmani
found no officer willing to meet him. Mahmud Shah first
offered the command to Yusuf Adil Khan ; but that aspiring
Turk was in no mood to fight one whose conduct was similar
to his own. At last one Sheikh Muwalid, an Arab, volunteered
to overthrow Ahmad Nizam Shah. At the same time he won
over to the royal cause one Zainuddin, the jaghirdar of Chakan,
an officer on whose help Ahmad Nizam Shah had counted. The
latter showed himself equal to the danger. In a surprise attack
on Chakan he destroyed the entire force of Zainuddin. Then returning with his victorious troops, he fell upon Sheikh Muwalid's
army, slew the general and captured his camp and baggage.
If it had been difficult before to find a commander to face Ahmad
Nizam Shah, it became still more so now. At last Mahmud
Shah found in one Jehangir Khan an obedient if not an efficient
officer. With eight thousand men he set forth to reduce the
redoubtable insurgent. Ahmad Nizam Shah fell back into the
western hills, securing his supplies through the Konkan passes.
There fortifying himself he awaited Jehangir Khan's attack.
The royalist general was loth to risk such reputation as he had
gained from Ahmad Shah's retreat. He did not assault the
rebel position but encamped twelve miles away. Not long
afterwards the rains broke. Jehangir Khan's vigilance and the
discipline of his troops insensibly relaxed. But in Ahmad
Nizam Shah's camp the qualities of the general sustained those
of the soldiers ; and everywhere reigned good order and prudence. On the night of the May 28, 1490, Ahmad Nizam Shah
with a picked force set out towards Jehangir Khan's camp.
The sodden roads deadened the noise of the advance and the
heavy clouds hid everything in darkness. As Jehangir Khan's
sentries slept, they were stabbed silently at their posts ; and
a few minutes later Ahmad Nizam Shah overwhelmed the royal
forces. Jehangir Khan and his staff fell fighting. Such officers
as surrendered were mounted on buffaloes and paraded in
derision before the army. Freed by this last victory from fur-

ther Bahmani attack, Ahmad Nizam Shah built a palace on the banks of the Sena River and called it Bagh Nizam. Round it grew a great city, which is now the headquarters of a British district. It is still called Ahmadnagar, or the town of Ahmad, and thus perpetuates the name of the great soldier who founded it.

Ahmad Nizam Shah fell ill and died in 1508. It is impossible not to admire the great talents and high character of the founder of the house of Ahmadnagar. Although of Brahman descent, he yet proved himself superior to every Musulman general against whom he fought. Although an absolute despot, he was continent and modest. Although himself the bravest of the brave, no king was ever more indulgent to the errors and even to the cowardice of his subordinates. It may be added that no Indian king, save Shivaji alone, was ever better served by his officers.

The late king's son, Burhan Nizam Shah, mounted the throne in his seventh year. Mukamil Khan, the prime minister of Ahmad Nizam Shah, became regent of the kingdom. He was a wise and capable man. Unhappily the vanity and insolence of his son Aziz-ul-Mulk led a body of Ahmadnagar nobles to conspire against the infant king. The king's nurse, Bibi Ayesha, a party to the plot, dressed her charge in a girl's clothes and carried him to the city where the conspirators awaited her. She was detected as she went. The boy king was recovered; and the disaffected nobles sought refuge with the king of Berar. They instigated him to attack the Ahmadnagar kingdom, which, so they urged, he would easily conquer from an infant monarch. But if the monarch was an infant, the regent was in the fulness of his powers, and completely overthrowing the Berar army near Ranuri forced the king to sue for peace (A.D. 1510).

In a few years Burhan Nizam Shah grew to manhood. He fell in love with and married a dancing girl named Amina and made her his chief queen. The marriage proved unfortunate for the kingdom. She taught the young king to drink wine and to regard with ill favour the rule of the regent. The latter resigned his office and left his master to manage his own affairs (A.D. 1523). Not many years later Burhan Nizam Shah con-

tracted a marriage with Bibi Miriam, the daughter of Yusuf Adil
Shah, the founder of the Bijapur dynasty, and sister of the reigning king, Ismail Adil Shah.   The Bijapur envoy promised to give
as her dowry the town of Sholapur and five and a half districts.
The promise however was repudiated by Ismail Adil Shah and
proved a constant source of enmity between the two kingdoms.
Burhan Nizam Shah revenged himself for the loss of Miriam's
dowry by neglecting her and by retaining Amina as his chief
queen.   The princess complained to her brother, whose ambas-
sador remonstrated strongly with the king of Ahmadnagar.
The latter's fury then knew no bounds.   He declared war
against Bijapur.   But in the absence of Mukamil Khan, the
Ahmadnagar troops proved unequal to their foes ; Burhan
Nizam Shah was completely defeated and suffering from
sunstroke was carried insensible from the field (A.D. 1524).

In 1537, one Shah Tahir induced Burhan Nizam Shah to become
a Shia.   His change of religion nearly lost him his kingdom.
With difficulty he quelled a furious Sunni tumult in Ahmadnagar,
only to learn that the kings of Guzarat, Bijapur and Khandesh
had decided to divide his kingdom between them.   Burhan
Nizam Shah extricated himself skilfully from the danger.   He
bought off the kings of Khandesh and Guzarat by some trifling
concessions and then drew to his standard a number of Shia
soldiers whom the king of Bijapur, a fanatical Sunni, had dismissed.   He next induced the kings of Berar, Golconda and
Bedar to join with Ramraj, king of Vijayanagar, and himself
in an attempt to destroy Bijapur.

Since I last mentioned Vijayanagar that state had passed
through many vicissitudes.   In 1490, one Narsinha Raya, a
kinsman of the reigning house, had usurped the throne.   He was
a man of ability and he and his successors increased the greatness of the Vijayanagar kingdom.   They were much helped by
the dissolution of the Bahmani empire and by the coming of
the Portuguese.   The latter, at enmity with the Musulmans,
gladly accepted the friendship of Vijayanagar.   They sold to
its king horses from Persia and powder from Portugal, and
from time to time aided him in battle.   With their help, King

Krishna Deva Raya recovered from Bijapur, in the year 1520, the fortresses of Raichur and Mudkal together with the Doab or the lands between the Krishna and the Tungabhadra. At this time Vijayanagar reached the summit of its glory. The Portuguese chroniclers have exhausted their vocabularies in describing the splendours of the capital. The streets, according to Paes,* were as wide as a tournament arena. Wall within wall guarded the citadel from hostile attack. Numerous lakes supplied the garrison with water. The shops overflowed with diamonds, sapphires and rubies. Its stores of provisions exceeded those of any other town in the world and its extent rivalled that of the city of the seven hills in the days of the Julian Cæsars. Upon Krishna Deva's death the royal power was usurped by the king's minister Timma, who ruled the country for forty years. On Timma's death his son Rama Raya, commonly known as Ramraj, married the daughter of Krishna Deva, imprisoned the lawful heir, Sadashiva, and in his stead proclaimed himself king of Vijayanagar. It was this sovereign whom the king of Ahmadnagar called to his aid. In 1548, Burhan Nizam Shah at the head of an allied army advanced to besiege Kalyani. As he besieged it, great bodies of Bijapur cavalry so harassed his communications, that in the quaint words of Ferishta, true believers and Hindus alike fasted in the month of Ramzan. In despair Burhan Nizam Shah made a dawn attack on the main Bijapur force. The hazard succeeded. The Bijapur army were so completely surprised that they lost all their guns ; while their king, who was at the time enjoying a warm bath, had to flee naked from the scene of his defeat. Kalyani afterwards capitulated, and so great was the demoralization of the Bijapur officers that the general who held Parenda suddenly deserted it. He had mistaken the buzzing of a mosquito in his bedroom for the trumpets of the Ahmadnagar troops, who were still forty miles distant. Burhan Nizam Shah recovered Sholapur and its five and a half districts. The allies then besieged Bijapur ; and it seemed likely that the Adil Shahi kingdom would be divided between Ahmadnagar and Vijayanagar, when Burhan

---

* See Sewell, *A Forgotten Empire*, p. 98.

Shah fell seriously ill. He withdrew with his troops to his capital, where he died. His body was embalmed and sent for burial to Karbela, the holy place of the faith to which he had been converted (A.D. 1553).

Hussein Nizam Shah, the eldest son of the dancing girl Amina, succeeded his father Burhan Nizam Shah at the age of only thirteen. The chief event of his reign was the destruction of Vijayanagar by a confederacy of four of the Musulman kings of the Deccan. Burhan Shah had left by his queen Miriam Bibi, princess of Bijapur, two sons, Ali and Miran Mahomed. On their father's death they fled to their uncle Ibrahim Adil Shah, king of Bijapur. He espoused their cause but suffered two reverses. He then implored the aid of King Ramraj of Vijayanagar. The Hindu king sent a large army under his brother Venkatadri, who soon severely defeated the enemy. Unhappily Ibrahim Adil Shah celebrated the victory with so many bumpers of country liquor that he fell ill. And as he put to death all the court physicians whose prescriptions did not instantly cure him, the survivors fled the country and left Ibrahim Adil Shah to die without their assistance (1558). His son Ali Adil Shah renewed the treaty with Ramraj. The two allies induced the king of Golconda to join them, and invading Ahmadnagar, laid siege to the capital. At last Hussein Nizam Shah was reduced to such straits that he was forced to order the execution of his best general, Jehangir Khan, to cede the fortress of Kalyani to Bijapur and to receive *pan* as an inferior from the hand of Ramraj. Hussein Nizam Shah's pride especially resented this last clause. After Ramraj had touched his hand, Hussein Nizam Shah called out in a loud voice for a basin of water. He then washed his hands in the most offensive manner possible. The generous Hindu would not avenge himself on one who was in his power. But the incident made any later reconciliation between the two impossible.

Five years later Hussein Nizam Shah, allying himself to the king of Golconda, tried to retake Kalyani. But Ramraj and Ali Adil Shah, joined by the kings of Bedar and Berar, attacked the besiegers, defeated them and again besieged Ahmadnagar.

ADILSHAHI KINGS OF BIJAPUR

(From a Miniature engraved in Lane's "Monumens de l'Hindoustan")

1. YUSUF ADIL SHAH
2. ISMAIL ADIL SHAH
3. IBRAHIM ADIL SHAH
4. BRAHIM ADIL SHAH
5. IBRAHIM ADIL SHAH II
6. MAHMUD ADIL SHAH II
7. ...

[To face page 101]

It would certainly have fallen, had not a quarrel broken out
among the allies. The Hindus, finding themselves in Musulman
territory, threw down the mosques and defiled the holy places.
Ali Adil Shah, scandalized at the insult to his faith, begged
Ramraj to raise the siege. Ramraj complied but vented his
ill will upon all the Musulman kings alike. He forced Ali Adil
Shah to cede him the districts of Etgir and Bagrakot. He took
Kowilconda, Pangal and Guntur from the king of Golconda. And
he showed his contempt for the kings of Bedar and Berar by
publicly slighting them and encouraging his officers to do the
same. Ali Adil Shah, who had long fretted at the insolence of
his Hindu ally, resolved to lay aside his quarrel with Ahmadnagar
and destroy Ramraj. Hussein Nizam Shah's hatred of Ramraj
proved stronger than his rivalry with Bijapur. He gave his
daughter Chand Bibi in marriage to Ali Adil Shah with Sholapur
and its five and a half districts as her dowry. Ali Adil Shah
gave his daughter Huddea Sultana to Hussein's son Murtaza. The
reconciled rivals allied themselves to the kings of Golconda
and Bedar, and all four declared war upon Ramraj (1564).
The latter regarded the hostile alliance with contempt. He
posted his army on the southern bank of the Krishna and defied
his enemies to enter the Doab. One night, however, the allies
skilfully crossed the great river. Next morning the armies
engaged. Ramraj, who was over seventy, would not ride,
but commanded the centre of his army from a raised throne.
His brother Venkatadri, who commanded the left wing, drove
back the Bijapur forces. His other brother Tirumal, commander
of the right wing, also drove back the army of Golconda. But
Hussein Nizam Shah, impelled by a furious hatred of the king
to whom he had humbled himself, cut his way through the
Vijayanagar centre until he reached Ramraj's throne and took
him prisoner. With malignant joy he had his captive's head cut
off and placed on a spear. A panic seized the Hindus. Ramraj's
brother Venkatadri fell on the field. Tirumal made no effort
to hold Vijayanagar, but retired south to the great fortress of
Pennakonda. Then alas for the great city with its mighty walls
and its sparkling lakes ; with its stone-paved streets and its

markets glittering with jewels and precious stones ! Hordes of robber clans rushed into the city to plunder the shops, the store-houses, the dwellings and the palaces. On the third day the Musulman armies arrived and completed the ruin. Street by street they slaughtered the inhabitants, broke in pieces the idols and desecrated the temples. When their work was done, Vijayanagar was a scene of utter desolation and such it has remained to this day.

Hussein Nizam Shah did not long survive the victory of Talikota, the name by which the great battle is known. Return-ing to Ahmadnagar he, as Ibrahim Adil Shah had done, killed himself by the excesses with which he celebrated his triumph (A.D. 1565).

The reign of his son Murtaza Nizam Shah is famous for his conquest of Berar. Early in his reign a treaty was concluded between Ahmadnagar and Bijapur. The principal articles were that Ali Adil Shah should be free to complete the conquest of Vijayanagar and that Murtaza Nizam Shah should be at liberty to conquer Berar, recently usurped by one Tufal Khan from the infant king, Burhan Imad Shah. Immediately upon the conclusion of the treaty, the Ahmadnagar army invaded Berar under the command of one Jenghiz Khan. He defeated Tufal Khan and took him and Burhan Imad Shah prisoners. Instead of placing the latter on the throne, Murtaza confined him and Tufal Khan and their families and dependants in a fort. But the prisons of princes are nigh to their graves. Shortly after-wards all the captives died suddenly, and Berar became a pro-vince of Ahmadnagar (A.D. 1575). The last years of Murtaza Nizam Shah were darkened by madness. He attempted the life of his son Miran Hussein. His brother Burhan conspired against him and then fled to Akbar's court. At last Prince Miran Hussein, who had hidden in Daulatabad, was recalled to Ahmadnagar by the nobles. He murdered his father and seated himself upon the throne (A.D. 1588).

This parricide profited the new king but little. His chief confederate in the late revolution had been the first minister, a Persian by name Mirza Khan. A conflict soon broke out between the new king, who desired to wield power, and the minister, who wished to retain it. Each tried every device to seize the person of the other. At last the king gave a banquet at the house of one of his favourites. To it he invited Mirza Khan, meaning to assassinate him. Mirza Khan excused himself on the ground of sickness but sent one Agha Mir to take his place. Agha Mir dined with the king, but rose during the meal complaining of internal pains and crying out that he had been poisoned. The king was deeply concerned and let him depart. An hour later a messenger came from Mirza Khan. He told the king that Agha Mir was dying and wished to see his master before he expired. The king with a few attendants went to the dying man's house to express his regret and protest his innocence. As he entered the house he was promptly captured by Agha Mir, supported by a body of troops. The king's plot had been met by a skilful counterplot. He was now in Mirza Khan's power and was thrown into a dungeon (A.D. 1589). Burhan Nizam Shah, the brother of Murtaza Nizam Shah, had, when fleeing to Akbar's court, left behind him his two sons Ibrahim and Ismail. Murtaza Nizam Shah had confined them in the fort of Lohgad to the west of Poona. The younger son Ismail was only in his twelfth year and, therefore, a suitable puppet for an aspiring minister. But as he was being crowned, there broke out a serious tumult caused by the hatred which the Deccan, or native-born, Musulmans had always borne to the foreign officials and mercenaries, ever since Ala-ud-din Shah Bahmani had pronounced the former to be perpetually inferior. The Deccani leader Jamal Khan demanded the release of Miran Hussein. Mirza Khan replied that he was unworthy to rule and had been deposed. The reply excited the Deccan Musulmans to fever pitch. " Are we the slaves of foreigners ?" cried Jamal Khan. " Are our kings to be deposed at their lightest whim ?" To the Deccan soldiers joined the Hindu mob. For they favoured the country-born Musulmans rather than foreigners from beyond the sea. Mirza Khan then had his wretched captive's head struck off and fastened to a pole. At this the mob began to dissolve. But Jamal Khan artfully fomented their fury.

" Will you," he cried, " men of Ahmadnagar, pardon your king's murder when you resented his deposition ?" The mob rallied and set fire to the gates of Ahmadnagar fort. Mirza Khan sought to escape, but was taken. He was mounted on an ass, paraded through Ahmadnagar city, and then beheaded. Jamal Khan next ordered a general massacre of the foreign soldiers, of whom a thousand were murdered in seven days. The rest fled to Bijapur (A. D. 1589).

The confusion into which the Ahmadnagar kingdom had fallen gave Akbar the chance of interference which he had long desired. He had sheltered Burhan Nizam Shah, the exiled brother of Murtaza Nizam Shah. He now helped Burhan Nizam Shah to defeat and slay Jamal Khan, depose his own son Ismail, and mount the throne with the title of Burhan Nizam Shah II.

The new monarch's reign was short, but in it he suffered two reverses. He tried to reduce the Portuguese fortress of Reva-danda. The attack was skilfully planned. The harbour was blocked to prevent any help from the sea, while the siege was pressed from the land side. The mutinous spirit, however, of the Deccan officers, who since the new king's reign had been out of favour, aided the besieged ; and when the Portuguese garrison were at the last extremity, sixty Portuguese ships, forcing by night the boom across the harbour, landed four thou-sand men with abundant arms and supplies. Next morning the initiative passed to the besieged. They attacked the besiegers, and although only half their number, killed twelve thousand of them and put the rest to flight. The king consoled himself by the thought that the fallen were mostly Deccan Musulmans and sought to re-establish his prestige by recovering Sholapur. This adventure also failed, and retiring to Ahmadnagar he died soon afterwards of dysentery (April 30, 1595).

Burhan Nizam Shah's eldest son Ibrahim Nizam Shah succeed-ed to the throne and appointed his father's former tutor, Mia Manju, his minister. The choice was wise, for the minister had capacity, but the disorder into which the state had fallen nullified his efforts. A turbulent Deccan noble named Yeklas Khan sought to revive the Deccan party and gathered round

him the native-born Musulman soldiery. The minister retaliated by forming a body-guard of foreign mercenaries. Faction
fights broke out in all parts of the city and the unhappy king's
authority vanished. The Bijapur king, on the pretext of
restoring order, invaded the Ahmadnagar territory. Mia
Manju endeavoured to persuade the Bijapur general Hamid
Khan that the time had come to make up the quarrels of the
two states, that they might better ward off the Moghul danger.
But Mia Manju's wise endeavours were frustrated by his own
king. The wretched boy had found consolation for the loss
of his power in ardent spirits, and in a drunken fit called on his
army to attack Hamid Khan. His troops obeyed. As he
charged at their head he fell struck by a cannon ball. Thus
after a reign of only four months the throne of Ahmadnagar
again became vacant (September, 1595).

Mia Manju, Yeklas Khan and some other leading nobles
now held council how the government of Ahmadnagar should
be carried on. It was at first suggested that the late king's
infant son Bahadur should be crowned and his aunt Chand
Bibi declared regent. This illustrious lady was the daughter
of Hussein Nizam Shah and had, while still a child, been married
to Ali Adil Shah, king of Bijapur. The daughter, wife and
sister of kings, she united in her person the highest qualities
of both the Bijapur and Ahmadnagar houses. When her
husband was killed in 1580, his nephew Ibrahim Adil Shah was
raised to the throne of Bijapur. To Chand Bibi was entrusted
the care of his person. The care of the state was entrusted to
a certain Kamil Khan. In no long time Kamil Khan aspired
to usurp the throne, and to seduce Chand Bibi. She scornfully
rejected her wooer's suit and planned his destruction. With
the aid of a certain Kishwar Khan, she overthrew the regency of
Kamil Khan. But Kishwar Khan had no sooner displaced
Kamil Khan than he began to follow his example. He assumed
the government of the state; and when Chand Bibi opposed
his ambition, he had her driven from the royal harem and confined in the fortress of Satara, destined long afterwards to be
the hereditary prison of Shivaji's descendants. But the power

7

of Chand Bibi made itself felt through the stone walls of a distant stronghold. The mob rose against Kishwar Khan as the jailer of their beloved queen and drove him from the city. They then released Chand Bibi, brought her back in triumph and once more entrusted to her care the person of the young king. In 1584, the widowed queen, disgusted at the turbulence of the Bijapur nobles, left that city to visit her brother Murtaza Nizam Shah. For ten years she resided at Ahmadnagar and her name was now put forward to conduct the administration. Mia Manju, however, desired supreme power and insisted that a certain Ahmad, the son of an impostor named Shah Tahir, should be placed upon the throne. Yeklas Khan met this intrigue by taking a beggar boy named Moti from the streets and declaring him to be the son of the late king. A fight ensued, in which the beggar boy's adherents won the day. Mia Manju then appealed to Prince Murad, the son of Akbar, to invade the country. On the appearance, however, of the Moghul vanguard, all Ahmadnagar called with one voice for Chand Bibi to defend them. Mia Manju fled and Chand Bibi, declaring her nephew, Bahadur, king, assumed the government on his behalf. Order now appeared where all had been disorder. The masculine queen with veiled face but sword in hand appeared everywhere to direct and to cheer the garrison. Prince Murad sought to mine the walls. Chand Bibi showed her troops how to countermine and with her own hands removed the powder from two of the mines. At last a third mine exploded and several yards of the fort wall fell. The chief officers sought to flee, but Chand Bibi, taking their place, shamed her generals into resolution. From four in the afternoon Moghul storming parties tried to force their way through the breach. But fired by the spirit of the gallant lady the Ahmadnagar garrison was invincible. At last the breach was choked with the corpses of the assailants. Night fell. The Moghul army withdrew to their camp and next morning saw to their wonder a new wall which the unconquerable queen had built during the night. The gallantry of Chand Bibi was now the theme of Prince Murad's camp and the chivalrous Moghul conferred on her the title of Chand

Sultana, or Queen in her own right. He also offered to withdraw his troops in return for the cession of Berar. Chand Sultana, as modest in success as she had been superb in danger, made the cession and the Moghul army retreated (1596).

The malady, however, of Ahmadnagar was beyond her cure. She appointed one Mahomed Khan as her Peshwa. In a few months he also sought to usurp the throne. The queen in despair wrote to her nephew Ibrahim Adil Shah of Bijapur to send to her some troops with which to reorganize the kingdom. Mahomed Khan in revenge begged the new governor of Berar, Khan Khanan, to come to his aid, promising to hold Ahmadnagar as the vassal of the Delhi emperor. Khan Khanan agreed. The Moghul horse neared the city. Then once again the mob rose, confined the usurper and restored the government to the dauntless lady. With her return to power the affairs of Ahmadnagar took a favourable turn (1599). In reply to her appeals armies came from Bijapur and Golconda. And although Prince Murad won against them a victory on the Godavari, dissensions in his own camp prevented him from turning it to advantage. In the following year an Ahmadnagar army actually penetrated Berar. But once more the factious spirit of the Ahmadnagar nobles thwarted the wisdom of the queen. Nehung Khan, an Abyssinian soldier of fortune, tried to overthrow the government. Faction fights broke out again in Ahmadnagar city. The Emperor Akbar, grasping the opportunity, took the field in person. Nehung Khan sought to oppose the Moghuls but was defeated and fled. And now for the last time the great queen sought to save her country. Besieged by the emperor, she for some weeks conducted the defence with all her former daring. At last she resolved to evacuate Ahmadnagar and retreat southwards with the young Bahadur Shah to the fort of Junnar among the western hills. The plan, if adopted, might have preserved the Ahmadnagar state intact for another forty years. But a eunuch named Hamid Khan, out of temper with Chand Sultana for disregarding his counsel, ran into the streets shouting to the garrison that the queen had betrayed them to the Moghuls. The credulous garrison rushed into the palace and killed her whose only wish was to serve their interests. With the heroic queen died the spirit of her soldiers. A few days later the Moghul army stormed the fort, put its defenders to the sword and carried off Bahadur Shah to Gwalior fort, where he died in captivity (A.D. 1600). Khandesh, which had fallen in 1599, was with Ahmadnagar made into a governor-ship for Akbar's youngest son Prince Daniyal. Although, as we shall see in a later chapter, the entire province did not submit until 1636, yet the fall of the Ahmadnagar fort may be deemed to mark the end of the Ahmadnagar kingdom.

A pathetic story still exists which shows how deep was the love which Chand Sultana inspired. The peasants of the western hills refused for many years to believe that she was dead. She had escaped, they said, through an underground passage and was hiding in some deep fold of the Sahyadri Mountains. When the time came she would again reveal herself, drive the Moghuls across the Vindhyas, and bring back once more the golden years of Ahmadnagar.

APPENDIX

It may assist the reader if he refers from time to time to the following table of the five Deccan dynasties :—

AHMADNAGAR

1. Ahmad Nizam Shah (d. 1508).

2. Burhan Nizam Shah (d. 1553).

3. Hussein Nizam Shah (d. 1565).

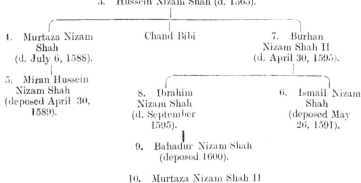

4. Murtaza Nizam Shah (d. July 6, 1588).

    Chand Bibi

7. Burhan Nizam Shah II (d. April 30, 1595).

5. Miran Hussein Nizam Shah (deposed April 30, 1589).

8. Ibrahim Nizam Shah (d. September 1595).

6. Ismail Nizam Shah (deposed May 26, 1591).

9. Bahadur Nizam Shah (deposed 1600).

10. Murtaza Nizam Shah II (d. 1631).

11. Hussein Nizam Shah (imprisoned 1633).

BIJAPUR

1. Yusuf Adil Shah I (d. 1510).

2. Ismail Adil Shah (d. 1534).

3. Mallu Adil Shah (deposed 1535).

4. Ibrahim Adil Shah I (d. 1558).

5. Ali Adil Shah (d. 1580).

6. Ibrahim Adil Shah II (d. 1626).

7. Mahomed Adil Shah (d. 1656).

8. Ali Adil Shah (d. 1672).

9. Sikandar Adil Shah (deposed 1686).

GOLCONDA

1. Sultan Kuli Kutb Shah (d. November 21, 1543).

4. Ibrahim Kutb Shah (d. 1580).   2. Jamshed Kutb Shah (d. 1550).

5. Mahomed Kutb Shah (d. 1612).   3. Subhan Kutb Shah (d. 1550).

6. Mahomed Kutb Shah (d. 1635).

7. Abdul Kutb Shah (d. 1672).

8. Abu Hussein Kutb Shah (captured 1687).

BEDAR

1. Kasim Barid (d. 1504).

2. Amir Barid (d. 1539).

3. Ali Barid Shah (d. 1582).

4. Ibrahim Barid Shah (d. 1589).

5. Kasim Barid Shah I (d. 1592).

6. Mirza Ali Barid Shah (expelled 1599).

7. Amir Barid Shah II (died 1609).

BERAR

1. Fateh Ulla Imad Shah (Imad-ul-Mulk) (d. 1504).

2. Alla-ud-din Imad Shah (d. 1527).

3. Daria Imad Shah (d. 1562).

4. Burhan Imad Shah (deposed 1568).

5. Tufal Khan (imprisoned 1575).

CHAPTER XI

THE PANDHARPUR MOVEMENT

A.D. 1271 TO 1640

No history of the Maratha people would be complete without a notice, however short, of the great religious movement of Pandharpur, a town on the lower reaches of the Bhima River. The story runs that Pandharpur was founded by one Pundalik. He was the son of a certain Janudev and his wife Satyavati. The parents lived at Pandharpur, which was then a thick forest called Dandirvan. After his marriage, Pundalik began to illtreat his parents, until to escape their torments they joined a body of pilgrims who were going to Benares.

When Pundalik's wife heard of this, she decided to go also ; and she and her husband joined the pilgrims on horseback while the old couple walked. At the end of each day's march, Pundalik forced his parents to groom the two horses. Thus Janudev and Satyavati came bitterly to regret that they had ever gone on a pilgrimage. At last the pilgrims reached the hermitage of a great sage named Kukutswami. There they resolved to spend the night. Soon all, wearied with the march, fell asleep, save only Pundalik. At dawn, as he still lay awake, he saw a company of beautiful women, clad in dirty raiment, enter Kukutswami's hermitage, clean the floor, fetch water and wash the sage's clothes. They then entered Kukutswami's inner room ; and after a short interval they came out again in beautifully clean clothes and, passing near Pundalik, vanished.

The following night Pundalik again saw the beautiful women enter the hermitage and act as before. He threw himself at their feet and asked them who they were. They replied that they were the Ganges, the Yamuna and the other sacred rivers of India in which pilgrims were wont to bathe. Their garments

were soiled because of the sins of which the pilgrims washed
themselves clean. They then turned on Pundalik and told him
that because of his treatment of his parents he was the worst
sinner of them all. They rated him so soundly that they effected
a complete cure. From the most cruel he became the most
devoted of sons.. He made his wife walk by his side while his
parents rode. By his filial conduct, he induced them to give
up the pilgrimage and return to Dandirvan. There no parents
were ever better served than Janudev and Satyavati were served
by Pundalik and his wife.

One day it fell out that the god Krishna, then king of Dwarka,
sat thinking of his early days on the banks of the Yamuna. He
remembered his sports with the milkmaids and how they, and
especially Radha, had wept when he had left Mathura. He so
longed to see Radha again that, although she was dead, he by
his divine powers brought her back to sit upon his lap. Just
then his queen, the stately Rukhmini, entered the room. Radha
should at once have risen to do her honour. She remained seated.
Rukhmini in a fury left, and fleeing to the Deccan, hid herself
in the Dandirvan forest. As she did not return to Dwarka, King
Krishna went to Mathura, thinking that she had fled thither.
From Mathura he went to Gokula. There he once more assumed
the form of a child, and round him began to play once more
the cows and the herdboys, the calves and the milkmaids.
They too joined in the search, and even Mount Govardhan
freed itself from its foundations and set forth with the gay
company to look for Rukhmini. At last they reached the banks
of the Bhima. Krishna left his attendants at a spot outside
the Dandirvan forest known as Gopalpura. Wandering alone
through the woods, he at last found Rukhmini. The queen's
celestial anger yielded to the endearments of the king. Reconciled, they walked together until they came to Pundalik's
hermitage. At this time Pundalik was busily engaged in attend-
ing to his parent's wants. Although he learnt that Krishna
had come to see him, he refused to do the god homage until
his filial task was done. But he threw a brick outside for his
visitor to stand upon. Krishna, pleased with Pundalik's

devotion to his parents, overlooked the slight to himself and standing on the brick awaited Pundalik's leisure. When Pundalik was free he excused himself to the god. The latter replied that, so far from being angry, he was pleased with Pundalik; and he ordered him to worship him as Vithoba, or him who stood upon a brick. A stately fane arose at the scene of the meeting of Krishna and Pundalik (A.D. 1228). In its holiest recess the god Krishna's image stands on the brick thrown to him by Pundalik. Close to his side stands an image of Rukhmini, whose flight was the cause of his visit to Pandharpur.

It was at this sacred place that the poet Dnyandev, the first of a long line of famous saints, took up his abode. According to the poet Mahipati, the world had become so sinful that the gods Brahmadeva and Shiva sought out Vishnu to devise some plan by which to purify it. They decided that all three gods together with Vishnu's queen Laxmi should take human forms. The parents whom they honoured by becoming their children were Vithoba, a Brahman from Apegaon, and his wife Rakhmai, the daughter of a Brahman of Alandi, a small town on the Indrayani River about twelve miles north of Poona. Vithoba and Rakhmai settled at Alandi. But although the union was in other respects happy enough, it was not blessed with children. In a fit of melancholy, caused by the death of his parents, Vithoba went to Benares and became a *sanyasi* or anchorite. This was a sin on his part, for no one who has a childless wife should take *sanyas*. Eventually his preceptor Ramanand happened to go to Alandi and met the unhappy Rakhmai. From her lips he learnt the true facts. He returned to Benares, drove Vithoba out of his hermitage and forced him to live with his wife at Alandi. Rakhmai welcomed him home and their reunion was blessed with the birth of four children—Nivratti, Dnyandev, Sopana and Muktabai, who were respectively the incarnations of Shiva, Vishnu, Brahmadeva and Laxmi.

The return of Vithoba to a married householder's life after he had taken a vow of asceticism deeply offended the Brahmans of Alandi. They outcasted him. And when he wished to have his eldest son invested with the sacred thread, they refused to perform the ceremony unless he could get the Brahmans of Paithan, a holy place on the Godavari, to give him a letter of purification. Nivratti with his two brothers and his sister went to Paithan. There the Brahmans heard their case and decided that there was only one penance for such a crime as the return of the anchorite to married life. The penitent must prostrate himself before every dog, pig, hare, ass or cow that he met, thinking all the time of the god Brahmadeva. Nivratti and his brothers annoyed the Brahmans by receiving the sentence cheerfully. The Brahmans asked Dnyandev what right he had to a name which being interpreted meant "the god of wisdom." Just then a buffalo passed, carrying a skin of water. "Let us call this buffalo Dnyandev," said the Brahmans; "he is every bit as wise as the real owner of the name." Dnyandev replied readily that they were welcome to call it by his name. For in the sight of Krishna men and animals were alike. The Brahmans retorted, "If the buffalo is your equal and you are really a learned man, let it recite the Vedas." Dnyandev rose and placed his hand on the buffalo's head. Straightway it recited all four Vedas without an error.

This miracle, followed by others, convinced the Brahmans of the saintly character of Nivratti and his family. They gave Nivratti a letter of purification and the Brahmans of Alandi had perforce to accept it. Investing Nivratti and his two brothers with the sacred thread they admitted him into the Brahman caste. At Alandi Dnyandev wrought many other miracles. At Newasa he wrote the *Dnyaneshwari* or Marathi commentary on the *Bhagwat Gita*, thus disclosing the teaching of Krishna to the humblest of the Maratha people. Besides the *Dnyaneshwari* Dnyandev wrote the *Amritanubhau* and the *Dnyaneshwar Naman*.

When his life-work was done, he wished to take *samadhi*, or in other words be buried alive at Pandharpur. The poet[*] Namdev has told the story of Dnyandev's end in beautiful and

---

[*] Namdev's *Charitra*, p. 198.

touching verses. One morning when Dnyandev and his brothers and sister were sitting in the temple of Krishna* at Pandharpur, he expressed the wish to be buried at the feet of Krishna's image. The god answered that if Dnyandev were buried at Pandharpur, his fame would be overshadowed by Krishna's. He must therefore be buried at Alandi. Dnyandev demurred. But Krishna reassured him that Alandi too was a holy place. Re-assured by Krishna, Dnyandev consented to take *samadhi* at Alandi. There amid a rain of heavenly flowers, Dnyandev entered a grave that had been dug for him. A deer-skin was spread for him to sit upon. A wood-fire was lit in a fire-place made for the purpose. Inhaling the wood smoke, Dnyandev became slowly unconscious. While he lay in a stupor, his dis-ciples closed the mouth of the grave and sealed him in his living tomb. Not long afterwards, his brother Sopana imitated, at Saswad, to the east of Poona, Dnyandev's act of self-immolation. Then Muktabai vanished in a lightning flash on the banks of the Tapti. Nivratti, the last left, took *samadhi* at Trimbakeshwar in the Nasik district.

Now Dnyandev was an outcaste Brahman. By his devotion to God he won his way to the caste and in the end became a saint. It therefore followed, so men said, that in the eyes of God caste must be as nothing and that all earthly disabilities could be overcome by the love and worship of Krishna. Thus Pandharpur came to attract pious men of all castes. The next great saint of Pandharpur was Chokhamela, a Mhar. Savata was of the *mali* or gardener caste. Raka and Gora were *kum-bhars* or potters. Rohidas was a *chambhar* or leather worker. Narhari was a *sonar* or goldsmith. Kabir was actually a Musul-man attracted from the north by the fame of Pandharpur. Namdev, the greatest of all, was a *shimpi* or tailor. They were all men of holy and austere lives. Their worship of Krishna was eminently pure and sane. Their preaching and their poems stimulated men's minds and led them to seek a refuge from their sorrows at Krishna's shrine. The spots

---

* Krishna is always worshipped at Pandharpur under the name Vithoba. But to avoid confusing my English readers I have retained the name of Krishna.

where Dnyandev and his brothers and sister died became cen-
tres from which the Pandharpur tenets were promulgated from
the Bhima to the Tapti and from Alandi to Saswad.   Men who
made pilgrimages to these shrines were drawn to each other
by their common knowledge of the Marathi speech and of the
doctrines of the Pandharpur saints.   In this way there came
into existence the beginnings of a national feeling.   In course
of time the Deccan governments, cut off from the recruiting
grounds of Afghanistan and Central Asia, began to employ
Maratha clerks, Maratha soldiers and Maratha financiers.
The Marathi language came to be the language not only of the
Ahmadnagar offices but of the Ahmadnagar court.   But while
the Musulman officials dissipated their vigour in vice and riot,
the Hindus, owing to the teachings of the saints of Pandharpur,
led clean and manly lives.   So it came about that the religious
movement made ready the path for the national hero who was to
free Maharashtra from the foreign yoke.   When he appeared,
great beyond human anticipation, religion gave to his genius a
fervour which he was able to impart to the comrades of his
youth and the peasants of his father's villages.   Thus inspired,
his half-trained levies fought with the valour of Cortez' companions or of Cromwell's cuirassiers.

CHAPTER XII

THE RISE OF THE BHOSLES

A.D. 1600 to 1637

WE must now return once more to the unhappy kingdom of Ahmadnagar. The fall of the city built round the palace of the great Ahmad Nizam Shah did not lead to the entire subjection of the kingdom. An Abyssinian named Malik Ambar, who had been a dependant of Jenghiz Khan, the conqueror of Berar, raised to the throne another descendant of Ahmad Nizam Shah and conferred on him the title of Murtaza Nizam Shah II. As Ahmadnagar could no longer serve as a capital, Malik Ambar made the head-quarters of his government at Khadki, or the Rocky Town, built by him under the shadow of the great fortress of Daulatabad. The Emperor Aurangzib in after years changed the name of Khadki to Aurangabad, by which appellation it is known to-day. Somewhat earlier, Prince Selim, the son of Akbar and afterwards the Emperor Jehangir, rebelled against his father. When the rebel had been won back by his father's clemency and patience, Prince Daniyal, Akbar's third son, to whom he had entrusted the government of Ahmadnagar and Khandesh, died of intemperance. These calamities broke the health of the great emperor and on October 5, 1605, Akbar passed away, leaving Prince Selim to succeed him. The new emperor mounted the throne with less difficulty than his successors. Nevertheless his eldest son Khusru rebelled and had to be defeated before Jehangir could feel himself master of upper India (1606).

The six years which had passed between the fall of Ahmadnagar and the defeat of Khusru had been most usefully spent by Malik Ambar, a man of consummate talents and energy. He introduced a new revenue system which made his government

at once rich and popular, and although he retained all the
power in his own hands, he yet won the love and esteem of
the young king. In A.D. 1610 he believed himself strong
enough to attempt the conquest of the entire Ahmadnagar
state. From 1610 to 1615 he was almost continuously successful.
He retook Ahmadnagar fort and not only recovered all the
Ahmadnagar kingdom except one or two districts in the extreme
north but also retook a large part of Berar.

The loss of territory and the defeats of his generals led
the emperor to appoint his eldest son Shah Jehan* to conduct
the campaign against Malik Ambar. Shah Jehan had already
won great distinction by his reduction of Udaipur and, now in
command of a numerous army, he soon inflicted a series of
reverses on Malik Ambar and drove him from Ahmadnagar
fort. The victorious course of the Moghul armies was then
checked by a curious intrigue at Delhi (A.D. 1621). Nur Jehan,
the all-powerful empress, had hitherto been a warm friend and
supporter of her stepson Shah Jehan. But having married
her daughter by her former husband to Prince Shahriyar, the
emperor's youngest son, she transferred her support to her
son-in-law.† She induced Jehangir to recall Shah Jehan from the
Deccan and to entrust to him an expedition against Kandahar,
recently taken by the Persians. Shah Jehan suspected an
intrigue and refused to leave the Deccan until some guarantee
of the emperor's good faith was given him. Nur Jehan artfully
inflamed her husband's mind against the insubordinate prince,
whose fiefs were confiscated and given to Shahriyar. At the
same time, several of Shah Jehan's friends were executed as
his fellow conspirators. Shah Jehan had now no hope save in
rebellion. He withdrew his army from the Deccan and marching
towards Agra fought an indecisive action with the royal troops
in Central India. Failing to obtain the first victory essential
to an insurgent, Shah Jehan retreated through Guzarat into
Khandesh, from Khandesh to Bengal and from Bengal back
into the Deccan. There he threw himself on the mercy of his

* Then known as Prince Kharram.
† Elphinstone's *History*, p. 563.

old foe Malik Ambar. The latter received him with open arms
and bade him besiege Burhanpur in Khandesh while Malik
Ambar reduced the northern districts of Ahmadnagar. But
the new allies could not make head against the imperial forces
led by the emperor in person. Shah Jehan implored his father's
forgiveness and would no doubt have been readmitted to favour
had not the emperor himself been rendered powerless by the
conspiracy of one of his nobles Mahabat Khan.*

The latter was the son of one Ghor Beg and had risen from a
subaltern's post to be the first soldier in the empire. His rise
excited the jealousy of Nur Jehan. Learning that the emperor
was planning his ruin, he skilfully seized, by the aid of a small
body of Rajputs devoted to his service, the emperor's person in
the very midst of his army. The army, which respected Mahabat
Khan as a valiant soldier, made no effort to save the emperor.
He was at last rescued by the skill and courage of Nur Jehan.
Gathering round her a loyal contingent, she, during a review,
attacked and cut to pieces Mahabat Khan's Rajputs. She then
released the emperor and restored his authority. Mahabat Khan
fled to join Shah Jehan. The latter's fortunes were at their lowest
ebb. He had quarrelled with Malik Ambar in order to win
back his father's favour; but he was unable to join Jehangir
because of Mahabat Khan's conspiracy. He was contemplat-
ing a flight to Persia when Mahabat Khan with his remaining
adherents reached his camp. Their coming did not at first
much advance the prince's fortunes. But in the following
year the death of his father from asthma enabled him to use
Mahabat Khan's contingent and establish himself firmly on the
Delhi throne.

In 1626 Malik Ambar had died, leaving to his son Fateh
Khan the regency of Murtaza Nizam Shah's kingdom. The
latter, owing to the troubles of Jehangir's reign, effected
a favourable peace with the Moghul general Khan Jehan
Lodi.† But Fateh Khan's power was soon overthrown

---

* *Memoirs of Jehangir*, Elliot and Dowson, Vol. VI, p. 30.

† The Musulman historians charge Khan Jehan Lodi with having accepted
a bribe. But the condition of the empire justified the treaty.

by the prince for whom Malik Ambar had created a kingdom. Murtaza Nizam Shah II had reached manhood and
resented the authority of one whose abilities were of the
commonest order. With the aid of an officer called Tukarrib
Khan he ended the regency and imprisoned Fateh Khan. But
the prince's abilities were even feebler than those of the fallen
regent and he was soon involved in troubles, which lasted until
his death. Khan Jehan Lodi, the Moghul commander with
whom Fateh Khan had made peace, was a personal foe of Shah
Jehan. Shortly after the latter's accession (A.D. 1628) he
openly rebelled, and after evading the royal pursuit made his
way to Daulatabad. Murtaza Nizam Shah in an evil moment
made the fugitive's cause his own and thus brought on himself
another Moghul War. Shah Jehan took the field in person,
defeated Murtaza Nizam Shah's army in front of Daulatabad,
and driving Khan Jehan Lodi out of the Deccan defeated and
slew him in Central India (1630). The death of Khan Jehan
Lodi did not end the troubles of Ahmadnagar. The Moghuls
continued their efforts against Murtaza Nizam Shah and the
horrors of war were doubled by the accident of a famine. At
last Murtaza Nizam Shah in despair turned to his former regent
Fateh Khan, and releasing him from prison placed him once more
in authority. This act completed the king's ruin. Fateh
Khan on reassuming power threw his master into prison. He
then put him to death, and placing Murtaza Nizam Shah's
infant son Hussein* on the throne, declared himself to be once
more regent on the child's behalf (1631).

At this point I must introduce to my readers a Maratha
noble named Shahaji Bhosle, famous both for his own merits
and as the father of Shivaji, the liberator of the Maratha nation.
His family claimed descent from Sajana Sing, the grandson of
Lakshman Sing, the ancestor of the house of Udaipur. One
of the family, Devrajji by name,† after a quarrel with the Rana
of Udaipur fled to the Deccan. There he and his descendants

---

* *Badshah Nama*, Elliot and Dowson, Vol. VII, p. 27.

† In the *Shivdigvijaya Bakhar* his name is given as Kakaji, a name not
to be found in the Kolhapur genealogical tree.

SHAHAJI, FATHER OF SHIVAJI

(To face page 123.)

assumed the name of Bhosle * from the family fief of Bhosavat in Udaipur. Another story is that two brothers, Khelkarnaji or Kheloji and Malkarnaji or Maloji, came together from Udaipur to offer their services as free lances to the king of Ahmadnagar. Khelkarnaji or Kheloji died in battle. Malkarnaji was drowned while bathing in a river. Malkarnaji's son Babaji purchased the Patilki or headship of the village of Verul near Daulatabad. Babaji had two sons, Maloji † and Vithoji, who were the real founders of the greatness of the Bhosle family. One evening during the harvest time, Vithoji had gone early and tarried late in his fields. Darkness had fallen, and his elder brother Maloji went to call him. As he went a black peacock and a *bharadwaja* bird crossed his path from left to right, ‡ and, cheered by the happy omens, he entered a deep wood. The night was dark but as he stumbled through the undergrowth he suddenly saw in front of him the divine figure of Bhavani or Parvati, the consort of Shiva. Maloji was about to faint with fright, but the goddess reassured him. She told him that in his house would be born an incarnation of the god Shiva her husband. He would restore the Hindu faith, drive the Musulmans from the land, and found a kingdom which would endure for twenty-seven gene- rations. The twenty-seventh king would be born blind and would lose his kingdom. She then pointed to an ant-heap and bade him dig in it. He would by doing so unearth a hidden treasure. At first Maloji was loth to obey her command. " The treasure," said the youth to himself, " must belong to some evil spirit. When he finds it gone, he will haunt me, or else our Musulman rulers will hear of my good fortune and rob m of my gold and my life as well." The goddess bade him fear nothing. " Go to Shrigonda," she said, " and deposit the money with Sheshaji Naik." The goddess disappeared and Maloji fainted.

---

* Other explanations are that Bhosle is derived from Ghoslah " a place" (Khafi Khan, p. 235) and " gharte " a bird's nest. The derivation given by me is to be found in the *Shivdigrijaya Bakhar*.

† Maloji was born, according to the Shedgavkar genealogical tree, in A.D. 1552.

‡ These are both fortunate omens.

8

In the meantime Vithoji had returned home, and missing
Maloji went to look for him and found him in a swoon.
Vithoji roused his brother, from whom he learnt what had
occurred. They went home and next morning the two
brothers went to the ant-heap, dug there, found the treasure
and took it to Sheshaji Naik at Shrigonda. To him also had been
vouchsafed a vision of Bhavani. She had revealed herself to
him and had bidden him keep faithfully the money entrusted
to him by Maloji. With it Maloji built a temple at Verul known
as Ghrishneshwar, and a temple and a tank at Shingnapur. In
1577 Maloji and Vithoji entered the service of a Maratha baron
named Jagpatrao or Vanangpal Nimbalkar, * the ancestor of
the present chief of Phaltan. They rose rapidly to the command
of several thousand horse, with which they harried Bijapur
territory. One day as they were bathing, they were surprised
by a Bijapur force. But with cool daring they rallied their
horsemen and routed their opponents. The fame of their success
reached the ears of Murtaza Nizam Shah I, then king of Ahmad-
gar. He summoned the two brothers, and gave them employment in his army, where they attracted the notice of the leading
Maratha noble at the Ahmadnagar court, Lakhoji Jadhavrao.
Through his influence Maloji obtained as a bride Dipabai, the
sister of Vanangpal Nimbalkar, his former master. For
many years the union was not blessed by any children.
Maloji built tanks, founded temples to the gods, and made
pilgrimages to the famous temple of Bhavani at Tuljapur,
but to no purpose. He visited the shrine of a Musulman
saint named Shah Sharif. † Then at last his piety and
patience were rewarded. In 1594 Dipabai bore her husband
a son, whom in grateful recollection of Shah Sharif they
named Shahaji. In 1597 a second son was born whom they
called Sharifji.

---

* This Vanangpal Nimbalkar had a great reputation for bravery, as may
be gathered from the Marathi proverb which is still current : " Rao Vanangpal, bara Vaziranch ь kal," Rao Vanangpal is a match for 12 vazirs.

† *Shedgavkar Bakhar.* Grant Duff says that Shahaji engaged the prayers
of Shah Sharif. But both the *Shivdigvijaya* and the *Shedgavkar Bakhars*
say that Maloji and his wife prayed at the tomb of the saint. He had long
been dead and buried.

Connected by marriage with an ancient Maratha house, fortunate in the possession of heaven-sent treasure, and now father of two sons, Maloji had reason to hope that Bhavani's prophecy to him might be fulfilled. He conceived the design of uniting his eldest son Shahaji to the daughter of Lakhoji Jadhavrao, his powerful patron.

The design seemed at first hopeless. Lakhoji Jadhavrao claimed descent from the ancient Yadava kings of Devagiri. He was *deshmukh* of Sindkhed and commanded in the Ahmadnagar service a division of 10,000 horse. In A.D. 1599 fortune favoured the aspiring adventurer. Shahaji was a very fine little boy, sturdy and intellectual above the ordinary. He became the inseparable companion of his father. One day, while still a child,[*] he went with his father to the house of his patron Lakhoji to celebrate the Holi festival. Present also was Jijabai, the daughter of Lakhoji, a little girl one year younger than Shahaji. It is usual at the Holi festival for guests and hosts to amuse themselves by squirting red-coloured water over each other's clothes and faces. The children mimicked the action of their parents. Lakhoji, his heart softened by the gay scene and attracted by Shahaji's beauty, exclaimed: "What a fine pair they will make!" Maloji at once drew the attention of the guests to the remark and called upon them to note that Lakhoji had betrothed his daughter Jijabai to Shahaji. Lakhoji appears at first to have been taken aback. But pressed by the other guests, he seems afterwards to have promised Maloji that his son Shahaji should have Jijabai as his bride.[†] The same evening Lakhoji told his wife Mhalsabai what he had done. The proud woman deeply resented the betrothal of her daughter to the son of one whom she remembered as her husband's client. She pressed Lakhoji strongly to break off the

---

[*] Grant Duff writes that Shahaji was then in his 5th year. The *Shivdigvijaya Bakhar* gives his age as 9 or 10. According to Maratha authorities Jijabai was born in 1595.

[†] Grant Duff insists that Lakhoji never consented then. But both the *Shivdigvijaya* and the *Shedgaokar Bakhars* say that he consented the same evening. I think that he must have done so. Otherwise Maloji would hardly have been able to keep him to his promise.

marriage. Next day Lakhoji invited Maloji to a dinner-party, making no reference to the engagement of their children. Maloji declined the invitation unless Lakhoji undertook publicly to recognize Shahaji as his future son-in-law. Lakhoji, smarting from Mhalsabai's reproaches. refused to do so. Maloji then left Ahmadnagar on a pilgrimage to Tuljapur, where, prostrate at the feet of Bhavani's image, he implored her divine assistance. The same night he had a dream in which she appeared before him. She promised him her constant help and assured him that he would come by the desire of his heart. Returning to Ahmadnagar, he challenged Jadhavrao to a duel.* Murtaza Nizam Shah II heard of the dispute and summoned both to attend his court and explain their conduct. Maloji stated his case, pleading that Jadhavrao had promised his daughter Jijabai to Shahaji, but now refused to keep his word. Lakhoji admitted that he had said something of the sort, but maintained that he had spoken in jest only. Murtaza Nizam Shah II, who liked Maloji and had no wish to drive a gallant soldier to take service elsewhere, pressed the match on Jadhavrao, and, to overcome the objections of his wife, promoted Maloji to the command of 5000 horse, gave him Poona and Supa in fief to support them, and further made him commandant of the fortresses of Shivner and Chakan with the title of Raja.† Jadhavrao could no longer withhold his consent and the marriage of Shahaji and Jijabai in 1604 was celebrated with great ceremonial and was honoured by the presence of the king in person. From this time until his death in 1619 Maloji increased in the favour of Malik Ambar.

When he died, his son Shahaji, who had grown up a gallant and capable soldier, succeeded to his estate. The next year Shahaji greatly distinguished himself in the fighting against the Moghuls. But in spite of his gallantry Malik Ambar was defeated. Lakhoji

*Duelling, according to Feris'.ta. was extremely common in the Ahmadnagar kingdom from the time of the first king. The story of Maloji's challenge to Jadhavrao will be found in the *Shivdigvijaya Bakhar*. The *Shedgavkar Bakhar* relates that Maloji attracted the attention of the king by throwing two dead boars into a mosque. There is nothing impossible in this tale either : I have myself known a man place a boulder on a railway track in Kathiawar and risk derailing a train simply to call attention to a private grievance, namely that his wife had run away.

† Grant Duff, Vol. 1, p. 92.

Jadhavrao and many other highly placed Maratha nobles deserted to Shah Jehan. Shahaji, however, remained faithful to Malik Ambar until the latter's death in 1626, and for three years afterwards continued in the employ of Murtaza Nizam Shah II. He vigorously supported the cause of Khan Jehan Lodi, but when the latter had been defeated and destroyed (1630) Shahaji deemed it prudent to make his submission to the emperor. He was summoned to Shah Jehan's presence, was graciously received and was not only confirmed in his fief of Poona and Supa but was given also some districts which were the private property of the regent Fateh Khan. When the latter in A.D. 1631 murdered his master, he at first set up Murtaza Nizam Shah's infant son Hussein as a pageant king and proclaimed himself regent on his behalf. But finding himself universally detested and his authority precarious, he sent his son Abdul Rasul to the emperor. Fateh Khan, so Abdul Rasul was instructed to say, had acted solely in the interests of Delhi. Murtaza Nizam Shah II had died suddenly and his son Hussein had, pending the emperor's pleasure, been seated on the throne. The emperor received the messenger with condescension. In return for the large present which accompanied Abdul Rasul, Shah Jehan accepted Fateh Khan's submission, confirmed his measures and restored to him the districts which had previously been taken from him and conferred on Shahaji. The latter was incensed at this treatment, and resigning the Moghul service, entered, with the help of Murar Jagdev, then minister, the service of the king of Bijapur.

Ibrahim Adil Shah II had died in 1626, in the same year as Malik Ambar. His successor was his son Mahomed Adil Shah. Ibrahim Adil Shah II had been an ally of the Moghuls and had in the lifetime of Malik Ambar agreed to divide with them what remained of the Ahmadnagar kingdom. Mahomed Adil Shah, either because* he had come under the influence of a certain slave Khavas Khan, or because he feared the immediate vicinity of so powerful a neighbour as the Delhi emperor, sent under his general Randulla Khan an army ostensibly to help the

* *Badshah Nama*, Elliot and Dowson, Vol. VII, p. 28.

Moghuls, who were then fighting against Murtaza Nizam Shah
II. But after making extravagant demands from their general
Azim Khan, Randulla Khan, acting on instructions from Bijapur, entered into negotiations with Murtaza Nizam Shah II.
Before the plot could mature, Azim Khan heard of it, and
making a surprise attack on the Bijapur army severely defeated
it. It was his despair at this defeat which prompted Murtaza
Nizam Shah II to call Fateh Khan to his aid, with the results
that have been already related.

When Shahaji entered the Bijapur service that kingdom was
still at war with the Moghuls. He pressed on Mahomed Adil
Shah an immediate attack on Daulatabad. The king agreed
and placed Shahaji in command of a large Bijapur force. Fateh
Khan in alarm wrote to Mahabat Khan the Moghul general*
and begged for his help. He, in return, undertook to surrender
Daulatabad and hold the rest of the kingdom as a vassal of
Delhi. Mahabat Khan willingly agreed and sent a picked force
under Khan Jaman his son* to throw themselves into Daulatabad
while he came afterwards with the main army. But quickly
as the Moghul cavalry rode, Shahaji‡ and his Bijapur troops
rode faster still, and reaching Daulatabad first, succeeded in
convincing Fateh Khan that his real interest lay in deserting
his Moghul allies and in making common cause with Bijapur.
If Fateh Khan resigned all claims to Sholapur and its five and a
half districts, Mahomed Adil Shah would let him retain Daulatabad and all that still remained of the Ahmadnagar state. Fateh
Khan, attracted by the offer, accepted it. And Shahaji at
once threw a garrison and provisions into the fortress. When
the Moghul advance guard reached its walls, they were greeted
with a salvo of artillery. Mahabat Khan was naturally enraged
at the treachery. He attacked Shahaji's troops, drove them
away, and getting between them and Daulatabad, regularly
invested it. Ever since its construction by Mahomed Tughlak

---

* *Badshah Nama*, p. 37.

‡ *Badshah Nama*, p. 38. Before starting on this expedition Shahaji
and Murar Jagdev weighed themselves against gold in a village called Nagargaon
on the banks of the Bhima. This incident has caused it to be known as
Tulapur to this day.

it had been regarded as impregnable, and Malik Ambar had greatly increased its strength. Nevertheless the imperial army, in which were large bodies of Rajputs, stormed its nine bastions one after the other and at the same time repulsed all Shahaji's efforts to relieve it. At last Fateh Khan, foreseeing the imminent fall of his stronghold, sued for, and was granted, terms. In return for a payment of ten lakhs of rupees he surrendered Daulatabad and the person of Hussein Nizam Shah, the son of Murtaza Nizam Shah II. Both were sent to Delhi. The property of the unhappy Hussein was wholly confiscated and he was imprisoned with Bahadur Shah in Gwalior fort. The traitor Fateh Khan received a grant of land valued at Rs. 20,000 per annum (1633).

Shahaji made one last desperate attempt to retrieve the fortunes of the campaign. When the Moghul general Mahabat Khan withdrew with his spoils and captives, he left a garrison in Daulatabad. The army was no sooner out of sight than Shahaji's troops occupied the besieger's entrenchments and tried to take the fortress by storm. But the commandant, Khan Dauran* was a veteran soldier. He fought several victorious actions against Shahaji and driving him back, succeeded in sending messengers to Mahabat Khan. The latter at once returned with all speed to Daulatabad, and Shahaji retreated towards Bijapur. He was however not yet at the end of his resources. Somewhere or other he discovered another infant descendant of Ahmad Nizam Shah and proclaiming him king, declared himself regent during the child's minority. At first he met with some success and with the help of the Bijapur troops defeated the Moghuls at Parenda and drove them out of Ahmadnagar into Khandesh.† There Mahabat Khan died of fistula and Shah Jehan resolved once more to take the field in person. So long as Bijapur was not crushed there would be, so the emperor felt, continued insurrections in the Ahmadnagar provinces. He therefore entered on a campaign against both

---

* *Badshah Nama*, p. 42.
† *Do.* p. 44.

Shahaji and the Bijapur king with an army of 40,000 men.
Of these, 20,000*men under Khan Dauran, the late commandant
of Daulatabad, were to attack and overrun the Bijapur kingdom,
20,000 men under Khan Zaman, the son of Mahabat Khan,
were to overwhelm Shahaji and then join forces with Khan
Dauran.† Shahaji, however, proved too skilful for his opponent.
Employing the same tactics for which Shivaji afterwards became
famous, Shahaji evaded pitched battles, but constantly out-
marching the imperial troops, inflicted repeated reverses on
their rearguard. At last Shah Jehan ordered Khan Zaman to
leave the pursuit of Shahaji and to join Khan Dauran in the
attack on Bijapur. Several indecisive engagements followed
between the Moghuls and the army of Mahomed Adil Shah.
At last both sides, weary of the war, came to terms. On May
6, 1636, Mahomed Adil Shah agreed to abandon Shahaji and
to help in his reduction. In return, he received Parenda,
Sholapur with its five and a half districts‡, the Ahmadnagar
Konkan as far north as Bassein, the country between the Bhima
and the Nira Rivers as far north as Chakan and also the
districts of Naldurga, Kalyani and Bedar in the Central Deccan.§

Shahaji had now to face both the Moghuls and the Bijapur
army. Nevertheless he conducted a most gallant defence. Khan
Zaman invested Junnar, the fort wherein Shahaji had made his
capital. Shahaji, leaving a garrison there, so harassed the
communications of the Moghuls, that had they been unaided
they would have had to raise the siege. To Khan Zaman's aid,
however, went Randulla Khan with the Bijapur troops.
Attacked both from north and south, Shahaji retreated skilfully
through the Sahyadris into the Konkan. There doubling on
his track, he retired through the same passes and reached the
Desh, while his pursuers still sought for him to the west of the
Sahyadris. When they learnt of his escape the combined
armies followed him with great expedition and at last brought

---

* *Badshah Nama*, p. 52
† Grant Duff, Vol. I, p. 115.
‡ Sholapur and 5½ districts had been ceded to Bijapur as Chand Bibi's
dowry on her marriage to Ali Adil Shah. Malik Ambar retook them in 1624
from Bijapur after his victory of Bhatvadi (*Shivdigvijaya Bakhar*).
§ For text of treaty, see Appendix, p. 122.

him to bay at Mahuli near Kalyan in the Konkan. There Khan
Zaman and Randulla Khan besieged him. After a prolonged
resistance Shahaji asked for terms (October, 1636). He was
granted them on condition that he surrendered the unfortunate
prince for whom he called himself regent and the six fortresses
still in his possession. He was then allowed to enter the service
of Bijapur and received back from that state the fiefs of Poona
and Supa, included by the late treaty within Bijapur. Upon
the surrender of Shahaji followed the complete subjugation of
Ahmadnagar. Berar had already been ceded by Chand Bibi
to Delhi. Bedar had been conquered by Bijapur. There thus
remained of the five kingdoms into which the Bahmani empire
had broken, only Golconda and Bijapur.

APPENDIX

TEXT OF TREATY BETWEEN DELHI AND BIJAPUR

(1) Adil Shah, the king of Bijapur, must acknowledge the overlordship of the emperor and promise to obey his orders in future.

(2) The pretence of a Nizam Shahi kingdom must be ended and all its territories divided between the emperor and the Bijapur king. Adil Shah must not violate the new imperial frontier nor let his servants hinder the Moghul officers in occupying and settling the newly annexed districts.

(3) The king of Bijapur was to retain all his ancestral territory with the following additions from the Ahmadnagar kingdom in the west, the Sholapur and Wangi Mahals, between the Bhima and the Sina Rivers, including the forts of Sholapur and Parenda ; in the north east the parganas of Bhalki and Chidgupa ; and that portion of the Konkan which had once belonged to the Nizam Shahis, including the Poona and Chakan districts. These acquisitions comprised 59 parganas and yielded a revenue of 20 lakhs of huns or 80 lakhs of rupees. The rest of the Nizam Shahi kingdom was to be recognised as annexed to the empire beyond question or doubt.

(4) Adil Shah must pay the emperor a peace offering of twenty lakhs of rupees in cash and kind. But no annual tribute was imposed.

(5) Golconda being now a state under imperial protection, Adil Shah must in future treat it with friendship, respect its frontier, and never demand costly presents from the king, to whom he must behave like an elder brother.

(6) Each side undertook not to seduce the officers of the other from their master's service, nor to entertain deserters, and Shah Jehan promised for himself and his sons that the Bijapur king would never be called upon to transfer any of his officers to the imperial service.

(7) Shahaji Bhosle, who had set up a princeling of the house of Nizam Shah, should not be admitted to office under Bijapur, unless he ceded Junnar, Trimbak and the other forts still in his hands to Shah Jehan. If he declined he was not to be harboured in Bijapur territory nor even allowed to enter it.

CHAPTER XIII

SHIVAJI'S BIRTH AND BOYHOOD

A.D. 1627 TO 1645

THE marriage of Shahaji to Jijabai appears, in spite of the differences between Maloji Bhosle and Lakhoji Jadhavrao, to have been for the first few years happy enough. In 1623, Jijabai bore her lord a son, three years after their marriage. He was called Sambhaji and became a great favourite of his father, just as Shahaji had been of Maloji. On April 10, 1627,* after an interval of four years, she bore Shahaji a second son. Several stories are told in support of the general belief that the baby boy was an incarnation of the god Shiva. A charming one is to be found in the *Shedgavkar Bakhar*. During the stormy years that followed the birth of Sambhaji, Shahaji, engaged in the warlike enterprises entrusted to him by Malik Ambar, found no time to pay his wife conjugal attentions. One night he dreamt that he saw a Gosavi or Hindu anchorite, clad in rags and smeared with yellow ashes, stand by his bedside and put a mango in his hand. "Share the fruit with your wife," said the anchorite, "and you will become the father of a son who will be an incarnation of the god Shiva. You must never force him to salute a Musulman and after his twelfth year you must leave him free to act as he pleases." When Shahaji awoke from his dream, he found a mango in his hand, visited his wife and shared it with her. The offspring of this reunion was the boy Shivaji, born on April 10, 1627. Convinced that the anchorite whom he had seen in his dream was the god Shiva, Shahaji gave the new-born child the name of Shivaji, just as Maloji had called Shahaji after the Musulman saint Shah Sharif. According to another story, Shahaji had a vision of Shiva after Shivaji's birth and was

* *Marathi Itihasanchi Sadhane*, pp. 42-43.

then told by the god that the new-born boy was his own in-carnation.* When Shivaji was born, his mother Jijabai was living in a house on the top of the Shivner fort close to Junnar. A ruined wall still stands on the site where the house stood and a marble tablet, inserted in it under the orders of the Bombay Government by the late Mr. A. M. T. Jackson, keeps alive the memory of the greatest of Indian kings and of one of the wisest and best of modern Englishmen.

Even Shivaji's early days were not free from peril and adventure. Before his birth, his grandfather Lakhoji Jadhavrao had joined the Moghuls, and Shahaji by refusing to follow his example had incurred his bitter enmity. The quarrel was taken up by the other nobles in the Moghul service. And although Lakhoji Jadhavrao died in 1629, treacherously assassinated at Daulatabad by Murtaza Nizam Shah II, the hatred borne by the Moghuls to Shahaji survived Lakhoji Jadhavrao's death. A certain Mhaldar Khan, originally appointed by Murtaza Nizam Shah II to be governor of Trimbak, deserted to Shah Jehan. Wishing to secure the favour of the emperor, he arrested Shahaji's wife (A.D. 1633). Jijabai succeeded in hiding Shivaji but she herself was confined in the fort of Kondana. During the three years, 1633 to 1636, in which Shahaji defied the Moghuls, they made every effort to find out Shivaji's hiding place, that they might hold him as a hostage for his father. But Jijabai's wit baffled them, and Shivaji remained safe until Shahaji's final surrender. Even then Shivaji could not enjoy his father's protection. In 1630 Shahaji had contracted a second marriage with Tukabai, a girl of the Mohite family. This family, although of ancient descent, was inferior in rank to that of Lakhoji Jadhavrao, and after his second marriage, Jijabai seems to have broken off all but formal relations with her husband.

When Shivaji was ten years old (1637), it became time accord-ing to the custom of the day to arrange his marriage ; for that purpose Jijabai took her son to Bijapur. There he was wedded to one Saibai, † the daughter of Vithoji Mohite Newaskar.

---

* *Sabhasad Bakhar*, p. 2.
† Another account makes Saibai daughter of Jagdevrao Nimbalkar.

Even at this early age the boy is said to have shown symptoms
of what his future career was to be. He made a public protest
when he saw some Musulman butchers driving cattle to the
slaughter house and he refused to bow to the king of Bijapur
in the manner required by the etiquette of the court. Fearing
that the unruly boy might injure his own prospects of advancement, Shahaji was glad to send Shivaji with his mother out of
Bijapur (A.D. 1638). He ordered Jijabai to reside at his fief
of Poona and Supa. To assist her in its management he appointed a trusted Brahman officer named Dadoji Kondadev.

It is hardly necessary to mention that Poona then had no
resemblance to what it now is. To-day two great rival cities
jostle each other on the banks of the two rivers, the Muta and
the Mula. A mighty cantonment seven miles in length stretches
from the cavalry lines at Ghorpuri to the artillery lines at Kirkee,
and, six miles in breadth, stretches from East Kirkee to the barracks at Vanavdi. To the west, overlooking the plain on which
fell the Maratha Empire, rises the beautiful palace erected by Sir
Bartle Frere. Through the whole length of the cantonment runs
the broad-gauge track of the Great Indian Peninsula Railway,
joining Poona on the west to Bombay and on the east to Calcutta
and all Central India. Wide roads shaded by gigantic banian
trees and bordered by riding paths are daily crowded with motor
vehicles and horsemen. In the heart of the cantonment are the
grounds and buildings of the Poona Gymkhana, famous for a
long series of struggles between the cricketers of Asia and Europe.
Directly to the north of the Gymkhana is the stone pile known
as the Council Hall, where the executive Government meet and
where the King's representatives hold their annual levees.
Opposite, to the east of the Council Hall is a gloomy building
in which the records of the Peshwas have lain for a hundred
years, wrapped in a sleep which is slowly yielding to the industry
of modern scholars. But the chief marvel and beauty of the
Poona cantonment is the great dam built in 1860 by the liberality
of Sir Jamsetji Jijibhai. The waters of the Mula, pent up by
a stone masonry wall, flow level with its banks throughout the
year. Fine trees fringe its borders for many miles up stream.

Along its course rise stately villas and over its waters flit boats plied by English and Indian rowers. To the north of the river may be seen the vast front of the Deccan College, of which the wide court-yards and red roofs bring back to memory the names of many famous men. To the south of the cantonment lies the city of Poona, a spot more interesting even than its rival to the passing traveller. In its very heart rise the giant bastions of the Shanwar Wada, which to-day overawe the spectator as they did in the days of Bajirao II. To the north of it stands the ancient palace of the Purandares, a noble family who boast with pride that the first Chitpawan Peshwa was once a petty clerk in their ancestor's office. To the east stands the home of the Rastes, which like the ancient dwellings of the Italian nobles is half a house and half a fortified castle. Behind the Shanwar Wada once stood the palace of Nana Phadnavis. Its site is now occupied by the buildings of the New English School. To the west the mighty temple of Onkareshwar looks down in its austere beauty on the last resting place of the Brahman caste of Poona.

In Shivaji's youth the scene was very different. Poona was then a cluster of tiny huts on the right bank of the Muta. It derived its name of " the meritorious town " from the sanctity which in India attaches to the confluences of rivers. About half a mile from the little hamlet, the Muta joined the Mula. But no dam then kept the Mula full. In the rainy season a vast volume of water due to the heavy rains in the western hills poured to waste down the Muta from Sinhgad and down the Mula from the Sahyadris. The two streams after joining flowed, often half a mile wide, into the Bhima, the Krishna, and lastly into the Bay of Bengal. Directly the rains ceased the Mula and Muta, from great rivers, dwindled to petty streams, which in April and early May almost wholly disappeared. Where the roads and the railways now run along the river's bank, there grew then a thick belt of undergrowth infested by wolves and panthers. To-day a canal system and a number of artificial reservoirs have turned the country round Poona into a smiling plain. In Shivaji's childhood it was a barren wilderness.

The wars between Ahmadnagar and Bijapur, between Bijapur
and the Moghuls, and those of Malik Ambar and Shahaji
against both had ruined the entire Deccan.* To grow a crop
was merely to invite a troop of hostile cavalry to cut it and
probably kill its owner. Nor was this the only danger. The
invaders usually carried away with them the children of both
sexes and the young women and forcibly converted them. The
father of the founder of Ahmadnagar and the first king of
Golconda were thus carried into captivity and made Mahomedans. Ramdas in his well-known sketch of a Hindu's life
mentions, evidently as a most ordinary event, that the
Hindu's young wife is carried away and married to a Musul-
man†. As Poona and Supa were Shahaji's private fief,
the malignity of his enemies applied itself deliberately to
their destruction. The rustic population had either fled
or perished. Wild beasts of all kinds took their place and
the few men who peopled the huts on the bank of the
Muta were fishermen, who lived by catching the fish in the
two rivers.

Such was the estate from which Jijabai, her son, and her
clerk, had to obtain their living. Ordinary persons would have
given up the attempt in despair. But Jijabai and Dadoji
Kondadev were not ordinary persons. Sooner than share with
a younger wife the affections of Shahaji, the proud lady was
ready, if need be, to starve. Dadoji Kondadev was a very
able man. A Deshasth Brahman, born in Malthan in the Poona
district,‡ he had, somehow, in the course of a varied service,
acquired a perfect knowledge of revenue administration. This
he now applied with signal success to the ruined fief. He
attracted cultivators from the hilly tracts and the neighbouring
districts by offering them rent-free lands. He kept down the
wild beasts by giving huntsmen rewards, probably from his
own savings. But when crops once more began to appear on
the barren plains, robbers and free lances began to carry off the

---

* In the last war between Bijapur and the Moghuls Mahomed Adil Shah
devastated all the country within 20 miles of his capital. The Moghuls to
punish him devastated as much again.

† Dasbodh.

‡ Ranade, p. 63.

harvests and enslave the villagers. Dadoji Kondadev met the danger by arming bands of hillmen from the Sahyadris, who, with a little training, soon made a raid on Poona a perilous undertaking. His success attracted Shahaji's notice and he added to Dadoji's charge two new estates recently given him by the Bijapur government. They are now known as the Indapur and Baramati talukas of the Poona collectorate. The Englishman who to-day visits Baramati will see along the banks of the Karha River, as far as the horizon, field after field of gigantic sugar-cane. In Shivaji's time no canals carried water to all parts of the taluka. Nevertheless, then as now, the soil was black and rich, and in good years yielded an abundant harvest. Of the resources of his new trust Dadoji made the fullest use. With the surplus revenue he planted mango and other fruit trees. Between Shirwal and Poona, where the mango orchards throve better than in other places, he founded a village and named it after his master's son. It is known as Shivapur to this day. To great energy, thrift and experience, Dadoji added what was rarer still in those times, namely, perfect honesty. A charming tale has been handed down which illustrates this. One day as Dadoji strolled through one of the shady groves at Shivapur, a large and luscious mango caught his eye. The day was hot ; he was tired and thirsty with labour. Unconsciously he stretched out his hand and plucked it. Then he realized too late that he had stolen fruit which belonged to his master. In an agony of remorse he begged his companions to cut off the offending right hand that had made him sin. They very properly refused and bade him think no more of the matter. Nevertheless it still so weighed on his mind that for many months he wore coats without a sleeve for his right arm. " For," so he would say, " if my right arm had had its deserts, it would have been cut off as a punishment." At last the story reached Shahaji's ears. He, not without difficulty, persuaded his retainer to forget his trifling fault and wear coats like other people.

Shivaji was between ten and eleven years old * when he first

* *Shivdigvijaya Bakhar.*

went to Poona with his mother Jijabai. Unhappily no portrait survives of the great king when he was still a boy. But he had suffered troubles early. He had long been separated from his father and to avoid captivity he had lived for years hidden in woods and caves. It is possible, therefore, that, although his cheeks were rounder and his skin smoother, he did not much differ in boyhood from the pictures which still exist of Shivaji in manhood. The brow is wrinkled as if with grave and constant thought. The cheeks are burnt with long exposure to sun and rain and deeply furrowed as if with anxiety and care. But the nose is curved like a falcon's beak. The eyes are large and bold. The thin lips are compressed with inflexible resolution. The whole face speaks eloquently of trouble bravely borne and dangers triumphantly surmounted. Shivaji's body was short but broad and strongly built. And a legend survives that, like those of Arjuna, the epic archer, the fingers of his long sinewy arms reached below his knees. Dadoji Kondadev had the good sense to understand that he owed a duty to his master's son as well as to his master's lands. He collected round Shivaji other boys of his own age. The best known were Tanaji Malusare, a petty baron of Umrathe village in the Konkan, Baji Phasalkar, the deshmukh of the valley of Musé, and Yesaji Kank, a small land-holder in the Sahyadris. Dadoji had Shivaji and his companions instructed in all the warlike exercises of the time. He had himself seen a good deal of fighting and no doubt supplemented the teaching of the paid instructors by tales of his own experiences in the field. He also realized that an exact knowledge of the wild lands in the Mawal, of the passes to the Konkan and of the folds in the Sahyadri hills was at least as valuable as skill in martial exercises or an acquaintance with the tactics of the day. Encouraged by Dadoji Kondadev, Shivaji and his companions wandered for days together through the Krishna valley, through the forests on the banks of the Koyna, along the winding course of the Indrayani, or followed the Bhima River to its source upon the shaggy sides of mighty Bhimashankar. But Dadoji Konda-dev was not only an efficient land agent and a veteran of Shahaji's

9

wars ; he was also, as became a Brahman, a profound scholar. He had built a roomy house for Jijabai and Shivaji, which he named the Raj Mahal, close to the right bank of the Muta, where stretches now the Municipal Garden to the east of the Shanwar Wada. There on winter evenings he would gather round him Shivaji and his friends and expound to them the teachings of Dnyandev and of the other saints of Pandharpur. When they grew weary of abstruse doctrines, he would take up the Sanskrit scrolls and by the smoky light of a wick soaked in oil, he would first read and then translate to them tales of Bhima the strong, of the archery of Arjuna, of the chivalrous courage of Yudhishthira. Or he would repeat to them the wise sayings of Bhishma, in which are contained the experience and wisdom of two thousand years of Indian war, statesmanship and government.

There were other influences too at work on Shivaji's character. The scenery round Poona is of the most inspiring kind. To the west are the tremendous barrier ranges of the Sahyadris. Only twelve miles to the south stands out the colossal fortress of Sinhgad. To the south-west may be dimly seen the peaks of Rajgad and Torna, which, when outlined against the setting sun, arouse even to-day emotion in the phlegmatic Englishman. But thirteen miles to the north of Poona lies Alandi, the spot where Dnyandev entered his living tomb and to which, now, as in Shivaji's time, thousands of pilgrims bearing yellow flags make their way from Pandharpur. But there was yet another influence more powerful than either Dadoji Kondadev's teachings or the grandeur of the landscape. Jijabai, fatherless, deserted by her husband and by her eldest son found a solace for her grief in Shivaji, the one possession left her. She lavished on her son all and more than all a mother's love. At the same time she bade him never forget that he was descended both from the Yadavas of Devagiri and the Ranas of Udaipur. She recited to him the Puranas with their marvellous feats of war and daring. But she wished to see him pious as well as brave. She made him pray constantly at the little village shrine which still may be seen in Poona not far from the site of Jijabai's home. There

too she welcomed Kathekaris or religious preachers to translate
and expound to him, better than even Dadoji could do, the
various virtues and merits of Krishna. ' Thus grew Etruria
strong '; and Shivaji at eighteen was a man tireless, fearless
and deeply devout.

It was now time for Shivaji to choose a career. As the son
of the former regent of Ahmadnagar, as the grandson of Lakhoji
Jadhavrao, as a near kinsman of the ancient house of Phaltan,
Shivaji was one of the natural leaders of the Maratha people.
There were several courses open to him. Like some of the
barons of the time he could live on Shahaji's estate, amuse his
leisure with strong drink, fill his zanana with the rustic beauties
of the neighbourhood and perform just as little military service as would enable him to retain such fiefs as he might inherit
from his father. But to the son of Shahaji and the grandson
of Maloji such a life probably never offered much temptation.
The second course was that favoured by Dadoji Kondadev.
He could go to Bijapur, join the king's service as a subordinate
of Shahaji, as Sambhaji had done, and with him rise to a high
place among the factious nobles who surrounded Mahomed Adil
Shah. But Shivaji was well aware of the weakness of the Bijapur
government. He knew that behind the glitter of the court
there were waste, mismanagement and incapacity. At Bijapur,
just as there had been at Ahmadnagar, there was a constant
and furious rivalry between the Deccan and the foreign parties.
Either faction, in order to gratify private spite, were prepared
to call in the Moghuls and ruin their country. Shivaji realized
that sooner or later a house so divided must fall a prey to the
disciplined Moghuls, whose forces were led by royal princes who
were among the first captains of the time. A third course open
to Shivaji was to seek his fortune at Delhi. The son of Shahaji
Bhosle would no doubt have received a high post in the Moghul
army. There his natural gifts would certainly have won him
most honourable distinction. But to adopt this course would
have been to desert his country and to stand by while Aurangzib's
armies enslaved the Indian peoples and insulted their religion
from the Bhima to Rameshwaram. There was yet another

course open to the young noble and that was to attempt the liberation of the Maratha race. It was a well-nigh hopeless task. After three centuries of slavery the wish for freedom was all but dead and lived, if at all, in a few hill tracts in the Mawal and the Konkan. He could expect no aid from other Maratha nobles. All that the Ghorpades, the Mores, the Manes, the Savants and others aspired to was their own advancement at court or the enlargement of their fiefs at the expense of their neighbours. Without resources he must raise an army. He must inspire it by his own words and acts with high ideals. He must fight against his own relatives and countrymen. He must incur charges of treason and charges of unfilial conduct. In the end, he would most likely see his hopes shattered, his friends butchered, and himself condemned to a cruel and a lingering death. Yet this was the course which Shivaji resolved to adopt. He did so, not with the rash presumption of youth, but after deep deliberate thought, after long discussion with the friends of his boyhood, with Dadoji Kondadev and with his mother Jijabai. Having once adopted it he never swerved from it until his work was done. More than 2500 years before, three immortal goddesses had called on another eastern prince to decide questions very similar to those which now confronted Shivaji. But far other than that of Paris was the judgment of Shahaji's son. He turned aside from the rich promises of Hera and the voluptuous smiles of Aphrodite and without a single backward glance placed the golden fruit in the hands of Pallas Athene.

CHAPTER XIV

THE RISE OF SHIVAJI

A.D. 1645 TO 1654

As early as 1643 Shivaji, then only sixteen years old, had begun the work of preparation.* In that year he appointed his own nominee as priest in the temple of Rohideshwar near the fort of Rohida in the Mawal, and won over to his side the affections not only of the hillmen of the neighbouring valleys but also of the Bijapuri officer Dadaji Deshpande.† By the year 1645, Shivaji's conduct led the Bijapur vazir to write a sharp letter to Dadaji Deshpande warning him against associating with Shivaji. This letter caused serious alarm to Dadaji's father Narsu, and Dadaji mentioned this in a letter to Shivaji. The latter in reply disclaimed all disloyalty to Bijapur but announced that the god Shiva, who resided in Rohideshwar, had promised him his help and that with it he would found an independent Hindu monarchy.‡

It was however in the monsoon of 1646 that Shivaji first seriously put his hand to his life work by the seizure of Torna.§ His choice no doubt fell upon Torna because it lay on the southern frontier of his father's fief. Attack would come probably from that direction. To the north the fief bordered on the Moghul province of Ahmadnagar. The western frontier was guarded by the forests and mountains of the Sahyadri range, through which no army would pass if it could help it. The

---

* As early as 1639 Shivaji had had a seal prepared with the inscription, " Although the first moon is small, men see that it will grow gradually. This seal befits Shivaji the son of Shahaji." Rajwade, *Marathi Itihasanchi Sadhane,* Vol. 15, p. 437.

† He took an oath to serve Shivaji. Rajwade, *Marathi Itihasanchi Sadhane,* Vol. 15, p. 269.

‡ Rajwade, *ibid,* p. 267.

§ Rajwade, *ibid,* p. 269.

eastern frontier was no doubt exposed, but to come by an eastern route from Bijapur to Poona was a long way round. The
fort of Torna had a commandant and a small garrison. But
during the heavy monsoon rains, when no military operation was
conducted, it was the custom of the Torna garrison to leave
the hill-top and live in the valley. Taking advantage of this
circumstance, Shivaji and his three chief companions Yesaji
Kank, Tanaji Malusare and Baji Phasalkar, with a following of
about a thousand men occupied Torna without bloodshed.
There, with the same good fortune that had attended his grandfather Maloji, he found, while digging in the fortification, which
had fallen into disrepair, a large hidden treasure. The Torna
commandant indignantly reported Shivaji's conduct to the
Bijapur government. But Shivaji had already made a counter-
charge. He complained to the king's ministers that the commandant had without leave deserted his post and that they had
far better entrust the fort to one as vigilant in the king's interest
as Shivaji was. He supported his complaint by a distribution
among the ministers of part of the Torna treasure. The commandant's report fell upon deaf ears and instead of satisfaction
he received a reprimand*. When Shivaji offered to pay a larger
rent than had ever been previously paid for the lands round
Torna, it was added to his father's fief. With the remaining
treasure Shivaji bought arms, cannon and ammunition, raised a
force of hillmen on the same lines as those upon which Dadoji
had raised his guards, and fortified another hill about six miles
away from Torna. It was then known as Morbad but he changed
its name to Rajgad or the king's fort, the name by which it is
known to-day.

The boldness of this act attracted all the youth of Poona
and the neighbourhood. Among those who now ardently
embraced Shivaji's cause were Moro Pingle, Annaji Datto,
Niraji Pandit, Raoji Somnath, Dattaji Gopinath, Raghunath
Pant and Gangaji Mangaji. They were all Brahmans and were
most of them sons of clerks appointed by Dadoji to help him
in the management of the estate. But Dadoji Kondadev, whose

---

* Khafi Khan, Elliot and Dowson, Vol. 7, p. 257.

ambition was that Shivaji should rise to distinction in the
Bijapur service and who was at once a loyal servant of Shahaji
and a loyal subject of Mahomed Adil Shah, protested vigorously.
He maintained that he, and not Shivaji, was the manager of the
fief, that Shivaji had acted without his sanction. Had Shivaji
sent a written request for leave to occupy Morbad, his father's
influence would possibly have secured it. As it was, the king
would not fail to punish Shahaji and Dadoji as well. But
Shivaji had already considered fully his acts. He believed
himself the trustee of a divine task. He had his mother's full
support. He bore patiently Dadoji's reproaches. But at the
same time he directed Moro Pingle to complete as rapidly as
possible the fortifications of Rajgad. Dadoji, finding his own
protests unavailing, called round him all the old clerks and
servants of the fief and bade them address Shivaji. He paid
as little attention to them as to Dadoji. At last the old man
wrote a formal letter of complaint to Shahaji at Bijapur.

The latter for the last ten years had troubled little or nothing
about his first wife and her son. In 1637, the year after he joined
the service of Bijapur, he was appointed under Randulla Khan
second in command of an army collected to subdue the south-
eastern coast of India. Ever since the battle of Talikota the
Golconda and Bijapur kings had tried to extend their power over
the territories of Vijayanagar and reduce the petty chiefs and
land-holders, who on its destruction had made themselves independent. But the wars with Ahmadnagar had diverted the
attention of Bijapur, and the kingdom of Golconda had so far
profited most by the fall of Ramraj. In 1637 Bijapur, freed
by the destruction of its ancient rival, resolved to conquer
as much as it could of southern India. Shahaji and Randulla
Khan spent the year 1637 in overcoming the resistance of a
powerful chief named Kemp Gauda, whose capital was Bengrul or
Bangalore. At the close of the year Randulla Khan was recalled
and Shahaji succeeded to the supreme command. The capacity
of the veteran general soon made itself felt and the Bijapur
army overran Kolar, Dood, Balapur and Sira. These districts
were conferred on Shahaji as military fiefs. After he had

conquered the whole plateau round Bangalore, he descended the
Eastern Ghats to subdue the ancient country of the Cholas.

As already related the invasion of Malik Kafir overthrew all
the dynasties of southern India. From this invasion Tanjore
never recovered. The rise of Vijayanagar was more fatal to
it even than the assaults of Malik Kafir. It lingered on, however,
in name until A.D. 1530. At that time the prince of Tanjore,
Vir Shekhar, was the deadly enemy of Chandra Shekhar, the
prince of Madura. After various turns of fortune Vir Shekhar
overthrew his foe and took Madura. Chandra Shekhar, to recover
it, called to his help Krishna Raya, king of Vijayanagar. The
result was the usual one in such cases. The Vijayanagar army
overthrew Vir Shekhar. The king annexed Tanjore and gave
it in fief to one Shivappa Naik, one of the royal princes. Chandra
Shekhar was for some time allowed to reign in Madura as a puppet
king. But before his death Madura had become the fief of a
certain Vishvanath Naik, a general of Vijayanagar. After Talikota,
Tanjore and Madura again became independent principalities.
In Shahaji's time Raghunath Naik was chief of Tanjore. He
passed his time in fighting with Vyankat Naik, the lord of the
great fortress of Jinji, and Trimal Naik, who owned the large
town of Trichinopoli to the south of the Coleroon River, the
name given to the Caveri before it reaches the sea. Shahaji,
taking advantage of their quarrel, reduced all three disputants
to a common obedience to the Bijapur government.

Shahaji, busy in the work of conquest and administration,
paid little attention to Dadoji Kondadev's complaint and does
not appear to have answered his letter. But the Bijapur government now began to look askance at Shivaji's conduct and called
on Shahaji for an explanation of it. Shahaji even then did not
treat the matter seriously. He wrote a soothing reply to
Bijapur and sent a letter to Shivaji in which he suggested that
he had better not fortify Rajgad. The evident indifference
of Shahaji, the obstinacy of Shivaji, and the fears which Dadoji
felt for the future of both preyed on his mind. He fell ill.
Shivaji, greatly attached to him, nursed him with filial devotion.
He sent for the best available doctors to treat him. But care

undid the work of their medicines. In a few weeks the old
man reached the threshold of death (A.D. 1647). He sent
for Shivaji and told him that his remonstrances had all been
in what he had thought to be Shivaji's interest. He then
summoned his principal subordinates. In their presence he
handed over the keys of the treasury to Shivaji and bade them
regard him as their master. Having thus indirectly given his approval to Shivaji's acts, he commended his family to the young
man's care and shortly afterwards breathed his last.* Dadoji's
dying words made a deep impression on those who were present
to hear them. But two of his chief subordinates were absent.
These were Phirangoji Narsala, the commandant of Chakan,
a fortified town to the north of Poona, and Sambhaji Mohite,
the brother of Tukabai Mohite, Shahaji's second wife, and commandant of Supa, a similar town to the south-east of Poona.
Phirangoji Narsala, on hearing that Dadoji Kondadev had
resigned his trust into Shivaji's hands, agreed readily to do the
same. Shivaji confirmed Phirangoji Narsala in his post and
increased his charge by adding to it some of the villages in the
neighbourhood. Sambhaji Mohite, however, was proof against
all persuasions. When Shahaji and Jijabai quarrelled on
Tukabai's account, Sambhaji Mohite took his sister's side and
bore no friendly feelings to Jijabai's son. He informed Shivaji
politely that the trust conferred on Dadoji Kondadev lapsed
on the latter's death to the trustor. He (Sambhaji Mohite)
must therefore await Shahaji's orders before he could acknowledge Shivaji as his superior. Argument was useless, so Shivaji
used force. With 300 picked men he made a sudden night
march to Supa, surprised Sambhaji Mohite in his bed, took his
guards prisoners and after enlisting in his own service those
who were willing, sent the rest together with Sambhaji
Mohite to Bangalore, the headquarters of Shahaji's government.
As it did not occur to the officers in charge of Indapur and

* Grant Duff, (Vol. I, p. 133), writes that Dadoji advised Shivaji to prosecute
his plans of independence, to protect Brahmans, cows and cultivators, to
preserve the temples of the Hindus from violation and to follow the fortune
which lay before him. But there is nothing so direct as this in the *Chitnis
Bakhar.* Ranade (p. 66), merely states, "The old man yielded and blessed
Shivaji before he died."

Baramati to dispute Shivaji's authority, Shivaji had now acquired complete control of his father's Poona estates. He was, therefore, at liberty to resume his former scheme and protect himself against attack from the Bijapur government. He had already, by the occupation of Torna and Rajgad, secured his south-western frontier. But twelve miles immediately south of Poona was the great fortress of Kondana. Whoever held it dominated not only the Muta valley but the Poona plain as far as Chakan. It was in charge of a Musulman commandant whose name has not survived. For a sum of money he consented to surrender it, and Shivaji after entering it changed its name to Sinhgad or the Lion's fort.

To the south-east of Sinhgad was, if possible, a still more stupendous natural stronghold. Its name was Purandar, another name for the god Indra, and it overlooked the plateau above the Sinhgad hills, in which lies Saswad, the burial place of Sopana. If it could be taken the whole of Shivaji's southern frontier would be safe. The Bijapur government had entrusted Purandar to a Brahman called Nilkanth Naik*. All that is recorded of him is that he had an ungovernable temper. On one occasion his wife objected to his conduct. He had her promptly blown from the mouth of a cannon. In youth he had been a great friend of Shahaji and his sons knew Shivaji well. The fiery old commandant died about the same time as Dadoji Kondadev; and the eldest son Pilo, without orders from Bijapur, not only assumed command of the fort, but usurped all the lands and revenues allotted to the commandant. The younger brothers claimed that they, as sons of the same father, had equal rights with Pilo. Whether the plea was good law in the case of a military fief may be doubted. But in any case they were entitled to a hearing, and as the Bijapur government was too slothful to grant them one, they appealed to Shivaji. What happened afterwards has been variously related. According to one authority† the garrison sent Shivaji a message advising him to seize the place himself and so end the quarrel.

---

* *Shivdigvijaya Bakhar* ; see also Ranade, p. 30.

† Ranade, p. 91.

According to a second authority* the brothers called in Shivaji
as an arbitrator. He, under pretence of examining the property in dispute, seized it.   According to a third authority,†
Shivaji, hearing of their differences, gave out that he was going
to attack the Nimbalkars of Phaltan. As he went he halted
at Saswad some six miles from Purandar. It was the Divali,
or the feast of lamps, and Pilo and his two brothers begged him
to join them in the festival. He accepted the invitation and
took part in the merry-making. Next day he proposed that he
and his hosts should bathe in the stream which flows through
Saswad. The brothers agreed and the young men spent the
morning bathing. When they returned to Purandar, Shivaji's
ensign flew from the battlements. His soldiers, in the absence
of the brothers, and with the connivance of the garrison, had
seized the fortress. But whatever the true story may be, we
need waste no pity on the brothers. The fortress, as such, was
worthless to them. They prized it merely for the salary which
the commandant drew. After its capture Shivaji offered them,
and they accepted, compensation elsewhere of greater value.
To Pilo Nilkanth he gave a wide tract of land below the fort
and round Purandar village and had a house built there for him.
Shankarraoji Nilkanth, the second brother, Shivaji made superintendent of his artillery, elephants and camels. The youngest
brother also entered Shivaji's service. Moro Pingle, whose
skill in fortification had recently been shown at Torna and
Rajgad, was appointed governor of Purandar.

Shivaji's southern frontier was now safe. But he had exhausted the Torna treasure and the revenues of his father's fief.
It was therefore absolutely necessary for him to obtain money.
Shortly after the capture of Purandar, chance enabled him to
supply this need. In the centre of one of the most fertile tracts
of the Thana collectorate is the rich town of Kalyan. It was
then the capital of a province entrusted to the care of a Musulman named Mulana Ahmad. Completely ignorant of Shivaji's
designs, he had collected the government rents of his charge

---

* *Shedgavkar Bakhar.*
† *Shivdigvijaya Bakhar.*

and had sent the money to Bijapur. With it went an escort large enough to guard it against an attack by a band of hill robbers. As the carts with their escort were winding their way through the Konkan, Shivaji, with a body of 300 horse, part of the former garrison of Supa, descended the Bhor pass west of Poona and surprised them. The guards could make no effective resistance and Shivaji made himself master of the treasure. Such an act meant, of course, open war with Bijapur. So Shivaji followed it up by a surprise attack on the neighbouring forts.* He took no less than nine. Of these the most important were Lohgad, Rajmachi and Rairi. Rajmachi is a stupendous hill at the foot of the Bhor pass. Rairi, which afterwards became Shivaji's capital, will be described in a later page. Lohgad stands above the Bhor pass and, with its twin fortress Visapur,† is a familiar object to travellers from Poona to Bombay. Strange legends are still told of this ancient fort. The best-known is the following. In early days, before the Bahmani kingdom had arisen and before Islam had become the state religion, six Musulman saints came to convert the Deccan. One of these was named Umar Khan, and his mission led him into the Indrayani valley. There, however, the fame of a Hindu anchorite who lived on the top of Lohgad hampered his missionary efforts. The Musulman resolved to remove his Hindu rival. He rode up the path until he reached a spot where the paths to Lohgad and Visapur bifurcate. He then alighted, and roaring a warning to the anchorite to depart, enforced his words by a violent blow of his spear against the hill side. Driven by the saint's muscular arm the spear passed through the edge of the cliff, leaving a gigantic window or flying buttress against its side. The anchorite, however, paid no attention. Umar Khan then climbed Lohgad, and on its summit found his enemy absorbed in beatific contemplation. Still louder Umar Khan bade him begone. Again the anchorite heeded him not. Umar Khan, exasperated, seized him by the

---

* Grant Duff gives the names of the forts as Kangooree, Toong, Tikona, Bhoorup, Koaree, Lohgad and Rajmachi.

† Visapur was not fortified until the time of Balaji Vishvanath.

leg and with superhuman force hurled him over the half mile which separates Lohgad from Visapur. Even then the anchorite did not fall to earth, but borne on by the prodigious power of Umar Khan's right arm, he fell at last in the very centre of the Visapur plateau. There a small temple was erected over his body by his Hindu followers. At the foot of Lohgad a number of clay horses mark where the Musulman saint alighted. Both temple and horses may still be seen by the curious.

While Shivaji took the forts, Abaji Sondev, one of Shahaji's old clerks, now a trusted officer of the young adventurer, rode with a body of horse to Kalyan, entered it without resistance, and made prisoner Mulana Ahmad. Shivaji, delighted with this success, followed Abaji to Kalyan, treated the captive governor with the utmost respect and sent him back honourably to Bijapur. Before he arrived there the news of Shivaji's conduct had reached the city. The king was naturally incensed at the rebellion of one whose father had risen high in the Bijapur service. A royal letter* was despatched to Shivaji censuring his conduct and ordering him to Bijapur. The king also directed Shahaji to use his influence with his son. To the former letter Shivaji replied curtly that he would go to Bijapur provided that all the territory in his possession should be conferred on him in fief. To his father Shivaji replied that he was no longer a child, but a man and master of his own destiny. He had now become an independent chief and regarded as his own both Shahaji's Poona estates and his recent conquests from Bijapur.

The king naturally refused to accept Shivaji's proposals. They were impossible in themselves ; and Shivaji's letter to his father showed that he did not expect their acceptance. Mahomed Adil Shah, instead of acting on Shahaji's advice and sending a force at once to overthrow the rebel, conceived the idea that Shivaji was really acting under his father's orders. This idea was fostered by the Musulmans at court, jealous of the position which Shahaji had reached by his industry and talents. The king resolved to seize Shahaji's person. It was, however,

* *Shivdigvijaya Bakhar.*

necessary to proceed cautiously. An unsuccessful attempt
would merely drive him into open rebellion. In the royal service
was an ambitious Maratha noble called Baji Ghorpade. The
family had once been known as Bhosle and were probably
connected although remotely with that of Shahaji. They had
later taken the name of Ghorpade after an ancestor who had
first used the ghorpad or large lizard for the capture of forts.
He had observed that the animal could not only climb a perpendicular rock, but could cling to it even if pulled with great violence.
The Maratha, acting on his observation, trained a ghorpad to run
up a wall in a given direction. Its training complete, he fastened
a rope ladder to its tail and made it run up the wall of a fort
which he wished to escalade. When the ghorpad had reached
the summit, a small boy was sent up the ladder. The ghorpad,
feeling the strain, dug its claws firmly into the earth. When
the boy reached the top, he released the ghorpad and fastened
the rope ladder to the ground with iron pegs. By means of a
ladder the storming party reached the top and overpowered
the garrison. This device was afterwards used extensively
by both the Ahmadnagar and Bijapur governments. The king
had recently conferred the fief of Mudhol on Baji Ghorpade and
he was now expected to show that he had deserved his promotion.
He was told treacherously to seize Shahaji's person and hand
him over as prisoner to the king. A few days later, Baji Ghorpade visited Shahaji and begged him to be present at a dinner-
party given in his honour. Shahaji accepted the invitation and
came on the appointed day. When Shahaji reached the outer
door Ghorpade's servants bade him doff his sword and shield and
dismiss his attendants. Shahaji, possibly suspecting danger,
refused to do so. Ghorpade then offered courteously to show
his guest over the house. Shahaji followed him until they
reached the most distant part of it. Suddenly Ghorpade shut
and bolted a door behind him, thus separating Shahaji's attendants from their master. At the same time a body of Ghorpade's
men hidden in the back of the house rushed on Shahaji and
took him prisoner. He was put in chains and sent to Mahomed
Adil Shah.

In the royal presence the unfortunate noble vainly protested his innocence. The king refused to believe him and ordered him to be bricked up in a wall. Masons were sent for. A niche large enough to admit a man was made. Into it Shahaji was placed and in front of him the masons began to build a fresh wall. As each layer added to its height the king shouted at his victim : "Confess your guilt and save your life !" At last the layers of bricks reached as high as Shahaji's chin, leaving only his face visible. As Shahaji still asserted that his son Shivaji had acted entirely without his authority, the king stopped the masons and left Shahaji as he was. But he told him to write to his son and threatened, in case Shivaji did not soon come to Bijapur, to close the small aperture that still remained. On receiving his father's letter Shivaji was in a cruel dilemma. If he went to Bijapur, he would almost certainly be executed. If he did not, his father would die in his place. A third course was, so it is said, suggested to him by his wife Saibai. He sent one of Dadoji's old clerks, Raghunath Pant, to Delhi to invoke the aid of Shah Jehan. That emperor had no love for Shahaji, who had so long defied his efforts to conquer Ahmadnagar. But the chance of picking a quarrel with Bijapur and above all of annexing that part of Ahmadnagar which had been resigned to Bijapur by the recent treaty was too good to be lost. The emperor sent direct to Shahaji a letter* dated November 30. 1649. In it he wrote that he overlooked the past and that he had sent word to his ambassadors to secure Shahaji's release and that he accepted him as a noble of the Delhi empire. He also conferred a dress of honour on Shahaji and gave a command in the imperial service to Sambhaji. The arrival of the letter at Bijapur must have caused Mahomed Adil Shah some hours of anxious thought. If he killed Shahaji, Shivaji would do homage for his recent conquests to Shah Jehan. The latter would gladly hold them as security for the Bijapur arrears of tribute and would further demand satisfaction for the death of Shahaji, now a subject of Delhi. Shahaji's friends Murar Jagdev, the first minister, and Randulla Khan, Shahaji's old

* See Appendix A, p. 149.

comrade in arms, interceded for him. The king relented, and releasing Shahaji from his brick coffin allowed him to move about in Bijapur city but forbade him to leave it. As Shivaji had achieved his object, he no longer wished to become a feudatory of Delhi. He begged that before he did so the emperor would graciously confer on him the deshmukhi revenue or tithes of Junnar and Ahmadnagar, which were his by ancient right. The emperor replied* courteously that he would attend to the matter when he returned to Court. Shivaji should then have his agent ready and fully instructed to argue his case.

The position now between Shivaji and the Bijapur government was one of stalemate. If Shivaji committed further aggressions they would certainly kill Shahaji. If Mahomed Adil Shah harmed Shahaji, Shivaji would call in Moghul aid. In the circumstances neither party wished to begin overt hostilities. But the Bijapur government made a secret attempt to capture their enemy.† Among the latter's conquests was the town of Mahad in the Konkan about 50 miles as the crow flies to the south-west of Poona. It is now the head-quarters of a taluka in the Ratnagiri district. It was even then an important place and Shivaji used often to visit it. This was known to the Bijapur government, and one Baji Shamraj was ordered to surprise him there and take him dead or alive. As the country immediately to the east of Mahad was a fief of a certain Chandra Rao More, Raja of Jaoli, he was made privy to the plot and he agreed to let Baji Shamraj conceal himself within his estates.

Chandra Rao More was one of the most important Hindu nobles under the Bijapur government. His chief town Jaoli, now a petty village, lay in the valley of the Koyna River, immediately below Mahableshwar, to-day the summer capital of the Bombay government. That plateau, which extends from the head of the Krishna valley to Panchgani, a distance of nearly 20 miles, is now intersected in every direction by broad red roads and by shady riding paths that lead the visitor to points and clearings, from which can be seen views

---

* See Appendix B, p. 149.
† Grant Duff, Vol. 1, p. 145. See also Ranade.

of unimagined splendour. In the summer months the chief officers of the executive government and hundreds of visitors from all parts of the Presidency come by motor car or carriage to enjoy the cool breezes that blow amid scenes which no other spot in the Bombay Presidency can rival. In May and early June when the fierce heat of the plains can hardly be borne by Europeans, the days in Mahableshwar are pleasant and the evenings chilly. In the morning heavy mists obscure the sun, ward off its rays and lie like coverlets of down upon the sleeping mountains. In the time of Shivaji the plateau was a trackless jungle known as the Nahar Forest. Its one inhabited spot was a village now called Old Mahableshwar. It lies on a narrow neck of land where five rivers are supposed to rise. The chief of these is the Krishna, which after a course of many hundreds of miles throws itself at length into the Bay of Bengal. Next to it in importance is the Venna or Yenna, a beautiful stream which, dammed up in the centre of the plateau, makes the Mahableshwar lake. The banks of the lake are covered with vegetable gardens and strawberry beds. From its south-eastern end the river issues again and a mile or two further on falls suddenly, at Lingmala, 1000 feet into the plain below, thus forming, especially after the monsoon rains, a waterfall of extraordinary beauty. The third is the Koyna River, the banks of which are still covered with dense forest and give shelter to sambhar and wild dog, panther and tiger. The Yenna joins the Krishna at Mahuli near Satara. The Koyna joins it at Karad. The Krishna, the Yenna and the Koyna flow eastward. The remaining two, the Gayatri and the Savitri, flow westward and mingle their waters with the Arabian Sea. According to local belief a sixth river may from time to time be seen by devout Hindu pilgrims. When every twelfth year* the planet Jupiter enters the sign of Virgo, the stately Ganges pays to her lowlier sisters a visit and for twelve months flows by their side in Old Mahableshwar. The sources of rivers are sacred in India as in many ancient countries, and Mahableshwar,

---

* This period is called the Kanyagat.

the source of no less than five, has been sacred from remote times. Amongst the earliest known pilgrims was Singhana, one of the greatest of the Yadava kings. In 1215 he built at the sources of the Krishna a small temple and dug a pond in honour of the god Shiva, who here is worshipped under the title of Maha-Bal-Ishwar, or god the mightiest.

The Yadava kings gave the Mahableshwar plateau and neighbouring valleys to the Shirkes, the family renowned by the defeat of Malik-ul-Tujar near Vishalgad. After their conquest by the Bahmani kings, the Shirkes held Mahableshwar as vassals. With the downfall of the Bahmani kingdom the Shirkes fell also. Yusuf Adil Shah, the founder of the Bijapur kingdom, offered the Shirkes' fief to Parsoji Bajirao More, one of his Maratha captains, and gave him 12,000 troops with which to conquer it. More was completely victorious. After a series of fights he drove the Shirkes from the lands which they had held for so many years. Besides the fief, Yusuf Adil Shah conferred on More the title of Chandra Rao, or Moon-lord, to be held by him in perpetuity. Parsoji's son, Yeshwant Rao, added fresh glory to the family fame. In the great defeat inflicted in 1524 on Burhan Nizam Shah I by Ismail Adil Shah, Yeshwant Rao captured the green standard of the Ahmadnagar army. For this feat More received the perpetual title of Raja and leave to keep the royal standard as a trophy. For seven generations the Mores governed Jaoli without leaving any enduring trace of their rule. The eighth in descent from Parsoji was one Krishnaji, called like his forbears Chandra Rao More. When harassed by a rising of the Kolis or the wild tribes of the valleys he vowed that he would, if successful, give the god Mahableshwar a silver image weighing half a maund. Either by the god's help or his own skill, he put down the rising, and in his gratitude he more than kept his promise. He not only had the silver image prepared but had a stately temple built, which stands to this day. Inside it is a pool into which the waters of the five rivers continuously flow. Beside them is a sixth channel reserved for the waters of the Ganges. Krishnaji had five sons, Balaji, Daulat, Hanmant, Govind and Yeshwant. The eldest, Balaji, succeeded to the title of Raja and Chandra Rao. The younger sons received a village each. To Daulat went the village of Shivthar ; Hanmant inherited Jor ; Govind, Jambli ; and Yeshwant, Bahuli. In Shivaji's youth Jijabai had taken him on a pilgrimage to Mahableshwar. While there she was attracted by the beauty of Balaji More's three daughters.* She asked for one of them as a bride for Shivaji. But Balaji More, who regarded the Bhosles as inferior to his own ancient house, declined the offer. When Shivaji later pressed More to join in the revolt against the Bijapur government, More again refused, pleading this time his loyalty to Mahomed Adil Shah. At the suggestion of the Bijapur government, More now allowed Baji Shamraj to use his fief as a base from which to surprise and kill Shivaji. The attempt failed as it deserved. Shivaji's spies were as well informed as those of Bijapur. He learnt of Baji Shamraj's design, and moving secretly from Mahad, fell upon his band as they lay in wait and drove them with considerable loss into Jaoli.

In 1653 Shahaji, after four years of restraint, was permitted to return to Bangalore. There he found everything in disorder. The chiefs whom his armies had subdued had revolted during his absence, and in one of the fights which ensued, his favourite son Sambhaji had fallen. A Musulman named Mustafa Khan claimed to have certain rights in the fortress of Kanakgiri, which had been conferred by the Bijapur government on Shahaji Bhosle. Instigated, if not actually aided, by a member of the royal household named Afzul Khan, Mustafa Khan overpowered Shahaji's garrison and occupied Kanakgiri. Sambhaji went there with a force but found Mustafa Khan prepared to resist. Sambhaji sent a letter to Mustafa Khan, urging him to refer the dispute to the king at Bijapur. While negotiations were proceeding, Mustafa Khan treacherously ordered his artillery-men to hit, if they could, Sambhaji and the knot of officers round him. The batteries opened fire and a cannon-ball, hitting Sambhaji, killed him instantly. The treachery profited Mustafa Khan but little. When Shahaji once more reached Bangalore he led another body of troops to Kanakgiri and stormed it. With

* Parasnis MSS. See also *Mahableshwar* by Rao Bahadur Parasnis

superb generosity he spared the life of his son's assassins. Towards Ghorpade of Mudhol, Shahaji displayed a different.spirit.
The king of Bijapur, anxious to protect Ghorpade from his
victim's vengeance, made both parties swear in his presence
never to molest each other and made them as a proof of friendship exchange with each other portions of their lands. Shahaji
kept his promise in the letter but not in the spirit. He sent
to Shivaji an epistle * in which he wrote, " Be careful to
complete the work which you have undertaken. By the grace
of the Most High may the wives of your enemies ever bathe in
their own warm tears. May God crown your hopes with success
and increase your prosperity. You will not fail to be courteous
always to Baji Ghorpade, for you know the great obligations
under which he has laid me."

Shivaji prized highly the words of approval contained in the
missive. He also grasped the real meaning of the last sentence.
And he resolved, when a fitting chance came, to comply with
Shahaji's wishes and exact full vengeance from Baji Ghorpade
of Mudhol.

* *Shivdigvijaya Bakhar.*

APPENDIX A

SHAH JEHAN'S LETTER TO SHAHAJI

After compliments, Shahaji Bhosle, be it known that the application sent by your son Shivaji has come before us. Since it contained expressions of sincerity and homage we bestowed upon it our royal favour. He made a representation to us in the matter of your offences and your release. Our victorious and world-protecting standards are now successfully turned towards our Imperial Court. We assure you of our favour and we order that your faithful heart should be at ease in all matters. When we reach the Imperial Court we will bring to our sacred notice all your requests and desires and will bring them to success. But the proper way of service and devotion is to send your own trusted servant, so that the world-compelling order guaranteed and adorned with the royal signature may be issued and sent with him.

Your son Sambhaji and others have also obtained royal favour. They will be gratified by their former appointments and favours. They should strive in all good faith and true servitude, which will secure them all objects and requests. Be free from anxiety. A dress of honour has been sent to you as a mark of our complete favour and approval. We hope that by its good-omened arrival you will become fortunate and you will understand from it that you are the object of the imperial condescension.

Written 5th Jilkad, 23rd year of the reign (1049). Seal of Morad Baksh, son of Shah Jehan.

APPENDIX B

SHAH JEHAN'S LETTER TO SHIVAJI

November 30th, 1649.

Deserving every kind of friendly feeling, recipient of great favour, worthy of magnanimous treatment, Shivaji Bhosle, imploring for imperial favour, be it understood, that your letter with Ragho Pandit has been received and has satisfied us. There appears in it a reference to Junnar and Ahmadnagar Deshmukhi, to which we have to say that you should be at ease about this. When we reach the royal camp in person, everything will be arranged satisfactorily.

CHAPTER XV

BEFORE carrying out Shahaji's injunction to punish Baji Ghorpade, Shivaji had his own quarrel to settle with Balaji More. He was, however, loth to destroy one whom he had known in boyhood and he resolved to make an effort to win over More by personal influence. He visited Jaoli himself and in an interview with Balaji More did his utmost by appeals to his religion and patriotism to gain to his side the reluctant noble. He merely wasted his breath. Balaji during the interview tried to secure * his visitor's person in order to hand him over, just as Ghorpade had handed over Shahaji, to the Bijapur government. But Shivaji, who had come prepared for treachery, broke loose from his assailants and made his escape. Shivaji now despaired of winning More's alliance. Nevertheless he did not at once declare war. He sent to Jaoli two envoys, Ragho Ballal Atre, a Brahman, and Sambhaji Kavaji, a Maratha, to lay before Balaji an ultimatum. Its terms were that he should at once join Shivaji and give him his daughter in marriage or take the full consequences of refusal. More at first affected to grant Shivaji's demands. Several interviews took place, but Balaji evaded a definite answer. At last it became clear that More was but amusing the envoys in order to gain time. On receiving their report, Shivaji with his army started as if to go to Purandar. By night he changed his direction and occupied Mahableshwar. Ragho Ballal Atre now demanded and obtained one more interview with More. What happened is obscure. It is probable that Shivaji's envoys charged Balaji

---

* The 'Mahableshwar Account,' Parasnis MSS. See also Rao Bahadur D. B. Parasnis, *Mahableshwar*, p. 19.

with double dealing and that the latter complained of Shivaji's invasion. High words were exchanged, swords were drawn and Ragho Ballal Atre and Sambhaji Kavaji killed More and his brother (1655). Then fleeing into the jungle they escaped to Shivaji. The latter had not authorized his envoy's acts. But as More's non-acceptance of the ultimatum was tantamount to a declaration of war, Shivaji determined to profit by them. He and his troops pushed on at once to Jaoli. They were joined by Balaji's brothers, who had long been on bad terms* with him because he had confiscated their villages. Balaji's minister Hanmantrao and Balaji's sons offered a gallant resistance. But their men lacked the discipline of Shivaji's force and the skill of his leadership. Hanmantrao fell fighting and Balaji's sons were overpowered and taken prisoners. Shivaji improved the victory to the utmost. He enlisted in his service More's own troops, and with their aid and that of the brothers, to whom he restored their villages, he overran in a few days the entire fief. In a remote part of it was the strong fort of Wasota, destined many years afterwards to be an English prison. It fell at the first assault and after its fall Shivaji met with no further resistance. He could now consolidate his conquest. He found at Jaoli a large treasure accumulated by successive generations of Mores. With part of it he improved the temple at Old Mahableshwar. The remainder he put to a more practical use, namely the fortification of Pratapgad†.

---

* The rhyme ' Milale barabhai ani budali Chandra Rai ' will be found in the *Shedgavkar Bakhar*.

† I have followed the *Shedgavkar Bakhar* here. Grant Duff makes Shivaji build Pratapgad temple later, see Grant Duff, Vol. 1, p. 204. I think that the former is right ; otherwise Shivaji could not have worshipped Bhavani before the battle of Pratapgad.

A tiny portion of More's treasure escaped Shivaji's observation. A number of gold coins had been concealed in an earthen pot and buried in a field in the Krishna valley. More than 250 years afterwards a cultivator accidentally unearthed the pot as he ploughed the field. He and his neighbours shared the coins among themselves. The find reached the ears of the Musulman chief constable of Panchgani. Unhappily for him he fell a victim to his own covetousness. Instead of reporting the matter to his superiors, he forced the villagers to surrender the treasure and thus misappropriated it to his own use. He was arrested. By a curious chance he was tried and convicted by the writer of these pages, then Sessions Judge of Satara, and sentenced to a long term of imprisonment.

A charming story has been preserved which explains his selection of Pratapgad rather than any of the other hills in the neighbourhood. It had been the practice of the Bhosle family to visit at least once a year the temple of Bhavani, or Parwati, at Tuljapur. After the vision in which she pointed out to Maloji the treasure from which the Bhosles' fortunes rose, she had become the special object of the family worship. But after Shivaji's rebellion it was no longer safe for him to make a pilgrimage to Tuljapur. For it lay far to the east of his territories. He therefore decided to build a temple at Rairi. For this purpose he sent all over India for a suitable piece of marble for the goddess' image. But one night he saw Bhavani in a vision. She told him that her wish was not to have a temple at Rairi but to live close to Mahableshwar. Shivaji should search until he found a hill known as the Bhorapya Hill. On its summit he should build a temple for her and a fort for himself. Next morning Shivaji searched for the Bhorapya Hill. A herdsman pointed it out to him about twelve miles to the west of the Mahableshwar plateau. When he reached it his vision was confirmed by the discovery of a stone on which was marked a 'ling,' the special mark of Shiva. Shivaji no longer doubted that his dream had come through the gates of horn and building a temple to Bhavani placed in it the marble idol prepared by him for Rairi. Round the temple Moro Pingle, at his master's orders, built a fortress. To it Shivaji gave the name of Pratapgad or "the Fort of Glory." The spot chosen by Bhavani did infinite credit to her judgment. From the Koyna valley Pratapgad rises over 1000 feet. But on the western side it drops yet another 1000 feet into the Konkan, and to him who looks at it from the Mahad road it offers a spectacle of the most imposing kind. At the same time it commands what is now known as the Mahad Ghat, the only pass by which the traveller can descend from the Krishna or the Koyna valley into the Konkan. The possession of this pass was of the utmost value to Shivaji, for it joined up his new conquest of Jaoli with his former conquests along the western seaboard.

GODDESS BHAVANI OF PRATAPGAD

(To face page 165.

Not long after the fall of Jaoli an incident happened which showed clearly the course which Shivaji had chosen for himself. In a village named Golewadi, not far from Wai but in Jaoli territory, lived a Maratha named Gole, who on Chandra Rao's death tried to make himself independent. Shivaji put down the rising and took Golewadi by storm. In the course of the fighting, Gole's daughter-in-law, a beautiful young woman, was taken prisoner and brought to Shivaji by one of his Brahman officers. Shivaji could have placed her in his zanana without incurring any reproach. Nevertheless, after praising the girl's beauty, he turned to his officer and said, " So fair is she that were it in my power, I should wish to be born as her son *." He then gave the lady presents such as she would have received had she visited her father or her brother and sent her back properly attended to her husband. To him he also wrote an assurance that the young woman was leaving his custody as pure as when she had entered it.

In 1656 a fresh war broke out between Bijapur and the Moghuls. Shah Jehan's third son Aurangzib had treacherously attacked and defeated the king of Golconda and forced on him a humiliating peace. The prince then turned his eyes towards Bijapur. He had long disliked the king, Mahomed Adil Shah, who had been on friendly terms with his eldest brother and rival Dara Shukoh. In November, 1656, Mahomed Adil Shah died, leaving as his successor his son Ali Adil Shah. The latter was only nineteen years of age and Aurangzib saw in the weakness of the young king a chance of revenging himself upon a dead enemy. He insinuated to the emperor that Ali Adil Shah was illegitimate. Bijapur was a tributary state. The succession, argued the prince, depended on the approval of Delhi. As Ali Adil Shah had without rights of inheritance and without the emperor's permission usurped the throne, he should be at once deposed. Shah Jehan yielded to this reasoning and ordered Aurangzib to attack Bijapur. The unhappy young king sued for peace in the humblest terms and offered to pay as ransom

---

* *Shedgavkar Bakhar.* A similar story is told in the Bombay Gazetteer of Shivaji and Mulana Ahmad's daughter-in-law. Both are probably variants of the same tale.

a crore of rupees. But Aurangzib's aim was to subvert the kingdom. He refused all terms, and overrunning Bijapur, pressed the siege of the capital with the utmost vigour. The king gave himself up for lost, when an event at Delhi completely changed his situation.

On September 8, 1657, the Emperor Shah Jehan fell seriously ill. His eldest son Dara Shukoh, who was at Agra with his father, assumed the government. Prince Shuja, Dara's second brother, was governor of Bengal. Prince Murad Baksh, his fourth brother, was governor of Ahmadabad. Both Shuja and Murad Baksh rebelled. Aurangzib, enriched by the wealth taken from the Golconda king, and general of the Deccan army, raised the siege of Bijapur and joined in the rising. What followed is too well-known to be related in detail. The emperor recovered from his illness and ordered his sons to return to their duties. They paid no heed to his orders, but attacking the imperial army under Dara Shukoh completely defeated it at Samaghar, one day's march from Agra. After the victory of the allies Aurangzib imprisoned Murad Baksh, defeated Shuja and beheaded Dara Shukoh (A.D. 1658). Then deposing Shah Jehan, he mounted the throne in his place. When Aurangzib first marched upon Bijapur, Shivaji welcomed him as an ally. He wrote a letter to the prince in which he begged that Aurangzib would, on the emperor's behalf, acknowledge his rights over the forts and territories conquered by him from Bijapur. Aurangzib, in a letter* dated April 23, 1657, replied in the most gracious terms. He recognized Shivaji as the lord of all the territories in his occupation and he called upon him as an ally to rejoice in his recent successes. "Day by day," wrote the jubilant Moghul, "we are becoming more victorious. See! the impregnable Bedar fort, never before taken, and Kalyani, never stormed even in men's dreams, have fallen in a day. Others would have tried for days together to take them, but would have tried in vain." But the victories which so gratified Aurangzib gave little pleasure to Shivaji. He had

---

* Original letter in Parasnis Collection.

resolved to free his countrymen from the Musulman yoke,
and the Moghuls, as the stronger, were more noxious to him
even than the troops of Bijapur. He tried to make a diversion
in favour of Ali Adil Shah by invading the Moghul provinces.
In May 1657 he attacked and plundered Junnar and Ahmadnagar.
But Aurangzib's close investment of Bijapur and the distress
of the king's government made Shivaji's raids of little importance. Believing that the Adil Shahi dynasty was on the verge
of extinction, Shivaji tried to make his peace with Delhi. He
wrote in a humble strain to Aurangzib. He admitted that he
had acted improperly, but craved the prince's pardon. If it
were granted, Shivaji would never again be false to his ally.
The letter appears to have reached Aurangzib shortly after
he had raised the siege of Bijapur and when about to enter on
his conflict with Dara Shukoh. The greatness of his new task
made him think but little of the raids on Junnar and Ahmednagar.
On February 24, 1658, he replied * that although Shivaji's
past misdeeds could hardly be forgotten, yet, since he had
repented of them, Aurangzib, as Shivaji would be pleased to
learn, would overlook his past misconduct. Provided that he
kept true to the alliance, Aurangzib would confirm to him not
only all that he had conquered, but all that in the future he
would conquer from Bijapur.

The departure of the Moghuls and the contest of the princes
for the imperial crown left Shivaji free to renew his campaign
against Bijapur. The boy king, saved almost by a miracle
from Prince Aurangzib, should at once have applied himself
to the reduction of Shivaji. But directly the Moghul peril
abated, the quarrels between the foreign and the Deccan nobles
rendered the government impotent. In Shivaji's territory
reigned everywhere energy and order. He now prepared for
an attack on Janjira (A.D. 1659).

Malik Ambar, when regent of Ahmadnagar, had seen the
advantages of a strong fleet with which to protect his commerce
with the Persian Gulf. He made a naval base on a rocky
island off the Konkan coast about twenty miles due west of

---

* Original letter in Parasnis Collection.

Rajgad ; and in command of his war-ships he placed a number
of his countrymen. These Abyssinians were wont to assume
the title of Syad and to claim a descent from the Prophet. This
title the Marathas corrupted into Sidi. Upon the partition of
the Ahmadnagar kingdom the rocky island passed with the
mainland to Bijapur. But it never received a name. It was
simply known as Jazira, or the Island. This Arabic word the
Marathas corrupted into Janjira, which serves it as a name to
this day. The Bijapur government retained the Abyssinian
sailors in their service, but placed over them their own officers,
to whom were also entrusted several forts on the mainland. At
the time of Shivaji the Bijapur governor was an Afghan called
Fatih Khan * and it was from his subordinates that Shivaji
had in his first direct attack on Bijapur taken the forts of Sala
Gossala and Rajri. Since that reverse Fatih Khan had shown
more alertness and his spies had carefully watched Shivaji's
movements. The latter nevertheless was confident of success.
He equipped an efficient force. into which he admitted 800
Afghan mercenaries, and defended the act by telling his somewhat scandalized followers that those who sought to found an
empire must have the sympathy and the help of all classes and
all creeds. He increased his cavalry out of the spoils of Junnar
and Ahmadnagar and appointed to command them Netoji
Palkar, a brave and enterprising officer. Shivaji had by this
time appointed, after the manner of the Bijapur and Ahmadnagar governments, a Peshwa or foreign minister. The holder
of the office was a Brahman called Shamraj Nilkant Ranjekar
and to him was entrusted the task of overthrowing Fatih Khan.
The appointment was a mistake. Shivaji should himself have
led the army in an undertaking so arduous. Shamraj proved
unequal to it. He was surprised and defeated by Fatih Khan
and his army dispersed. Shivaji strained every nerve to repair
the disaster. He sent a large body of fresh troops and ordered
Ragho Ballal Atre to assume the command in place of the
beaten general. Ragho Ballal Atre not only checked the pursuit

---

* Both Grant Duff and Ranade call Fatih Khan a Sidi. But this is incorrect.
He was an Afghan officer of Bijapur (*Khafi Khan*, Elliot and Dowson, Vol.
VII. p. 289).

but soon forced Fatih Khan to act on the defensive. Moro
Pingle succeeded Shamraj as Peshwa, and Shivaji, Pingle and
Netoji Palkar spent the monsoon of 1659 in equipping a force
large enough to overwhelm Fatih Khan in the following winter
and seize Janjira.

Shivaji however was forced to change his plans to meet a new
and formidable danger. Shamraj's repulse before Janjira had
put fresh heart into the Bijapur government. The young
king at his mother's suggestion called on the nobles of his court
to volunteer for the command of an army destined to destroy
Shivaji and his followers. The first to step forward was one
Afzul Khan, a man of great stature and strength. He was the
son of the dowager queen's brother, who was superintendent
of the royal kitchen. He was the same man who, as I have
already mentioned, instigated Mustafa Khan's rebellion, in
the course of which Shivaji's elder brother Sambhaji fell. Afzul
Khan had also been governor of Wai on the upper reaches of
the Krishna and he knew well the country round Jaoli. The
king gladly accepted his services and placed him at the head of
a fine army composed of 12,000* horse and well equipped with
cannon, stores and ammunition. His instructions were to take
Shivaji dead or alive. Failing that, he was to recover Shivaji's
recent conquests from Bijapur. Afzul Khan made the boastful
reply that he would not only take Shivaji prisoner, but would
make him ride on his own horse back to Bijapur.

In spite of these brave words, evil omens, so the Maratha
chroniclers love to relate, repeatedly warned Afzul Khan against
the enterprise. As he reviewed his army before the first march,
Fatih Lashkar, the picked elephant of the Bijapur stables, died†.
When Afzul Khan went to say good-bye to his priest ‡, the
latter recoiled in horror, for he could see in front of him only a
headless figure. Nothing daunted by these omens, Afzul Khan
set out in September 1659 from Bijapur. He seems to have first

---

* Grant Duff estimates the force at 5,000 horse and 7,000 foot ; all the
Hindu writers estimate it at 12,000 horse.

† Ballad of Afzul Khan.

‡ *Shedgavkar Bakhcr*

intended to turn Shivaji's southern fortresses by a wide flanking march. He, therefore, marched almost due north from Bijapur to Tuljapur. This was, and is still, a favourite shrine of Bhavani and was, as I have said, especially dear to the Bhosle family. Knowing this, Afzul Khan resolved to desecrate it. The priests suspected his intentions and before his arrival moved the goddess' image to a place of safety. Unable to destroy the image, Afzul Khan had a cow killed and its blood sprinkled throughout the temple.* In the meanwhile Shivaji, hearing of Afzul Khan's advance, had retired with his troops from Rajgad to Jaoli, where the difficulties of the country would enable him better to meet the Bijapur army. Afzul Khan at once altered his line of march and turned south-west, crossing the Bhima River at Pandharpur. Here also he desecrated the temples and threw the image of Pundalik into the water. The idol of Krishna standing on a brick was saved from his fury by the vigilance of the Brahmans. From Pandharpur, Afzul Khan marched through Rahimatpur to Wai, where he amused himself by preparing a cage for Shivaji's confinement. At the same time he sent a messenger to Shivaji inviting him to a conference at Wai. But Shivaji by now had had some experience of Bijapur ways. Vishvasrao,† a Prabhu by caste and the chief of Shivaji's secret service, had already made his way dressed in a fakir's garb into Afzul Khan's camp and had heard him boast that he meant to entrap Shivaji and take him prisoner to Bijapur. This information Vishvasrao at once communicated to his master. When Afzul Khan's envoy, Krishnaji Bhaskar, ‡ reached Pratapgad, Shivaji affected to believe his words and expressed himself as anxious to meet the Khan as the latter was to meet him. "The Khan," said Krishnaji, "will use his influence with the Bijapur government to obtain not only forgiveness but formal cessions of all lands in your occupation." "If that is so," replied Shivaji, "and the Khan is really well-affected towards me, I shall gladly meet him at Jaoli. But I

---

* Ballad of Afzul Khan.

† *Shedgavkar Bakhar.* His full name was Vishvasrao Nanaji Muse Khorokar.

‡ Krishnaji Bhaskar was Kulkarni of Wai and Diwan of Afzul Khan. He sent him to Shivaji.

fear to go as far as Wai. Here I can make every preparation for his reception."

Krishnaji Bhaskar spent the night at Pratapgad. In the course of it Shivaji managed to have a secret interview with him. Shivaji told Krishnaji his suspicions and implored him to swear by all that a Hindu held holy and to disclose on oath what the Khan's real intentions were. Did he mean, as Shivaji's spies had warned him, to entrap him, or did Afzul Khan mean really to befriend him at the court ? Krishnaji confessed that Shivaji's suspicions were well-founded and that Afzul Khan intended treachery and nothing else. Shivaji retired to his own quarters and the same night he saw in a vision the goddess Bhavani. She complained to him of the desecration of the temple at Tuljapur and as her champion, she called upon him to avenge her. By next morning Shivaji had made up his mind. He knew now what Afzul Khan had really planned and he resolved that if Afzul Khan attempted treachery he alone should suffer. He publicly sent by his own officer, Pantoji Gopinath, a formal invitation to Afzul Khan to meet him at Pratapgad a fortnight later. This would give him the time needed to prepare a road along which the Bijapur general and his army should pass. After the envoy had left, Shivaji impressed all the villagers and cut through the forest a wide road over the Radtondi pass. It was then a tree-clad shoulder of the Mahableshwar plateau. It is now the daily meeting place of scores of carriages and is known as Bombay Point. All along the road Shivaji had stores of food placed, so that the Khan and his army should want nothing. At the same time he posted men throughout the jungle off the road, so that no movement of Afzul Khan should pass unnoticed. In the meanwhile Afzul Khan's envoy, Krishnaji Bhaskar,* together with Shivaji's agent, Pantoji Gopinath, had reached Wai and had given Shivaji's message. Krishnaji Bhaskar added to it, " The king is timid. He dare not come to you for the interview. If you but go to Jaoli and assure him of your protection you will easily

---

* Grant Duff calls the envoy Pantoji Gopinath. This is incorrect. He was Shivaji's officer. (*Shivdigvijaya* and *Shedgavkar Bakhar*.)

induce him to return with you to Bijapur." Afzul Khan, confident in his troops and in his own personal strength, sent back a message to Shivaji accepting his invitation.

When the fortnight had elapsed, Afzul Khan struck his camp and marched over the Mahableshwar plateau. At each halting place he found ample provisions for his troops, who marched gaily along, ignorant that thousands of hostile eyes watched them from the neighbouring thickets. They descended the Radtondi pass, but as they went, yet another ill omen warned Afzul Khan of approaching disaster. The elephant which carried the royal standard stopped dead and refused to move.* But the Bijapur general was as blind to omens as the Greek warriors who marched against Thebes. The standard was placed on another elephant's back and the army, reaching the Koyna valley, encamped at Par, a small village at the foot of Pratapgad.

The interview was fixed for the following evening and the place chosen was a spot about a quarter of a mile from the fort walls. Shivaji had a shamiana erected and furnished with rich carpets and costly hangings. In the morning he bathed and ate his breakfast as usual. In the afternoon he lay down and slept, as if no danger awaited him. After rising he visited the temple of Bhavani and implored her help. Next he took into his confidence his comrade Tanaji Malusare, the Peshwa Moro Pingle and Netoji Palkar. They were ordered to post troops round the flanks and rear of the Bijapur army so as to cut off all possibility of retreat in case Afzul Khan attempted treachery. The signal for their attack was to be a blast on a horn. Shivaji then called a council and named in the event of his death his young son Sambhaji as his heir and Netoji Palkar as regent. Last of all he visited his mother Jijabai. She begged him not to meet Afzul Khan. Shivaji, however, stood firm in his resolve. "The Hindu gods," he said, "angered with Afzul Khan, will, if need be, fight on my side." At length Jijabai gave way, blessed him, and as he left her said, "Be careful, my son, be careful and take vengeance for Sambhaji your brother."

---

* Afzul Khan Ballad.

Shivaji then prepared himself to meet the treachery which he anticipated. He put on a coat of chain armour. Over it he put on a gold-embroidered coat. On his head he fastened a steel cap and wound over and round it a long cloth turban. Into his left hand he fitted the steel points known as *waghnakh* or tiger claws. He concealed a small dagger known as a *vinchu* or scorpion in his right sleeve. Then fully equipped he began to descend the hill accompanied by Jivba Mahala, Sambhaji Kavaji and a third whose name has not survived. In the meantime Afzul Khan was being carried up Pratapgad in a palanquin. At his side went Krishnaji Bhaskar. Behind them followed a large body of armed men. Krishnaji pointed out that if the Khan hoped to dupe Shivaji, he had better leave his soldiers behind. Afzul Khan agreed and reduced his escort to the same number as Shivaji's. One of these, however, was a famous swordsman named Sayad Banda. Shivaji, seeing Sayad Banda, sent a messenger to say that he feared his presence and offered to dismiss one of his attendants, if Afzul Khan left Sayad Banda behind. Afzul Khan consented and Sayad Banda halted. Shivaji then sent away his third attendant and accompanied only by Jivba Mahala and Sambhaji Kavaji advanced to greet the Khan, who had now entered the shamiana. Shivaji appeared to be unarmed and Afzul Khan, who carried a sword, thought that the moment had come to seize him. He addressed Shivaji in insulting tones and asked how a common peasant like him came to have the riches displayed in the shamiana. Shivaji replied hotly that that was his business, and not Afzul Khan's, whose father was nothing but a cook.* The Khan, enraged at the taunt, seized with the left arm Shivaji by the neck, forcing his head under his armpit. At the same time the Khan with his sword tried to stab him in the stomach. The coat of mail turned the point. Nevertheless Shivaji was in great peril. Although expecting treachery he had yet been taken unawares. To use a term from the prize ring, he was in chancery ; and by a common trick of

---

* Afzul Khan Ballad. Shivaji's taunt referred to the post of superinten-dent of the royal kitchen held by Afzul Khan's father.

11

Indian wrestlers Afzul Khan was trying to dislocàte Shivaji's neck by twisting his head. As he afterwards said when relating the scene to a friend,* he was on the point of fainting. Had he done so he would have been lost. Suddenly he thought of his divine mission. Hope and courage returned. He swung his left arm round the Khan's waist as he raised his right arm for a second blow. The steel claws bit deeply into the Khan's stomach and as he winced with the pain, Shivaji freed his right arm and drove the dagger into his enemy's back. Afzul Khan broke away and aimed a mighty blow at Shivaji's head, which cut through the turban and the steel cap, inflicting a slight scalp wound. Shivaji snatched a sword from Jivba Mahala, who carried two, and struck the Khan through his left shoulder. He fell, calling for help. Sayad Banda and his other attendants rushed up. They placed Afzul Khan in a palanquin and tried to carry him back to Par. But Shivaji and Jivba Mahala overcame Sayad Banda ; and Sambhaji Kavaji, running after the palki bearers slashed at their legs until they dropped their burden. Sambhaji then cut off the dying man's head and brought it back to Shivaji. The latter blew his horn. From every corner of the thick jungle poured out bodies of foot-soldiers and squadrons of cavalry. The battle was ended in a few seconds. The Bijapur horsemen, completely surprised, were ridden over by Netoji Palkar before they had time to mount. Those who tried to escape on foot were cut off by Shivaji's infantry. Numbers fell ; but at Shivaji's orders all who surrendered were spared. The Maratha prisoners were allowed to enlist in Shivaji's service. A body of 300 cavalry, including Fazal Mahomed, Afzul Khan's son, managed with the help of one Khandoji Khopade to escape to Karad. But the entire camp, treasury, stores, horses, elephants and cannon of the Bijapur force fell into Shivaji's hands. Much of this booty he distributed as rewards among his troops. On Pantoji Gopinath he bestowed the village of Hivare. To Vishvasrao, the spy who had first

* Ramdas. Shivaji said that his courage returned when he thought of Ramdas ; but I take it that he meant that he thought of Ramdas and all that Ramdas stood for—the Hindu temples, gods and castes.

warned him against Afzul Khan's treachery, he gave a large sum in gold. Then carrying in one hand Afzul Khan's bleeding head, he went to see his mother. She had watched the scene from the top of Pratapgad and when he came with the ghastly trophy, she blessed him and thanked him for avenging Sambhaji's death. The dead man's head Shivaji buried on the top of the hill as an offer to Bhavani and built over it a tower which he called the Afzul Buruj or tower of Afzul Khan. The general's sword is still preserved as a trophy by Shivaji's descendant. The gold-headed pole which supported his tent was given by the conqueror to the Mahableshwar temple, which it yet adorns. And the tomb erected by Shivaji, where the dead man's body was reverently buried, may be seen to-day on the slopes of Pratapgad.*

---

* For a further discussion of the Afzul Khan incident, see Appendix, p. 164.

APPENDIX

The account given by me of the Pratapgad battle differs so widely from that given by Grant Duff, that I think it necessary to go into the matter more carefully than I could do in the previous chapter, for fear of spoiling the narrative.

In Grant Duff's story, Shivaji is made to bribe Afzul Khan's envoy, Pantoji Gopinath, and with his help to lead Afzul Khan into a trap deliberately laid for him and treacherously to murder him. With all deference to that learned and eminent writer, I cannot but think that on this occasion he has been less than fair to Shivaji. Pantoji Gopinath was Shivaji's officer and not Afzul Khan's. The bestowal therefore on him of Hivare village was not a bribe at all and could not have influenced the real envoy, Krishnaji Bhaskar. The story of Shivaji's treachery was taken by Grant Duff from Khafi Khan. Now Khafi Khan's account should in my opinion be wholly discarded. His bias against Shivaji is such that he never speaks of him except as "that vile infidel" or "that hell dog." His description of the scene too is ridiculous. According to him, Shivaji begged forgiveness in abject terms and "with limbs trembling and crouching." If Shivaji had thus overacted his part, he would certainly have roused suspicion in the Khan's mind. Again Khafi Khan's story could not have been based on any eye-witness's evidence. All the Musulmans near enough to see what happened died with Afzul Khan. It may be of course said that if Khafi Khan's account should be rejected on account of his bias, so also should the *Bakhars*. But this is not so. Owing to a curious mental attitude of the writers of the *Bakhars*, they have gone out of their way to impute unscrupulous acts to Shivaji in the belief that thereby they proved his cleverness and subtlety. It is certain that if Khrishnaji Anant Sabhasad, the author of the *Sabhasad Bakhar*, had believed that Shivaji had begun the attack on Afzul Khan, he would have gloried in the act. Now both this *Bakhar* and the *Shivdigvijaya Bakhar* agree that it was Afzul Khan who was guilty of the first treacherous attack. In this they are supported by the *Shedgavkar* and *Chitnis Bakhars* and by the Afzul Khan Ballad. Indeed Grant Duff has later admitted that all the Hindu authorities lay the blame of the attack on Afzul Khan. But he has not given any reasons for rejecting them in favour of Khafi Khan's account. To my mind, however, there is one conclusive ground for preferring them to the Musulman historian. There is a passage in the life of Ramdas by his pupil Hanmant in which the latter, a contemporary of Shivaji, writes that at their first meeting after the death of Afzul Khan, the king spoke to Ramdas as follows :—" When at our interview Abdulla (*i.e.* Afzul Khan) caught me under his arm, I was not in my senses and but for the Swami's blessing I could not have escaped from his grip." Now had Shivaji torn Afzul Khan's stomach open with his *waghnakh* and stabbed him with his dagger, he would have been in no danger and would have needed no blessing. A man as badly wounded as Afzul Khan had been was bound to collapse in a minute or two. From this it follows that Afzul Khan must have seized Shivaji when unwounded. It was, therefore, Afzul Khan and not Shivaji who was guilty of treachery

CHAPTER XVI

MUDHOL, PANHALA AND SAVANTVADI

A.D. 1660 to 1662

THE news of Afzul Khan's death and the complete destruction of his army produced the wildest consternation in Bijapur. The dead general was the first cousin of Ali Adil Shah; and the queen mother, at whose suggestion Afzul Khan had been appointed to the command, felt her nephew's death most deeply. She refused for several days to eat or drink. And not only she, but the king and the whole Bijapur court, put on mourning robes for Afzul Khan.[*] Nor were the tidings that daily reached the capital calculated to allay their grief. Shivaji's army, swollen by the enlistment of the Bijapur Hindus, spread over all the Bijapur districts in the neighbourhood of Jaoli and over the southern Konkan. The Dalvis, an ancient Maratha family in the Bijapur service, were driven from Shingarpur. Panhala, a great fort near Kolhapur, surrendered without a siege to Annaji Datto. Pavangad and Wassantgad fell immediately afterwards. Rangna and Khelna were carried by assault. Shivaji changed the name of the latter place to Vishalgad, by which name I shall hereafter call it. The Bijapur government, in the hope of checking Shivaji's triumphant progress, ordered Rastam Jaman, the commandant of Miraj, at once to move towards Kolhapur and drive the rebel back to Jaoli. It was a counsel of despair, because Rastam Khan's striking force numbered only 3000 men. Shivaji allowed him to come close to Panhala and then fell upon him with a greatly superior army. Rastam Jaman was completely defeated[†] and he had considerable difficulty in escaping back to Miraj. Shivaji, after the victory, rallied his cavalry and leading them to Bijapur plundered

[*] *Sabhasad Bakhar.*
[†] *Khafi Khan*, Elliot and Dowson, Vol. VII, p. 260.

the royal territory up to the very gates of the city. Retreating
with his plunder to Vishalgad he deposited it there and descended
into the Konkan (January, 1660). There he levied a heavy
contribution from the town of Rajapur, captured the fort of
Dabhol, which had been conceded to him by Aurangzib and
returned in triumph to Rajgad.

Ali Adil Shah now resolved to stake the whole resources of
his kingdom on an attempt to avenge the disaster of Pratapgad.
He felt it useless to entrust the duty to any of his hereditary
nobles. Intrigue, jealousy and evil-living had rendered them
incapable of acting vigorously. The king therefore selected
Sidi Johar, an Abyssinian mercenary, and conferred on him
the title of Salabat Jang. As his second in command, he named
Afzul Khan's son Fazal Mahomed, a high-spirited young man
who had escaped from Pratapgad and who longed to retrieve
his own honour and his father's death. The king collected an
army of 10,000 horse, 14,000 foot and efficient artillery. He
instructed Sidi Johar to recover Panhala. At the same time
he ordered Fatih Khan to issue from Janjira and retake the Konkan. The Savants of Savantvadi undertook to harass Shivaji
by an attack on his south-western frontier.

The little country of Savantvadi, or the home of the Savants,
lies along the Sahyadris. It is bounded on the north by the
Malwan taluka and on the south and west by the Portuguese
districts. During the greatness of the Vijayanagar kingdom,
Savantvadi had been governed by the Vijayanagar viceroy of
Goa. At the close of the fifteenth century Savantvadi fell to
the arms of Bijapur, but a local dynasty known as the Desais
of Kudal were allowed to continue as governors. In 1554 a
national hero of great talents, named Mang Savant, revolted
against Bijapur, and driving out the Musulman garrisons
remained independent until his death. His son was overthrown ; but the family retained a large part of the district
as Jaghir until 1627, when Khem Savant, a descendant
of Mang Savant, once more made himself independent. In
1640 he was succeeded by his son Som Savant, and
Som Savant, eighteen months later, by his brother Lakham

Savant. The latter, to make himself secure, murdered the
Desai of Kudal, who still retained a part of Savantvadi. But
the outcry against the slayer of a Brahman was so terrible,
that in A. D. 1650 he tendered his allegiance to Shivaji. Under
the title of Sardesai, Shivaji confirmed to him as his vassal
the possession of the whole South Konkan. After the defeat
of Shamraj by Fatih Khan of Janjira, Lakham Savant
had wavered in his allegiance ; but upon seeing the skill with
which the disaster had been repaired, he executed a fresh instru-
ment, by which he bound himself to pay half the revenues of
the South Konkan and Savantvadi to Shivaji, and to maintain
for his use a force of 3000 infantry. But Lakham Savant was
a faithless ally. He now tried to secure the king of Bijapur's
pardon by attacking his overlord when defending himself against
Bijapur and Janjira.*

Assailed from three sides, Shivaji skilfully distributed his
forces. Ragho Ballal was sent to keep in check Fatih
Khan. Baji Phasalkar marched with an infantry force to
repell the invasion of Lakham Savant. Shivaji threw himself
with a strong garrison into Panhala and ordered Netoji
Palkar to harass Sidi Johar until the monsoon burst. Then
Shivaji hoped the Bijapur army would retire. At first Shivaji's
arrangements proved successful. Neither Fatih Khan nor
Lakham Savant was able to effect anything against the troops
opposed to them. Sidi Johar invested Panhala, but Netoji
Palkar's cavalry cut his communications incessantly, while the
garrison made repeated sorties. Picked bodies of Mawal infantry
crept along ravines round Panhala and nightly rushed the
besiegers, causing them heavy losses. But the investing army
was large and Sidi Johar a veteran commander. He drove
in the outposts of the garrison until he commanded and blocked
all the ravines. At the same time his own light horse operated
vigorously against Netoji Palkar. Fatih Khan, by a skilful
use of his fleet, won some successes against Ragho Ballal, while
Savant Kaya, a relative of Lakham Savant, fought a drawn
battle against Baji Phasalkar, in which both commanders lost

* Bombay Gazetteer, Vol. X, p. 440.

their lives[*]. The monsoon, during which Shivaji had expected Sidi Johar's retirement, burst, but the stout old Abyssinian paid no heed to the teeming rain and he pressed the siege with unremitting energy. Shivaji's situation was now extremely serious. Famine was beginning to make itself felt among the garrison. September had come and the dry season would soon be at hand. The fall of Panhala would then be certain, and its fall meant his capture and the ruin of all his hopes.

But if his situation was grave, never was his mind more resourceful or his courage higher. He sent a messenger to Sidi Johar, informing him that he was anxious to surrender and proposing a personal interview. The Abyssinian, who was a man of honour, granted it. He received Shivaji with all courtesy and the two leaders spent the day negotiating for the surrender of Panhala. In the evening some points remained unsettled. They were reserved for the following morning. Shivaji was permitted to return unmolested to Panhala. The besiegers were convinced that next day would see the fall of the great fortress and considered themselves entitled to a little relaxation after months of toil and exposure. The sentries slept at their posts. The dinners of the officers were more convivial than usual. About midnight Shivaji and a body of chosen troops left Panhala. They descended, not by any of the regular roads, but by a different path known as " Shivaji's Window." In perfect silence they picked their way through the sleeping enemy and taking a westerly direction began to march, as only Maratha hillmen can, towards Vishalgad.[†] It was impossible long to conceal the flight of a large body of

---

* *Sabhasad Bakhar.*

† I have already (see *Tale of the Tulsi Plant*, 2nd edition, p. 29) expressed the opinion that Shivaji fled to Vishalgad and not to Rangna. I rely chiefly on (1) local tradition, (2) the *Vishalgad Bakhar*, (3) the greater distance of Rangna from Panhala. As regards (3) it is reasonable to suppose that Shivaji, other things equal, would have fled to the nearest fortress. Now Vishalgad is 40 miles from Panhala, while Rangna by the shortest road is over 60. Nor is Vishalgad any less strong than Rangna. Both descend into the Konkan. Thus neither can he starved out. Again the road to Vishalgad is through a dense forest, through which infantry can move as quickly as cavalry. The road to Rangna lies through open country. Had Shivaji taken it, he would have soon been overtaken by the Bijapur horse. It is no doubt true that both Grant Duff and Ranade mention

troops. Before it dawned, Shivaji's escape had been discovered and Fazal Mahomed begged and obtained leave to pursue him with a force of cavalry. Sidi Johar promised to follow him with a large body of infantry. In the wooded country through which Shivaji led his force, men on foot can move as quickly as men on horseback. Nevertheless desire for revenge lent wings to Fazal Mahomed. About noon his leading squadron sighted Shivaji's foot soldiers. The position was critical. Vishalgad was yet six miles off and his men were worn with want of sleep and fatigue. But the great king's coolness did not desert him. He detached half his troops to form a rearguard and placed it under the command of one Baji Deshpande with orders to resist to the last at a place called Pandhar Pani, or the White Water. In the meantime Shivaji with the main body of his troops would make for Vishalgad with all expedition. When he had reached it, he would fire five guns as a signal. Baji Deshpande was then to break off the fight and retire as best as he could to Vishalgad. The officer to whom the perilous post of rearguard commander was entrusted had recently been in arms against Shivaji. He was of the same family as the Deshpandes of Rohida, who had helped him in his early days. But Baji Deshpande had served Chandra Rao More ; and in the contest between him and Shivaji, Baji had stood by his master even after his death. Eventually Baji had joined Shivaji's service. He was a Kayastha Prabhu and a few words about that most attractive and lovable caste may not be out of place.

Rangna as the place to which Shivaji fled. But both these eminent writers appear to have relied on the *Chitnis Bakhar*. On the other hand the *Shivdigvijaya Bakhar* is curiously ambiguous. It says that Shivaji first went to Vishalgad and then to Rangna. But Shivaji could not have started before 11 p.m., and according to Grant Duff he was overtaken before noon. In other words he would have had to cover a hundred miles in thirteen hours, marching continuously at a rate of nearly eight miles an hour. This was an impossible speed even for Mawal infantry. It is further noteworthy that the *Shivdigvijaya Bakhar* says (1) that Deshpande fought his rearguard action at Pandhare Jalav, clearly the same place as Pandhar Pani, which is only six miles from Vishalgad, and (2) that afterwards the Musulmans encamped at Gajapuri and besieged Shivaji at Vishalgad. Lastly it must not be forgotten that Shivaji had stored his recent booty at Vishalgad. He would naturally fall back there so as to protect it. In these circumstances, I think, there is good reason for affirming that Shivaji escaped to Vishalgad and not to Rangna.

Its members account for their origin by the following tale.
A certain Sahasrarjuna, otherwise known as Kritavirya, was
once king of the Haihiyas and had a thousand arms. In his
kingdom lived a sage called Jamadagni, who, wishing to attain
perfect freedom from all human passions, cast them from him.
Among them was Anger. Before leaving Jamadagni, Anger
warned him that he was making a mistake, for without anger
man could achieve nothing. Jamadagni, however, intent
only on attaining complete *sanyas*, heeded not the warning
and bade Anger depart with the other passions. Some days
later king Sahasrarjuna came to Jamadagni's hermitage. The
sage was out. But his wife bade the king welcome. He
repaid her hospitality in churlish fashion by stealing her sacred
calf. This act led to a dispute between the sage and the king.
But as Jamadagni had lost all power to get angry, he was unable
to lift his hand against his royal foe. The latter gave him
twenty-one wounds on the head and killed him. Now among
Jamadagni's sons was one Rama, called Parashurama, or Rama
with the axe, a weapon given him by the god Shiva. He was
the sixth incarnation of the god Vishnu and when he heard of
his father's death he took a fearful vengeance. For each
wound that Jamadagni had received, he cleared the earth once
of the Kshatriyas or warrior class to which Sahasrarjuna
belonged. Among his victims was Sahasrarjuna's son
Chandrasena. His wife, who was pregnant, fled to the hermitage of the sage Dalabhya. Parashurama heard of the flight and
following her demanded her of the sage. The latter complied so
readily that Parashurama promised to give him any boon for
which he asked. The sage at once asked for the life of the
child still in the princess' womb. Parashurama granted the
boon but stipulated that the child, if a boy, should become a
writer and not a warrior, and that instead of Kshatriya he
should call himself Kayastha, as he had been spared in his
mother's *kaya* or body. Whatever truth may underlie this
legend, it is certain that Kayastha Prabhus unite the qualities
both of warriors and writers. They are brave and loyal,
laborious and intelligent.

On this occasion Baji Deshpande proved himself worthy of his caste. He gladly accepted the post of honour and occupying a height near Pandhar Pani awaited the attack of the Musulman cavalry. These Baji Deshpande, favoured by the precipitous ground, repulsed without difficulty. After some delay some Musulman infantry came up and relieved the cavalry. Nevertheless Baji Deshpande and the rearguard successively repulsed two attacks. At noon a still larger contingent of infantry arrived. Fazal Mahomed led it up the slope in person. The rearguard began to give ground, but the gallant Deshpande rallied them until he fell, covered with wounds.* Just then the boom of five guns was heard from Vishalgad and the dying hero knew that his task was over. His men lifted his body and retiring in good order bore it safely to Vishalgad.

Sidi Johar, disheartened at Shivaji's escape, encamped at Gajapuri, a village near Vishalgad. After some delay, due to uncertainty as to what course to pursue, he resolved to besiege Vishalgad. That fort, however, cannot be invested from the western side. For it falls 2000 feet sheer into the Konkan, whence Shivaji could easily obtain provisions. Sidi Johar tried to mine the eastern fortifications, but Shivaji detecting the mine countermined and destroyed the Bijapur sappers. At last Ali Adil Shah, furious at this second failure, relieved Sidi Johar of his command and assumed it himself. The royal army, inspirited by the king's presence, achieved several successes. He renewed the siege of Panhala, which fell, together with all the other forts recently captured by Shivaji except Rangna and Vishalgad. These two on the very edge of the Sahyadris are exposed to an intensely heavy rainfall. Ali Adil Shah therefore resolved to leave them until the following dry season. When the monsoon broke he withdrew to a town called Chimulgi on the banks of the Krishna. Shivaji to compensate himself for the loss of his fortresses attacked Danda Rajpuri, a port a few miles to the north-west of Janjira. Two reasons prompted his action. The first was the wealth of the port, from which he exacted a large contribution. The second was the presence

---

* *Shivdigvijaya Bakhar.*

of some English factors, whom he rightly or wrongly suspected of helping Fatih Khan to defend Janjira. He took them prisoners and did not release them until he had obtained a considerable ransom. During the monsoon Shivaji laid siege to Janjira. This time he led the besieging force in person. Nevertheless he was unable to effect his purpose. Fatih Khan's ships held the sea and the island was too far from the mainland for Shivaji's artillery to produce any effect. At last Shivaji, so the story runs,* had a dream in which he saw Varuna. The Sea-god spoke to him and said, " Janjira will never fall into your hands. To take it is beyond your strength. I shall give you another island on which to erect a fortress equal to Janjira." When Shivaji awoke he resolved to raise the siege and, believing an island off Malwan, known as Sindhu Durg, to be the island of which the Sea-god had spoken, fortified it and made it a naval base.

Shivaji had another and perhaps a better reason for raising the siege. The Savants of Savantvadi proposed to the court of Bijapur a further plan of campaign. If they were supported by the Bijapur army and by Baji Ghorpade of Mudhol, they undertook to engage Shivaji with success. The king agreed and sent one Bahlol Khan with a force to co-operate with the Savants and Baji Ghorpade. Had Shivaji waited until the confederates had completed their preparations, the Savants' scheme might have succeeded. But that was not Shivaji's way. He went back to Vishalgad, which is about equidistant from Mudhol in the Doab and Savantvadi in the southern Konkan. There, in the winter of 1661-62, he learnt from his father that Baji Ghorpade was at Mudhol with only a small force.* Instantly Shivaji with 3000 horse stole forth from Vishalgad. With extraordinary swiftness he reached Mudhol, completely surprising his father's enemy. Now was the time to take vengeance, and he took it to the full. Baji Ghorpade fought bravely, but he, his followers and his sons were all killed. Shivaji marched through the fief stripping it of everything portable and destroying the rest. As he wrote in a letter† to his father informing him

---

* *Shivdigvijaya Bakhar.*   † See Appendix, p. 178.

of his victory, the booty was enormous. The king of Bijapur
sent a reinforcement under one Khawas Khan to replace the loss
of Baji Ghorpade and his troops. But Shivaji intercepted
Khawas Khan and to use his own words drove him back "sad
and despondent" to Bijapur.

That government had at this time to suffer further ill fortune.
Sidi Johar, who had so nearly succeeded in ending the war
by the capture of Shivaji, deeply resented his supersession and
disgrace. He at first retired to his own estate and then began
to intrigue with the Hindu nobles of the Doab, who, fired by the
example of Shivaji, had risen against Ali Adil Shah. That
king, unaware of Sidi Johar's treachery, appointed him to
command an army to suppress the rising. This gave the angry
general the chance which he sought. So far from acting against
the Doab nobles, he not only helped them as far as he could,
but entered into a correspondence with Shivaji himself. The
prince, however, was too prudent to be drawn into a distant
expedition. Nevertheless Sidi Johar thought the time fitting for
rebellion and attacked the Phaltan contingent, when separated
from the main Bijapur army by the Tungabhadra River.
The treachery failed. The Phaltan chief rallied his men and
eventually repulsed Sidi Johar, who not long afterwards was
assassinated by his own soldiers. But although his rebellion
was unsuccessful, it yet caused the rising in the Doab to spread
in every direction. The great stronghold of Raichur, so often
lost and retaken by the troops of Vijayanagar, defied the king's
authority. So, too, did the lesser fortress of Torgal. Ali
Adil Shah was forced to recall the army sent to co-operate with
the Savants of Savantvadi. Those unhappy chiefs were now
left to bear the full weight of Shivaji's anger. In vain they
called in the aid of the Portuguese. The latter sent them a
force too small to be of any use.* And Shivaji, falling upon
the allies, dispersed their army and overran the whole fief of
the Savants. They fell back on the fort of Phonda to the
south-east of Goa. But Shivaji blew up one of the bastions
and the fort became untenable. The unhappy Savants had now

---

* Shivaji's letter, see Appendix, p. 178.

no hope save in the clemency of the conqueror. "We are
Bhosles like yourself," they pleaded ;* "extend to us therefore
your protection. Take half our revenue and leave to us the
other half. If you do so, we shall equip three thousand men
and serve always as your allies." Shivaji accepted the terms
but insisted on the surrender of Phonda fort, and from that
day forward Savantvadi was his vassal state. The Portuguese,
however, had incurred Shivaji's wrath by aiding the Savants.
He invaded the country round Goa, and forced the Governor-
General to sue for peace and to supply him with muskets,
ammunition and cannon (A.D. 1662).

The king of Bijapur, with the Doab unsubdued, his ally the
chief of Mudhol dead, the Savants in Shivaji's power, was in
no state to renew the war. Nor had Shivaji any wish to prolong
it. He had throughout his life but one aim and that was to
free the Maratha race from Musulman rule.† The portion
subject to Bijapur he had freed. He now wished to keep it
free from the Moghuls by forming a triple alliance between himself and the states of Bijapur and Golconda, which might defy
Moghul aggression and enable him to liberate that portion of
Maharashtra which had been conquered by the Delhi emperors.
When both sides are anxious to end a war, peace usually comes
without much difficulty. A convenient mediator was at hand
in Shahaji. He had neglected his son in his youth but now
felt intensely proud of him. And nothing delighted him more
than the successful attack on Mudhol and the fall of Baji Ghorpade. On the other hand Shivaji also felt proud of his distinguished father and on hearing that the Bijapur government
had appointed Shahaji as their envoy, sent him by a messenger
a cordial welcome.

Shahaji set out on his journey with no less pomp and circumstance than if he had been about to visit Delhi. He first consulted astrologers, and learning that the stars were propitious.
he took with him his second wife Tukabai and her son Vyankoji.

---

* Shivaji's letter, see Appendix.
† Ranade, pp. 87, 88. So long as we bear this aim in mind, Shivaji's
conduct with regard to both the Delhi and Bijapur governments is clear.
If not, it is difficult, if not impossible, to understand it.

Shahaji first journeyed to Tuljapur, where he did homage to
Bhavani for the favours which she had lavished on her son.
From Tuljapur he visited Shingnapur, where he worshipped
at the family shrine of the Bhosles and the tomb of his father
Maloji. Next he went to Pandharpur and prostrated himself
before the image of Vithoba, which had, by the vigilance of the
priests, escaped the destructive fury of Afzul Khan. Thence
he travelled to Jejuri, a famous shrine of the god Khandoba in
the Poona district.

By arrangement with his father, Shivaji was to await him at
Jejuri. On hearing of Shahaji's near approach, Shivaji sent
his Peshwa, Moro Pingle, to meet him. After an interval
he set out himself, accompanied by his mother Jijabai and
his two wives Saibai and Soyarabai. But while Moro Pingle
rode on until he met Shahaji, Shivaji and the ladies with him
halted at the temple and there awaited Shahaji's cavalcade.
He made fitting offerings to the gods, and when Shahaji arrived
he prostrated himself at full length and laid his head upon his
father's feet. Shivaji's two wives next greeted with profound
respect their father-in-law : and Jijabai greeted her husband.
The salutations over, Shahaji entered his palanquin, but
Shivaji would neither enter one nor mount his horse. He
walked back to Jejuri village, barefoot to do his father honour.
When father and son reached the pavilion erected for Shahaji's
reception, Shivaji refused to sit down in his father's presence.
But standing in front of him with hands across his breast he
repeatedly implored Shahaji's pardon for the youthful disobedience which had led to his father's imprisonment. Shahaji,
deeply touched, embraced his son and said that all was forgiven
to one who sought to free his countrymen. He pressed his
son to continue in his appointed task and begged him after
he had himself passed away to extend to Vyankoji his love and
protection. From Jejuri father and son went to Poona. There
the terms of a treaty between Shivaji and Bijapur were settled.
The Bijapur government granted all Shivaji's demands (A.D.
1662). He was left in possession of his conquests from Kalyan

in the north to Phonda in the south, and from Dabhol in the
west to Indapur in the east, and his complete independence
was acknowledged. Both parties undertook to defend the
other from foreign aggression. And Shivaji took a solemn
oath not to molest Bijapur during Shahaji's lifetime.

Shivaji entertained in royal style Shahaji's party during the
rainy season. When the monsoon had abated Shivaji took
Shahaji with him to Rajgad and Purandar, Lohgad and Rairi.
When they reached Rairi, Shahaji's experienced eye took in
its extraordinary strength. Lying to the west of the Sahyadris,
it is surrounded on every side by a sea of mountains. It rises,
however, higher than any of its neighbours. To climb it to-day,
when undefended, is a most arduous task. To storm it, if
properly fortified and garrisoned, was to Shivaji's contempor-
aries an absolute impossibility. Shahaji urged his son to change
his chief stronghold from Rajgad to Rairi. Shivaji, convinced
by his father's reasoning, agreed. He changed the name of
the great hill from Rairi to Raygad and appointed Abaji Sondev
to fortify it and to build on its summit public buildings and a
palace for himself. At its base, but elevated some hundred
feet above the plain, he was to erect a dwelling place for Jijabai.
When the work of fortification was complete Shivaji issued a
proclamation. By it he offered a bag of gold and a gold bracelet
worth 100 pagodas to anyone who would ascend the fort by any
other path than those which passed through the fort gates.*
A man of the Mhar caste came forward and undertook with
Shivaji's permission to try. If he succeeded, he would plant
a flag at the top. Shivaji smiled and bade him try. But the
Mhar proved equal to the task. Climbing by a path known to
him from boyhood he disappeared from Shivaji's view. Not
long afterwards the watchers saw the Mhar's flag fluttering
on the summit. He then descended, prostrated himself at his
prince's feet and received the promised reward. Shivaji closed
the path by a gate still known as Chor Darwaja or the thief's
door. Not long afterwards another event occurred which
showed that Abaji Sondev's work was not yet complete. A

---

* *Khafi Khan*, Elliot and Dowson, Vol. VII, p. 288.

cowherd's wife named Hirakani or Diamond had entered Raygad
fort to sell milk to the garrison. Engaged in the task, she had
not noticed that night was falling. When she tried to leave,
she found the gates closed and the guards obdurate. In her
house below she had a child and a mother-in-law. Sooner
than neglect the one or incur the wrath of the other, she scrambled
down the hill side at the risk of her life and reached home the
same night. Shivaji heard of the feat and built a bastion to
close the path which she had taken. The bastion he called the
Hirakani Tower, thus immortalizing the name of the venturous
herdswoman. All ways to the fortress closed, Shivaji moved
his treasures and state papers to Raygad and from this date it
became the seat of his government. In the meantime Shahaji,
•after an affectionate parting with his son, and laden with
presents, had returned by Bijapur to the headquarters of his
own fief.

APPENDIX

SHIVAJI'S LETTER TO SHAHAJI

In your last letter you wrote to me as follows :—

" Far from helping the cause of his faith, Baji Ghorpade of Mudhol became party to the insidious schemes of the Mahomedans and Turks, and by foul and treacherous means he brought us to Bijapur. What terrible danger faced us there you well know. It seems that the Almighty has in his infinite wisdom decided to carry out your aspirations, to establish the Maratha power and protect the Hindu religion. Therefore it was that the peril was averted.

At present, inspired by malignant motives, Khawas Khan has marched against you, and ready to serve him Baji Ghorpade of Mudhol and Lakham Savant and Khem Savant are with him. May God Shankar (Shiva) and Goddess Bhavani grant success to you.

Now it is our desire that we should be fully revenged upon them and as we are fortunate to have such an obedient son, ready to carry out the wishes of his father, we command you to do this work. Baji Ghorpade has gone ahead to Mudhol with his men."

On hearing this from you, we went with an army to Mudhol, left the territory in ruin and took his thanas (garrisons). On learning this, Baji Ghorpade gave battle to us, in which he with other notable men fell. It was a great battle. We marched up and down the country and plundered it. Our gain on this occasion was enormous. We then proclaimed peace and brought the territory under our control. At this time Khawas Khan was coming upon us. With our army we fell upon him, defeating him and turning him back sad and despondent to Bijapur. Our next work was to crush the Savants. Fort after fort came into our possession. On we went, completely devastating their territory. They ceased to receive help from Goa, but the killedars of Phonda fought for them. By means of explosives, we blew up one of the bastions of the fort. Thus we became masters of their territory.

We next turned our arms against the Portuguese and took a part of their territory. They sued for peace and presented us with guns. The Savants could no longer consider themselves safe in Portuguese territory. For they sent one Pitambar as their Vakil to us. " We are," they pleaded "likewise the descendants of the house of Bhosle and you ought to care for our interest. You should take half the revenue of our possessions and the other half we shall devote to the expenses of our troops with which we shall serve you." Their requests are granted. Thus it is by your blessings that everything ended as you desired and I have great pleasure in submitting this account to you.

CHAPTER XVII

At this point it will not be out of place to sketch the lives of two men who each in his own way exercised an influence upon the Maratha prince. I have in an earlier chapter endeavoured to show how the religious movement of Pandharpur helped the military movement headed by Shivaji. The two saints who were at this time the chief vehicles of that teaching were Tukaram More and Ramdas.

Tukaram More was a *vani* or grocer by caste and came of a family of petty traders, who lived at Dehu, a beautiful little village fourteen miles to the north-east of Poona. The earliest known ancestor of Tukaram was one Vishvambar, who is said to have erected a temple to Krishna and Rukhmini on the banks of the Indrayani. He left two sons. They abandoned the family business, took service in the Ahmadnagar army and fell in action. This unfortunate mishap stamped itself on the family. For six generations afterwards, the Mores were deeply religious and closely attached to the worship of the god Vithoba of Pandharpur. Tukaram's father was one Boloji and his mother was named Kankai. Their eldest son was Savji, their second son was Tukaram. Their third son was Kanhoba. The date of Tukaram's birth is uncertain. According to Mr. Rajwade he was born in *Shake* 1490 (A.D. 1568-1569). According to Sir Ramkrishna Bhandarkar he was born in *Shake* 1530 (A. D. 1607-1608). His eldest brother Savji developed from earliest youth so strong a taste for the ascetic life that Boloji found it impossible to take him into his shop as an assistant. So when Tukaram was only thirteen years old, his father initiated him into the secrets of the grocery trade. For the next five years Tukaram helped to keep the accounts. When he grew older he received as a bride a girl called Rakma. His wife however grew delicate. Boloji therefore married Tukaram to a girl called Jijabai, the daughter of one Appaji Gulve, a Poona money-lender. On her marriage, Tukaram gave her the name of Avalai. When Tukaram was eighteen years old, his father Boloji died. Kankai died soon afterwards. The unhappy Tukaram was left to carry on the family business, to support his two wives, his eldest brother Savji, whose ascetic life rendered him useless as a bread-winner, and his youngest brotherKanhoba, who was still a child. Tukaram's gentle nature proved unequal to the task. He was too soft-hearted to take rigorous measures against his debtors. So they one after another repudiated their debts. Before the shop could recover from this shock, there came a famine. Tukaram became a bankrupt. His delicate wife Rakma died of privation. Her little son Shivaji did not long survive her. Savji left Dehu to go to some distant shrine and was never heard of again.

These calamities completely changed Tukaram's life. From being an active although a too kind-hearted business man, his thoughts turned, as Savji's had done, to religion and he became a whole-hearted devotee of Vithoba of Pandharpur. Indeed, but for his wife Avalai's influence, he would have disappeared like his elder brother. Her name has become equivalent to a scold or termagant, the Maratha synonym of Xanthippe. Yet there is no doubt that she saved Tukaram. For him and for their children she worked like a common labourer. She begged food and money for them from her parent's house. And if she at times lost her temper, this is not surprising. She was never sure that her husband would not give what she had begged to a passing tramp. One day indeed while she was bathing, he gave away her clothes. But Tukaram's devotion to the god Vithoba came, in course of time, to have its reward. Once a farmer employed him to drive the birds away from his crop. Tukaram, however, soon became lost in his dreams of the Pandharpur god. And when the farmer returned he found that the birds had eaten up almost his entire crop. He dragged Tukaram to the village headman and made him execute a bond for two *khandis* of grain, that is to say a bumper crop, and in return to take over the produce of the ruined field. The transaction over. Avalai made Tukaram reap what remained. He did so and to the amazement of the villagers and the disgust of the farmer, the reaped crop amounted to eighteen *khandis*. The god had worked a miracle on his worshipper's behalf. Avalai was overjoyed. But her joy was shortlived. Her husband resolved to return to Vithoba what Vithoba had given and devoted the proceeds of the crops to repairing the temple which his ancestor Vishvambar had built many years before.

Avalai made a last effort to give her husband a fresh start in business. She borrowed Rs. 200 from her father and sent Tukaram with a party of hawkers to sell the goods bought by her with the money. All went well until the hawkers reached Supa. There Tukaram witnessed the eviction of a poor indebted Brahman. Tukaram gave at once his goods to satisfy the Brahman's creditors. Then slipping away from his companions, he walked to Pandharpur, where he joined the crowd of devotees who worshipped before Vithoba's image. The villagers of Dehu were now satisfied that Tukaram was a lunatic. When he returned home, they put a necklace of onions round his neck, mounted him on a donkey and paraded him through the streets to be mocked at by the crowd. The unhappy Tukaram fled from the village and hid in the Bhambunath hills. His brother Kanhoba went in search of him and having found him begged him, either to return to Dehu and manage the family business or to let him do it. Tukaram went back with him. The brothers agreed to divide the bonds passed to their father by his debtors. The division complete, Tukaram flung his share of the bonds into the Indrayani. He then went back to his former hiding place in the Bhambunath hills. His wife Avalai tracked him out and daily brought him his dinner. One day a thorn entered her foot and made her faint with the pain. Touched with Avalai's devotion he returned home with her. But it was impossible for him to take up again the petty cares and duties of a grocer. In the silence of the hills there had come to him the poet's inspiration, and from the day of his return to that of his death, he never ceased to write poems either in praise of Vithoba or narrating incidents in his own life. They are written in the *Abhang* metre. They are rudely constructed, but full of force, and above all they embody to the fullest extent the pure teaching of the doctrines of Pandharpur.

Ramdas was a later contemporary of Tukaram.* He was the son of a certain Suryajipant and his wife Ranubai. For a long time they had no children. But they prayed diligently to the Sun-god for offspring. At last he appeared to them and promised that they should have two sons. One of them would be an incarnation of himself, the other of Maruti the Monkey-god, who helped the divine hero Ramchandra. A year afterwards Ranubai gave birth to a son, whom she named Gangadhar, and three years later she gave birth to a second son, whom she called Narayan in honour of the Sun-god. From their earliest years both children showed a taste for religion and it is said that to Narayan, when only five years old, was vouchsafed a vision of Maruti. According to the custom of the time Gangadhar was married when seven years old. A year or two later Narayan's marriage was arranged. But from his earliest years Narayan showed an intense dislike for the married state. At last he compromised by promising his mother that he would do or say nothing until he came to that part of the ceremony when the cloth which separates the married pair is withdrawn. She hoped that then Narayan would feel it too late to go back. When the priests however were about to repeat the verses that complete the ceremony, they as usual cried out to the audience 'Savadhan,' 'Be on your guard.' Narayan instantly fled from the room and was not found for some days afterwards. Suryajipant and Ranubai now gave up the idea of marrying their son, and let him wander about the various shrines of India. Numerous stories exist of the miracles performed by him while yet a child. Of these the most interesting is the following, for it shows the great capacity of him with whom Shivaji was so much associated.

---

* The account of Ramdas is taken from his life by his disciple, Hanmant Swami.

One day Narayan went to beg at the house of the Kulkarni of Shahapur near Karad. He found the ladies in a state of great perplexity. A Musulman officer from Bijapur had just arrested the Kulkarni on a charge of misappropriation and had taken him away to the capital. Narayan overtook the officer and his victim and went with him. At Bijapur he posed as the Kulkarni's clerk and so perfect was his knowledge of accounts, that he was able to convince the authorities that the charge was false.

When Narayan grew to manhood he established himself at Chaphal in the Satara district. There he built a temple to the hero-god Ramchandra, and believing himself to be an incarnation of the Monkey-god Maruti, he changed his name from Narayan to Ramdas, which, being interpreted, means 'the slave of Rama.' Gradually the fame of the new saint spread over Maharashtra and attracted to Chaphal a number of disciples. In course of time it reached the ears of Shivaji. The latter had just started his wonderful career. One day a Hindu *gosavi* or mendicant advised him to take a *guru* or spiritual preceptor, as that was the surest way to obtain salvation. The young hero consulted Bhavani and from her learnt that Ramdas was his destined *guru*. Shivaji at once went to Chaphal. Ramdas was not there when Shivaji reached it; so he had to return home with his wish ungratified. Not long afterwards he again went to Chaphal. Once more Ramdas was absent. But the prince wandered in search of him to Mahableshwar, Wai and Mahuli. At last Ramdas, who knew that Shivaji sought to find him,* wrote him a letter. It was in verse and may be translated as follows :—

> " O Meru of Resolution, O Helper of many, of unchanged resolve, rich and master of your passions ! O thou who pourest benefits on others, whose qualities are incomparable ; Lord of men, horses and elephants ! Lord of forts, earth and ocean ! Leader and king, who art strong always. King triumphant and famous, powerful and

---

* The date of Shivaji's meeting with Ramdas is the subject of much controversy. It seems to have occurred in 1649 (*Itihas Sangraha*).

generous, meritorious, virtuous and wise. Possessed ever
of conduct and judgment, generosity and faith, knowledge
and character. Bold and generous, grave and daring,
swift to execute. Thou who by thy vigilance didst spurn
kings. The holy places were broken. The abodes of
Brahmans were polluted. All earth was shaken. Religion
had fled. Narayan resolved to protect the gods, the faith,
the cows, the Brahmans and inspired thee to do so. Near
thee are many wise pandits, great poets, men skilled in
sacrifice and learned in the Vedas ; men quick and shrewd
and fitted to lead assemblies. None of this earth protects
the faith as thou dost. Because of thee some of it has
lingered in Maharashtra. A few have sheltered themselves
with thee and still some holy acts are done. Honour to
thy glory ! It has spread all over the earth. Some evil
men thou hast killed. Some have fled in terror. Some
thou hast pardoned. King Shiva the fortunate ! I have
lived in thy country. But thou didst never ask for me.
Thou didst forget me ; why, I do not know. Thy councillors
are all wise, the faith incarnate. What can I say to thee ?
It behoves thee to keep alive thy fame as the establisher
of religion. Many are the affairs of state in which thou
art busied. If I have written unreasonably, may I be
pardoned !"

Shivaji's desire to see the saint was stimulated by the praises
contained in his letter. He again went to Chaphal and not
finding him, pressed one of his female disciples to disclose the
saint's hiding place. She at last told the king that Ramdas
was at Shringanwadi. She then offered her visitor food.
But Shivaji vowed that he would eat nothing until he had seen
the object of his search. He procured a guide and at last found
Ramdas. He was sitting under a tree and was composing
verses for his famous *Dasbodh*. The king begged his pardon
for his remissness in the past. In return the saint blessed the
king. Shivaji then asked Ramdas to give him advice on the
art of government, and after some little time he received a
second metrical letter which may be translated as follows :—

"I bow to Ganpati the remover of obstacles. I bow to
Saraswati, to the virtuous, to the saints, to the family
gods, to Rama. If my hearers so wish, let them profit.
If not, let them disregard my writing; I have written for
the sake of your government. He who governs wisely
obtains happiness. If your labours are untiring, you win
in the end.

"First learn to know men. If you find a man is a
worker, give him work to do. If he is useless, put him
aside. To see, to understand, to labour, in this there
is nothing amiss. Achievement depends on the quality
of the worker. If he be industrious but at the same time
obstinate, still be in your greatness indulgent. But if he
be indolent and treacherous, then execute him. Learn
correctly the thoughts of all. To keep men pleased, to
keep the wicked sternly at a distance, these are the signs
of good fortune. If a man has helped you reasonably,
suffer him a little but not so that wrong may follow. Trans-
gress not the bounds of justice. If they be transgressed,
evil ensues. If there is no justice, there is no remedy. He
who has wearied in ill fortune, he whose head has been
turned by good fortune, he who has proved coward in the
hour of need, such are not true men. In evil times be not
despondent. Try every remedy; in the end all will be
well. Keep all men under proper control. Then the
wise will value your rule. If there be no proper control,
the government grows weak. Do not go in the van of the
battle. Such is not true statecraft. There are many
whom you can send as generals. Have many officers.
Do not appoint all to one task. Give them in your wisdom
separate tasks. If a leader's pride is fired, he will not
look to his life. Gather together many leaders and then
strike. When the sheep see the tiger's claw, they flee
on all sides. What can the proud buffalo do, big though
he be? Let kings observe the religion of kings. Let
Kshatriyas observe the religion of Kshatriyas. Let your
horses, weapons and horsemen be ever your first thought :

so that when your picked troops approach, your enemies,
great though they be, shall flee away.

 " Thus I have spoken a few words on the art of government. When the minds of lords and servants are one it
is good."

When Shivaji wished to return home, he presented the saint
with a large sum of money, but Ramdas distributed it among
his cowherds. The prince urged Ramdas to live with him.
Ramdas declined but he gave him as a farewell gift a cocoanut,
water, earth, a few pebbles and some horse dung. These Shivaji
took with him to his mother. Jijabai asked scornfully the
meaning of such a present. Her son with rare insight had
penetrated the sage's meaning. The water and the earth
meant that Shivaji would conquer Maharashtra. The pebbles
meant that he would hold it by means of his fortresses. The
horse dung meant that he would win his greatest victories by
means of his cavalry.

Unable to induce Ramdas permanently to live with him,
Shivaji looked about for a more pliant saint. He heard of
Tukaram. That holy man, after his return to his village, had
again suffered persecution, but had overcome it. The verses
which he had composed on the Bambhunath hills were eagerly
read and learned by the peasantry and petty traders. But the
Brahmans who lived on the alms of pilgrims to the various
shrines resented the competition of one who was of a Sudra
caste. One day, as Tukaram sat on the banks of the Indrayani
composing verses, some Brahman mendicants seized his books
and flung them into the river. But the god whom he loved
saved them and restored them, dry and uninjured after thirteen
days of immersion. Another time when Tukaram went to
a village called Vagholi, a learned Brahman scholar, named
Rameshwar, induced the herdsmen to drive Tukaram away.
Not long afterwards the same Rameshwar was attacked by some
ailment. He went to Alandi and prayed at Dnyandev's shrine
that he might be cured. One night he saw in a dream the great
teacher. He told Rameshwar that this ailment had come to
him as a punishment for his treatment of Tukaram. Let

Rameshwar ask Tukaram's pardon and treat him with honour instead of contumely and the ailment would go. Rameshwar obeyed the saint's command and was cured of his illness. In his gratitude he sang far and wide the praises of Tukaram. In this way Shivaji came to hear of him. He sent a messenger and a body of horse to convey Tukaram to him. But the saint felt that the camp of a high-spirited and warlike prince was no place for him. He declined the invitation in a metrical letter, of which I give the first five stanzas* :—

"Torches, umbrellas, and horses, these are not among things good for me. Why, O lord of Pandhari, dost thou entangle me among such ? Honour, ostentation, and aping other men's ways, I court as the dung of swine. O God, says Tuka, run to set me free from this !

"Thou providest me the very things that I dislike ; why dost thou persecute me when I have surrendered my soul to thee ? I feel that I should avoid society and keep the world far from me. I should seek a solitary place and utter no sound. I should look on mankind, wealth and my body as though they were vomit. Yet it rests with thee, Lord of Pandhari, says Tuka.

"The creator has founded the universe, therein are various designs and diversions afoot. A child of one design, you are devoted to Brahma and knowledge of Brahma ; you are faithfully loyal to your teacher. Part of your love I learnt when I saw the writing in your letter. Shiva is your name, the sacred name that has been given to you ; you have the right of the umbrella, you are one of the threads that keep the world together. Vows, rites, austerities, contemplation, mystic arts ; all these you have studied and dispensed with. Your mind is bent on meeting me ; this is the chief import of your letter. Listen, O Lord of the earth, to this my answer ; I have written out my prayer and purpose. Let me wander in the forest indifferent to all things. Let the sight of me be vile and

---

* The translation is taken from the admirable work of Messrs. Nelson Fraser and Marathe.

inauspicious. My unclad person is covered with dust ;
I live on fruit, for I have no food to eat. My hands and
feet are emaciated ; my skin is pallid ; what comfort could
there be in looking on me ?   It is my pressing request that
you will not even talk of seeing me.

" See how humble my speech is ; this is a boon from him
who dwells in my heart. Yet I am not a wretch who need
seek a boon from you ; I have a refuge in Pandharpur.
Pandurang watches over me and feeds me ; since that is
so, why need I care about others ? You wish to see me :
what matters this request ?   I have turned to nothingness
all desires. Freedom from desire has been bestowed on
me ; I have renounced every impulse of activity. As a
chaste wife longs to meet her husband, so let me live
joyously in Vithal (Krishna).   The universe to me is
Vithal and nothing else ; in you too I see him. I looked
upon you as Vithal (Krishna) but one difficulty keeps me
from you. Fix your thoughts on the good teacher, Ramdas ;
he truly is an ornament of the world ; do not swerve from
him. If your impulse carry you in many directions how
can you serve Ramdas ? Tuka says, O Father, O sea of
wisdom, faith and love are the vessel that carry the faithful
across the stream of life.

" What would it profit me to enter your presence ?   The
fatigue of the journey would be wasted. If I must needs beg
my food, there are many whom I may ask for alms.   In
the lanes are rags to furnish me with shelter. The rock
is an excellent bed to sleep on. I have the sky above me
for a cloak. With such a provision made, why need I
fix my hopes on anyone ?   It would be a waste of my days.
Should I come to your palace seeking honour, what peace
of mind should I find there ?   In a king's palace the wealthy
are respected ; the common herd meet with no respect.
If I saw there fine apparel and men wearing jewels, it would
at once be the death of me. If you are disgusted when you
hear this, still, God will not scorn me. Let me tell you
this surprising news, there is no happiness like the beggar's.

Austerity and renunciation are the greatest things : wealthy
men fettered by desire live miserably. Tuka says you are
opulent and honoured but the devotees of Hari (Krishna)
are more fortunate."

This refusal only whetted Shivaji's wish to see Tukaram.
He left his camp, and joining Tukaram led with him for several
days the life of a religious devotee. From this condition he was
rescued by the influence of his mother Jijabai. The blood
of ancient kings boiled in the proud woman's veins at
the thought that her son should give up a hero's life for that
of a wandering beggar ; and her entreaties, joined to those of
Tukaram, induced Shivaji to return to his duties as a warrior
and a prince.

Yet although both Tukaram and Ramdas refused to live
as religious preceptors with Shivaji, he never lost touch with
them. Several times afterwards he attended *Kirtans* or religious recitations given by Tukaram. This on one occasion
nearly cost the king his life. He had invited Tukaram to visit
Poona and recite a *Katha*, or sacred story, at the temple where
Shivaji as a child so often worshipped. Somehow the news
of his design reached the ears of his enemies. A body of Afghans
stole forth with orders to take Shivaji as he listened to Tukaram.
The Afghans surrounded the temple and searched for the prince
among the audience. With admirable coolness the saint continued his recitation and Shivaji sat perfectly still listening to
it. Nevertheless he would surely have been taken, but for what
is believed to have been the divine interposition of the god
Krishna. As the Afghans searched, a man in face and in
clothes closely resembling Shivaji rose and slipping through the
guards ran out of the door. The Afghans rushed out of the
temple to seize him. But he ran with incredible swiftness
towards Sinhgad. And although mounted Afghans ran close
to his heels, they never could quite catch him. On reaching
the forest at the base of the great fort he dived into a thicket
and disappeared. In the meantime Tukaram continued his
story. When it was over Shivaji and the rest of the audience
returned home unmolested.

But it was to Ramdas that Shivaji was peculiarly associated. Tukaram indeed did not long survive his meeting with Shivaji. One day as he was leaving his home he told his wife Avalai that he was going to Vaikuntha, the god Krishna's heaven. He went to the banks of the Indrayani and, so it is believed, flung himself into the river either in a state of religious excitement or because he suffered from some incurable disease. At any rate he never returned home again. His followers believed— and the belief still finds in the Deccan wide acceptance—that the chariot of the hero-god Ramchandra descended from heaven and bore Tukaram back in it to the skies (A.D. 1649). Ramdas, on the other hand, outlived Shivaji and whenever the busy monarch could spare a few moments, he loved to visit the saint and hear from his lips sacred verses and religious discourses. Many touching stories exist which show how close was the friendship which the prince and the saint bore each other. One day, it is said, Shivaji, then at Pratapgad, heard that Ramdas was at Mahableshwar. He at once rode off to see him. On reaching Mahableshwar he learnt that Ramdas was no longer there. Shivaji plunged into the woods to overtake him. All day the king wandered vainly through the wild hill country. Night fell but still he searched for Ramdas by torch light. At last when the eastern sky began to pale, Shivaji came upon Ramdas in a tiny cave. He lay there groaning and seemed to be in great pain and sick unto death. Shivaji in great distress asked Ramdas how he might help his suffering friend. The saint replied that there was but one cure in the world for such a malady as his. " Tell me what it is," said Shivaji, "and I will get it for you." " Nay," replied Ramdas, " to get it for me might cost you your life." " No matter," cried the generous hero. " Gladly would I give my life to save yours." " Then," said Ramdas, " the medicine which alone can save me is the milk of a tigress." Sword in hand went forth into the jungle the dauntless prince. In a short time he saw some tiger cubs in a thicket. He entered it, and catching them, sat down by them to await their mother's return. An hour later the tigress came, and seeing her cubs in Shivaji's hands, sprang

upon him. The prince boldly faced the raging beast and told
her that he but wished to give the dying saint a draught of her
milk. The saint's name cowed the tigress. She let Shivaji
go and allowed him to draw some of her milk and take it away
to Ramdas' cave. There he gave some of it to Ramdas. His
pain instantly left him. Then Ramdas in turn made Shivaji
drink the rest of the milk. At once the scratches inflicted by
the tigress when she first sprang on Shivaji healed. And the
king and his retinue rode back with Ramdas to the temple at
Mahableshwar.

Another time, so it is said, Shivaji was at Satara. Ramdas,
who was at Mahuli at the confluence of the Krishna and the
Yenna, went to beg upon Jaranda Hill, a holy spot a few miles
to the east of Mahuli. The king was also visiting the Jaranda
temple and met Ramdas. The saint asked for alms. Shivaji
wrote some words on a piece of paper and dropped it into the
Swami's lap. Ramdas picked it up and read in it a grant by
Shivaji of his entire kingdom. The saint affected to accept
the grant and for the whole day Shivaji, having no longer any
property, acted as his servant. At the close of the day Ramdas
asked Shivaji how he liked the change from kingship to service.
Shivaji replied that he was quite happy, no matter what his
state, provided that he was near his preceptor. Ramdas then
returned the grant and said. " Take back your kingdom. It is
for kings to rule and for Brahmans to do worship." Nevertheless
Shivaji insisted that the saint should bestow on him his sandals
as Rama had done to his brother Bharata, so that the
world might know that Ramdas and not he was the true
king. He also chose for his flag the orange brown banner
which the pilgrims carry when they go to worship Krishna
at Pandharpur.*

Another time, so it is said, Shivaji begged Ramdas to live
with him always and let him serve him as he had done for a
single day at Jaranda. Ramdas asked him in return whether,
instead of serving him, Shivaji would grant him three boons.
Shivaji said that he would do so gladly.

---

* This is known in history as the Bhagva Zenda.

The boons asked for were :—

(1) Shivaji should in the month of Shravan, or August, honour Shiva by giving feasts to Brahmans and by distributing images of the great god, whose incarnation he was deemed to be :

(2) He should distribute *dakshina*, or gifts of money, to Brahmans in Shravan ;

(3) He should honour the hero-god Ramchandra by ordering his subjects when they met to say to each other by way of greeting, " Ram Ram."

Shivaji granted all these boons and " Ram Ram " are still the words of greeting used by Deccan Hindus when they meet.*

Yet another time Shivaji was building a fort at Samangad in Kolhapur territory. As he watched it, he felt a natural pride that he should be able to support all the workmen that the work needed. Just then Ramdas came up. Shivaji, after saluting him, walked with him round the base of the fortress. On their way they passed a boulder. Ramdas called to some stone-cutters and bade them break it in pieces. The stone-cutters did so. In the heart of it was a cavity half filled with water. Out of the water jumped a frog. Ramdas turned to Shivaji and said, " O King, who but you could have placed water in the middle of the stone and thus saved the frog ?" Shivaji disclaimed any connexion with the matter. But when Ramdas insisted, he guessed that the saint was rebuking him for his vanity. He at once acknowledged his fault and admitted that it was god who had alike provided for the needs of the frog and for those of the workmen at Samangad.

But if Ramdas dared to rebuke the great king to his face, he refused always to go beyond his own sphere of action. Peter the Hermit, having inspired a crusade, aspired afterwards to lead it. The foolish Scotch ministers led their countrymen to ruin on the field of Dunbar. But when Shivaji, on hearing of Afzul Khan's march from Bijapur, asked for Ramdas' advice, the wise Brahman bade the king pray for counsel to Bhavani.

---

* The old form of salutation was the " Johar." It is still used by the Mhars and depressed castes.

He knew that if God had given him power to move men's hearts by verse and prayer, God had given to Shivaji other and greater powers, and that his resourceful mind, if left to itself, would find a key to every difficulty.*

Ramdas would have liked always to lead the wandering life, such as had been his before Shivaji first sought him. But the king insisted that he should make his head-quarters at some easily accessible spot. He bestowed on the saint the fortress of Parali, a wild hill some six miles south-west of Satara. Ramdas reluctantly accepted the gift and built there a temple to Maruti. For the use of the temple the king assigned to Ramdas the revenue of Chaphal and 32 other villages. As he grew older, Ramdas came to spend more and more of his time at Parali. It was there that Shivaji paid him his last visit. It was there that Sambhaji, reeking with the blood of Rajaram's friends, sought but was denied an interview. At last the wise old Brahman felt his end approaching. His disciples felt it also and gave way to grief. But Ramdas' courage never forsook him. He rebuked their tears and composed for them the following verses :—

> "Although my body has gone I shall still live in spirit. Grieve not. Read my books. They will show you the way to salvation. Heed not unduly the wants of the body. Fall not into evil ways, and to you the doors of salvation will open. Keep ever in your heart the image of the god Rama."

A few minutes later the dying saint called out the words "Har! Har!" † twenty-one times. Then his lips whispered the words "Ram! Ram!" His eyes sought the image of the hero-god, and a flame, so it seemed to the onlookers, left his mouth and entered that of the image. His disciples called to

---

* Ramdas' words were :—"You are a king and control the affairs of your state. I dwell in the forest and (in state matters) you cannot depend upon me. Set your hand to the task and act as you think you should act. I have already told you how to obtain the guidance of the goddess (Bhavani). Bear my words in mind. The goddess cares for you. By her blessing you have attained the kingship. Consult her before you act, tell her your troubles and act on her advice."—Hanmant's *Ramdas Charitra.*

† A name of Shiva.

him, but he was dead.* He had survived Shivaji less than a year. Ramdas' body was burnt to the north of Parali upon a pyre of *bel* and *tulsi* wood. His ashes were then gathered and taken to Chaphal, and after some interval were, at Sambhaji's cost, conveyed northward and cast reverently into the Ganges River.

---

* Ramdas died at 12 noon on Magh Vadya 9 in Shake 1603 (A.D. 1681).

CHAPTER XVIII

SHIVAJI, allied to the Bijapur king, in whose plighted word he trusted, thought himself strong enough to attempt the liberation of the Marathi-speaking subjects of the emperor. Nor was a good ground for hostilities lacking. In May, 1661, the Moghuls had occupied Kalyan in the Konkan, the town which Shivaji had taken from Mulana Ahmad. He had been unable to recover it at the time. He now sent Netoji Palkar with a force of cavalry and Moro Pingle with a strong body of infantry to plunder the Moghul territories from Ahmadnagar to Aurangabad. A curious story exists* that the imperial officers complained to Shaistekhan, the governor of the Moghul Deccan, that they were unable through fear of the Marathas to send to Aurangabad, the provincial capital, their revenue collections. In reply the governor sent them a sarcastic letter. " Although you are men," he wrote, " you fear to meet the Marathas. I am sending you a woman who will not fear to do so." At the same time he collected troops and placed over them a certain Rai Bagin †, the wife of one Udaram Deshmukh. In spite of her sex she was a skilful and daring soldier. Nevertheless Shivaji attacked her, took her prisoner and dispersed her army. Shortly afterwards Shivaji defeated near Ahmadnagar another force sent from Aurangabad under a Rajput officer.‡ He then swept the Moghul Deccan as far as its capital and levied contributions from every town of importance.

Aurangzib, on hearing of Shivaji's successes, urged Shaistekhan, who was his own maternal uncle, not to stand on the

---

* *Shedgavkar Bakhar.*

† *Shivdigvijaya Bakhar.* The *Sabhasad Bakhar,* which Grant Duff has followed, makes Rai Bagin take part in the fight at Khadase.

‡ *Shivdigvijaya Bakhar.*

defensive but to invade and conquer the territories which
Shivaji had taken from Bijapur. Shaistekhan, agreeably to
these orders, collected such Moghul forces as were then in the
Deccan. He left one Mumtaz Khan at Aurangabad and placed
his second in command Jaswant Sing, Maharaja of Jodhpur,
in charge of his reserves. He himself marched to Ahmadnagar
and after a short halt marched thence due south to Pedgaon.*
From Pedgaon he sent Jadhavrao of Sindkhed,† a Maratha
noble, ahead with his cavalry. Several sharp skirmishes took
place between him and Shivaji's horse. The imperial cavalry
were in the main successful. And as Shivaji fell back on Rajgad,
they occupied first Supa and then Poona. Shivaji as a counter-
move threw himself into Sinhgad, only thirteen miles away.
It was no doubt Shaistekhan's intention eventually to invest
Sinhgad. But before doing so he wished to clear his communications. Chakan lay on the high road between him and Junnar,
the nearest town large enough to furnish him with supplies.
The commandant of Chakan was still that Phirangoji Narsala
who had, on Dadoji Kondadev's death, acknowledged Shivaji
as his master. He now proved himself a gallant soldier. His
defence was favoured by the heavy rains of the Sahyadris,
which were then falling, and by the efforts of Netoji Palkar's
cavalry to harass the besiegers. Nevertheless the conduct of
the garrison and of Phirangoji Narsala deserves all praise. On
dark, rainy nights they made desperate sallies and frequently
rushed the Moghul trenches. In the end, however, the garrison
were driven back into Chakan and after a siege of 50 or 60 days
the Moghuls exploded a mine which carried away a bastion and
the men defending it.‡ The Moghuls placed their shields in
front of their faces and tried to cut their way through the breach.
Phirangoji, however, was not yet willing to surrender. He had
prepared an earthwork inside the fort wall and there he and
his men stood desperately at bay. All that day the Moghuls

---

* In Ahmadnagar district.

† Khafi Khan.

‡ "Stones, bricks and men flew into the air like pigeons." *Khafi Khan*,
Elliot and Dowson, Vol. VII, p. 262.

assaulted the work in vain. And during the following night both the besiegers and the besieged slept close to each other among the ruins of the bastion. Next morning the Moghuls received reinforcements and drove the garrison back from the trenches into the citadel. Invested there and without supplies, Phirangoji Narsala capitulated. Shaistekhan received him with all honour and offered him a post in his own service. Phirangoji Narsala declined, and Shaistekhan suffered him and the remnant of his garrison to return to Shivaji. As the brave commandant bade Shaistekhan farewell the latter told him that if ever he wished to join the Moghul service, an honourable post awaited him. Phirangoji returned to Shivaji. The latter, received his lieutenant cordially, and made him commandant of Bhupalgad.†

By this time Shivaji had withdrawn from Sinhgad to Rajgad. There he received a letter from Shaistekhan. It contained a Persian stanza in which Shivaji was derided as a monkey, whose only safety lay in his mountain forests. In return Shivaji sent Shaistekhan a Sanskrit couplet.‡ Therein he asserted that he was not only a monkey but Hanuman himself—the prince of monkeys ; and he vowed that he would destroy Shaistekhan just as the monkeys had helped king Rama to destroy the demon Ravan. Shaistekhan after this exchange of compliments returned from Chakan to Poona, where he occupied Shivaji's old house, the Raj Mahal. He was however well aware of Shivaji's resourcefulness and courage and posted a ring of patrols all round Poona. He then dismissed every Maratha horse soldier from his cavalry and forbade all Hindus, whether civilians or soldiers, to enter or leave Poona without a pass. He did not venture to dismiss his Maratha infantry for fear of reducing too greatly his army. His neglect to do so proved his undoing. In April, 1663,§ Shivaji, Yesaji Kank, Tanaji Malusare ‖

† In Satara district.

‡ *Shivdigvijaya Bakhar.*

§ Grant Duff fixes the date by a letter from the English factors imprisoned in Rajapur, dated March 12, 1663.

‖ These were the two friends of his early manhood.

and 200 picked men disguised themselves as foot soldiers in the Imperial service and obtained permission from the Kotwal for a marriage party to enter the town. In front went a boy dressed as a bridegroom.* Behind him walked Shivaji and his companions, beating drums and playing *sannais* † to keep up the disguise. About the same time another band of Shivaji's men, dressed as foot soldiers, entered by another gate of the town dragging with them a number of their comrades, whom they declared to be prisoners of war and whom they beat unmercifully. Outside, but at some distance from Poona, several thousands of Shivaji's infantry concealed themselves, so as to cover his retreat in case of mishap. The two bands that entered the town met at a given spot and changed their garments. About midnight Shivaji posted the bulk of his men, about 500 in number, at various points in the city. He himself, with Tanaji Malusare, Yesaji Kank and some 20 others, went to the Raj Mahal. They tried first to pass through the main entrance.‡ But it was well lit and some watchful eunuchs guarded it. Shivaji therefore turned back and entered the cook-house. There some of the cooks were at work; others lay asleep. Shivaji and his men noiselessly strangled the former and stabbed the latter to the heart in their sleep.

It was all done so skilfully that no alarm was raised. With pickaxes Shivaji's men next removed some mud and bricks which blocked a window opening into the women's apartments. A servant, whose bed was against the wall, awoke and roused Shaistekhan. The general, too drowsy to hear anything, swore at the servant for awaking him unnecessarily and again went to sleep. A minute or two later some of his maids ran in to say that a hole was being made in the wall of their room. Shaistekhan, awake at last, sprang from his bed and seized a spear and his bow and arrows. But by this time Shivaji's party had opened the window and were pouring through it. Shaistekhan

---

* Khafi Khan.
† A kind of fife.
‡ *Shivdigvijaya Bakhar.*

shot the first man through the body with an arrow. But the
Maratha, before he fell, slashed off Shaistekhan's thumb. The
next Shaistekhan killed with his spear. But another party
of Shivaji's men had by now overpowered the eunuchs and had
forced their way through other doors. In vain Shaistekhan's
servants beat drums for help. Shivaji's men bolted the doors
behind them. Shaistekhan's son, Abdul Fatih Khan, rushed
at the Marathas, but after killing two or three was himself cut
down. His gallantry, however, enabled two maid-servants
to drag Shaistekhan, faint with pain, to a place of safety. An
unfortunate nobleman in his train and similar to him in age and
appearance tried to escape by a rope ladder. But the Marathas
saw him, and believing him to be Shaistekhan, killed him and
cut off his head. Shivaji, thinking the Moghul general dead,
opened the doors and after collecting all his men, fled as fast
as possible out of Poona. Before they could be overtaken,
they had joined the main body of infantry left as supports,
and with them Shivaji retreated to the Katraj Ghat, the pass
which crosses the range of hills of which the fort of Sinhgad
forms the western extremity. To the trees that grew along the
top of the Katraj hill the Marathas fastened blazing torches,
so that the Moghuls might believe that a large army was encamped upon its summit. Shivaji then led his men due west and went
back as swiftly as he could to Sinhgad. The Moghuls had by
this time heard of the raid and seeing the lights on the Katraj
pass marched there with all expedition. On reaching the foot
of it they made a careful disposition of their force and with
barren valour stormed the empty summit, thus giving Shivaji
and his men the necessary time to reach their stronghold.
Shaistekhan some hours later followed them to the fort of
Sinhgad. This however was mere bravado. He had no siege
guns with him. The rainy season was close at hand, when the
rise of the Muta River, which has its source near Sinhgad, would
make siege operations extremely difficult. The Khan's folly was
duly punished. Shivaji allowed the Moghul army to come close
to the fortress and then fired into them point blank with his
heavy artillery. Numbers fell, and Shaistekhan's riding elephant

was killed by a cannon-ball.*   The Moghul general had no
alternative but to order a retreat to Poona. But even so he
did not escape from his difficulties. As the Moghuls retired,
their cavalry were ambushed by a party of Maratha horse
under Kadtoji Guzar,† Netoji Palkar's most brilliant lieutenant,
and were driven back with great loss upon the main body.‡

On Shaistekhan's return to Poona, Jaswant Sing, his second
in command, called on his chief to express his regret. Shaistekhan was now beside himself with pain and vexation. Instead
of accepting the Maharaja's condolences with courtesy, he
remained for some moments silent and then said,§ "I thought
the Maharaja was in His Majesty's service when this evil befell
me." The Rajput prince, who commanded the reserves and
was therefore in no way responsible for the mishap, left the Raj
Mahal in a fury. Shaistekhan reported his conduct to Aurangzib
and declared that all his Hindu subordinates were in league
with Shivaji. After sending this letter, Shaistekhan, in a fit
of childish temper, evacuated Poona and marched with most
of his troops back to Aurangabad, exclaiming that he would
trust no one and that, if he stayed, the loss of his head would
soon follow the loss of his thumb. He, however, ordered Jaswant
Sing to hold Junnar and Chakan. The Maharaja did his best
to repair the effect of his superior's imbecility, by attempting
when the rains ceased to invest Sinhgad. But his forces were
inadequate. He therefore raised the siege and fell back on
Chakan. On receiving Shaistekhan's letter the emperor censured
both him and Jaswant Sing. But he recalled the former and
gave the command of the Deccan army to his son, Prince
Muazzim (July 15, 1663).

After his failure to take Sinhgad, Jaswant Sing remained
inactive. His enemy, however, was planning a counter-attack
on one of the richest possessions of Aurangzib. In South Guzarat,
near the mouth of the Tapti River is the town of Surat. Unlike

---

* *Shivdigvijaya Bakhar.*
† Better known as Prataprao Guzar.
‡ Grant Duff, p. 197.
§ *Khafi Khan*, Elliot and Dowson, Vol. VII, p. 271.

AURANGZIB

[To face page 215.]

most of the great cities of the East it has no very ancient history. It was sacked by Mahomed Ghori, the conqueror of Delhi, and by Mahomed Tugh'ak while engaged with the rebellious nobles of Guzarat. But its inhabitants trace its prosperity to a certain Gopi, either a Nagar or Anavala Brahman. He was the son of a poor Brahman widow who lived in the latter half of the 15th century. While still a lad, he resolved to leave his native town and boldly to seek his fortunes at Delhi. Although a Hindu, he was an accomplished Persian scholar and he hoped to get a clerkship in one of the imperial offices. For some days he sought employment in vain. Nevertheless he continued to frequent the public buildings on the chance of a vacancy. One evening the chance came. A high official brought for perusal an important Persian letter. It was so late that the expert Persian readers had all left and the script was so crabbed that the official could not himself decipher it. Nevertheless he sat by a candle vainly trying to master its contents. At last he saw Gopi sitting near him and in despair he asked his help. Without even taking the letter in his hand, Gopi, to the official's astonishment, told him at once its full purport. While the other was trying to spell out word by word the baffling hieroglyphics, Gopi had read them through the paper held up against the light. The official at once appointed Gopi to a high and well-paid post, wherein he soon accumulated a respectable fortune. Taking it with him, he returned to his native town and induced other rich merchants to settle there also. The place grew beyond all recognition, until at last Gopi, now its first citizen, asked the leave of the king of Guzarat to call it Suraj, after his wife, who had stood by him through both ill fortune and prosperity. The king agreed, but changed Suraj into Surat so that the lady's name might agree with the heading of certain chapters in the Koran.

In A.D. 1512, the Portuguese, jealous of the trade and wealth of the new emporium, took and sacked it. Thereupon the king of Guzarat ordered a fort to be built. But the fort was badly constructed and in A.D. 1530 and 1531 the Portuguese ships again entered the Tapti and plundered the town. The king of Guzarat then resolved to build a castle on the banks of the river and entrusted the work to a Turk called Safi Agha. The Portuguese bribed him to delay the work. Nevertheless he completed it about 1546. It was strongly fortified on the river side, and on the land side it was protected by a ditch six feet wide, and had a rampart 35 yards wide. In 1573, Akbar conquered Surat and in the same year made a treaty with the Portuguese, who soon became the chief merchants of Surat and the masters of the Arabian Sea. But in 1580, an irreparable calamity overtook the little country, whose innumerable heroes had spread her fame to the farthest corners of the civilized world. Philip II inherited the crown of Portugal, and as the appanage of the Castilian kings, Portugal shared in their misfortunes. In 1579, Holland had revolted and soon every Portuguese possession was either conquered or threatened by hardy sailors from the mouth of the Scheldt or from the shores of the Zuyder Zee. In 1616, a Dutch merchant, Van den Broeck, came to Surat. Two years later the Moghul emperor gave the Dutch the right to build there a small permanent settlement, known in the parlance of the time as a factory.

About the same time as the Dutch, came another race from the fog-wrapped islands that divide the North Sea from the Eastern Atlantic. On December 31, 1600, the English queen Elizabeth granted a charter to a number of London merchants, who had associated themselves together under the title of the East India Company. In 1612, Mr. Kerridge, in the *Hoseander*, arrived at Surat. He was well received by the inhabitants, but was attacked by the Portuguese. The English repulsed the attack, and in 1612 the Emperor Shah Jehan gave them leave to build a factory. On the heels of the English and the Dutch followed the French. In 1620, the French Admiral Beaulieu dropped anchor in the Tapti, anxious to buy Surat cloth and sell it to the natives of Sumatra. And in 1642 a French factory rose in Surat similar to those built by the English and the Dutch. The enterprise of the foreign merchants and the shiploads of European commodities which every year they brought to the Tapti soon made Surat the richest emporium in the Moghul Empire.

SKETCH MAP SHOWING PLACES MENTIONED IN THE ACCOUNT OF
SHIVAJI'S CAMPAIGNS.

Shivaji's plan was, as usual, a masterpiece both of daring and foresight. He gave out that he intended an attack on the Portuguese at Bassein and erected two camps between that port and Choul. While he gathered there a large army, his chief spy, Bahirji Naik, made his way to Surat and brought back a full report of the condition and geography of the town. At the same time Shivaji, disguised as a mendicant, explored the roads that led from the Northern Konkan through the Dharampur State into South Guzarat. He then returned to the two camps, and taking from them 4000 picked cavalry, he left them again so secretly that none outside his staff knew of his departure. Passing through the territories of the Dharampur chief, whom he had won to his cause, he suddenly appeared on January 5, 1664. some 10 or 12 miles from Surat. The Governor timidly sent a messenger to inquire what Shivaji's intentions were. He also called on the Dutch and English merchants to assist in the defence of the town.† Both, however, refused to do more than defend their own factories. But the Dutch sent two messengers to watch the movements of the invading army. They were caught and detained, as was the Governor's messenger, while Shivaji and his cavalry rapidly approached the mud walls of the city. The Governor and the garrison made no efforts to man them but withdrew into the castle. The inhabitants, deserted by their ruler, took to the river boats or fled into the open country. Shivaji then sent a message to the Governor, summoning him and Haji Sayad, Viraji Bohri and Haji Kasim, the three richest merchants in the town, to attend his camp and to ransom Surat ; otherwise he would burn it down.‡ The cowardly Governor refused to leave the shelter of the castle walls. So after some time had elapsed, Shivaji ordered his troops to plunder the empty city. A body of Marathas tried to storm the English factory but were gallantly repulsed. The same night a Mr. Anthony Smith, unaware of Shivaji's arrival, rode into Surat from Suvali.

† Dutch account in Valentyn's *Lives of the Moghuls*.
‡ English factor's letter in Forrest's *Selections*, Vol. I, p. 24.

He was seized and taken to the king. Shivaji sent him as a messenger to the English and about the same time he sent a Greek merchant named Nicholas Kolostra* to the Dutch, to demand ransoms for their factories. The Dutch replied that they had no money. The English sent back a haughty refusal denouncing Shivaji as a rebel. With the small force that the king had at his disposal, he very wisely did not attempt the reduction of the two strongholds, defended as they were by resolute men and containing little or no treasure. He also received kindly a French Capuchin monk named Father Ambroise, who bravely went to the Maratha camp and implored the king's protection for the members of his flock. But the Marathas collected or dug up without interruption the property left behind by the rich and timid Surat merchants.† On January 10, after he had gathered property worth several thousand pounds, the king received news that a Moghul army was advancing to relieve the city. He at once rallied his troops, loaded the plunder of Surat on the horses of the unfortunate inhabitants and vanishing as swiftly as he had appeared, brought the treasure of the great town to store it safely in the fort of Raygad.

On the return from the Surat expedition, Shivaji heard of his father's death. After peace had been made with Shivaji, the Bijapur government were free to devote their whole strength to the task of stamping out the rebellion of the Doab nobles. A number were forced to capitulate. But the chiefs of Bednur and of several other places along the Tungabhadra offered a stout resistance. At last the Bijapur government directed Shahaji to undertake the reduction of the insurgents. The gallant old soldier readily complied. He defeated them in a pitched battle, and investing Bednur, forced the chief to surrender all his lands except Bednur itself and the district round it. Having crushed the rebel leader, Shahaji marched along the north bank of the Tungabhadra overcoming all resistance. At last he reached

---

* Dutch account.

† Aurangzib was so pleased with the conduct of the Dutch and English that he reduced the customs duties payable by them from 3½ to 2 per cent. According to Bernier (*Travels*, pp. 188-9), Shivaji spared the home of a Hindu broker because he had been very charitable.

the village of Yergatanhalli in Basavapatan and there pitched
his camp. The country round swarmed with game and Shahaji
thought that his recent efforts had earned him some relaxation.
He left his camp for a day's black buck hunting. Having
wounded a buck, he galloped after it at full speed. As he rode,
a creeper caught his horse's foreleg. It fell, and Shahaji, thrown
violently, broke his neck. His attendants galloped up on seeing
the accident, but life was extinct before they reached their
master (January, 1664). They at once sent word to his son Vyankoji, who hastened to the Doab from Tanjore, cremated Shahaji's
body and performed his funeral rites. The Bijapur government
expressed most handsomely their appreciation * of the dead
man's services and bestowed his fiefs of Bangalore and Tanjore
on Vyankoji. When the news reached Shivaji, both he and
Jijabai were deeply affected. The latter indeed was with
difficulty restrained from committing *sati*.† And only Shivaji's
entreaties that she should remain with him a little longer and
help him in his holy work induced her to alter her resolve.
Shivaji found a different solace for his grief. He resolved to
avenge Shahaji's death by attacking the Doab nobles, whose
rebellion had indirectly caused it.* He sent into the Doab a
force of cavalry and guns and levied a large contribution. The
Bijapur government, to whom the rebels had for several years
caused continuous trouble, in no way resented the invasion.
On the contrary they granted the village wherein Shahaji had
fallen as an *inam* ‡ to his son. Thither Shivaji went and
after distributing large sums in charity erected a building over
the spot where Shahaji had fallen. And for many years lamps
burnt in it day and night to honour and to comfort the dead
man's spirit. §

Shahaji's renown has like Hamilcar's been overshadowed
by that of his more famous son. Nevertheless the achievements
neither of Hannibal nor of Shivaji could well have been accomplished but for the work done by their fathers before them.

* *Shivdigvijaya Bakhar.*
† Ranade, p. 63.
‡ Shivaji collected the revenue. Bijapur retained the jurisdiction.
§ See letter in Parasnis MSS. The tomb is now in ruins.

Hamilcar, from his Sicilian stronghold, first showed his countrymen that with mobility and good generalship, the Carthaginian
army could hold its own against the superior discipline of the
Roman legion. Shahaji first showed the Deccan that Hindu
troops under a Hindu leader could with rapid movements and
local knowledge prove a match for the picked forces of Delhi
or Bijapur. Indeed, had Shahaji been opposed to only one
of these two powers, he would most likely have re-established
the kingdom of Ahmadnagar and have governed it through a
puppet king. This, however, would have been but a doubtful
blessing to the Maratha people. Shahaji's kingdom would have
inherited the Nizam Shahi traditions of cruelty, treachery and
murder. His failure enabled Shivaji to found a government
entirely new and, if it be regarded as a whole, singularly free
from the political crimes which mar the histories of most Indian
states and which were not infrequent among the early kings
of Scotland and of England.*

On Shahaji's death, Shivaji assumed the hereditary title of
Raja granted by the king of Ahmadnagar to Maloji.   He
established a mint at Raygad to show his complete independence
of Bijapur and struck, in his own name, both gold and copper
coins.† He also began to make use of the fleet which he had
built or collected at Malwan to plunder all ships issuing from the
imperial ports. Unfortunately some of these were ships filled
with Mecca pilgrims. This brought on him the wrath of both
Delhi and Bijapur. A large Bijapur force debouched from
Panhala and invaded the Konkan. It at first gained some
successes but was eventually defeated and driven back into
Bijapur territory. Shivaji, fearing Moghul invasion from the
north, did not pursue the beaten army. He had recourse to
his fleet and plundered the whole Bijapur coast as far as Gokarna
and returned to Raygad to await the expected Moghul attack.

Aurangzib recalled Jaswant Sing of Jodhpur and sent in his
place Jai Sing, a Rajput veteran who at one time had fought

---

* The only royal murder in Maratha History was that of Narayan Rao
Peshwa by his uncle Raghunath Rao.

† *Shedgavkar Bakhar.* See also *Khafi Khan*, Elliott and Dowson, Vol.
VII, p. 271.

for Prince Dara, and Diler Khan, an Afghan soldier of eminent merit (March, 1665). Aurangzib entrusted a large army to each of the generals and they worked together in perfect harmony. Diler Khan invested Purandar while Jai Sing blockaded Sinhgad* and raided with his cavalry the country between it and Rajgad.

Before the present European war, Purandar was a charming little hill station. It stood over 4000 feet above the sea and, lying well to the east of the Sahyadris, did not suffer from such heavy rains as most of the mountain forts of Maharashtra. Neat bungalows built by enterprising merchants of Poona could be leased at far lower rents than those demanded in more lordly Mahableshwar. The presence of a garrison ensured a constant supply of stores and a small but pleasant society. A broad road 28 miles long took the visitor from Poona over the Sinhgad range through Saswad to the foot of Indra's Hill.† Thence a wide bridle path enabled him to walk or ride comfortably to a narrow plateau some 1300 feet above the plain. A carriage road led round the hill, past the barracks and hospital, the bungalows and offices. A little church embowered in roses gave the English stranger a surprise, so closely did it resemble a house of prayer in some far off Surrey village. From the south a path climbed 400 feet to the summit of Purandar, whence could be seen the entire Saswad plateau. To the north-east stood a peak half a mile, as the crow flies, from the top of Purandar. It was easily accessible and formed a convenient spot for teas or picnic parties.

In Shivaji's time the ledge on which to-day stand bungalows and barracks was the lower fort. On the summit of Purandar was the upper fort or citadel. The peak to the north-east was known as Rudra Mal or the Rosary of Shiva and formed a separate fort. It added nothing to the strength of Purandar. But as it completely commanded the lower fort and partly commanded the upper fort, it had to be defended. It was strongly fortified and long walls enabled the garrison to retire

* *Sabhasad Bakhar.*
† Purandar, as I have said, is another name for Indra.
14

on Purandar, if too hardly pressed. In 1665, Shivaji had
appointed as commandant of Purandar one Murar Baji, a
Prabhu and therefore of the same caste as Baji Deshpande, the
hero of the rearguard action near Vishalgad. He had with him
a force of 1000 men, but a great number of peasants from the
surrounding districts had fled to the fort for refuge. A separate
force garrisoned Rudra Mal. The defenders, animated by
Murar's spirit, offered a most stout resistance. Diler Khan,
however, exploded a mine under one of the bastions of the
lower fort and carried it immediately afterwards. The storming
party, led away by their success, attempted in their onset to
rush the upper fort also. Murar Baji instantly counter-attacked.
With 700 men he charged down the hill side, killing no less than
500 Afghan infantry, and drove the besiegers in headlong flight
to the foot of the hill, where Diler Khan from the back of an
elephant was watching the attack. The latter with great
coolness shot Murar Baji through the body. Thereupon, the
garrison, after a loss of 300 men, retreated to the upper fort.
Not long afterwards, Diler Khan obtained a further success
by scaling Rudra Mal.

Shivaji now became seriously alarmed. He had long been
accustomed to consult Bhavani, the patron goddess of his house.
And lately he had employed one Balaji Abaji, a Prabhu
refugee from Janjira, to record words which he spoke when, as
he believed, he was inspired by the divinity. On this
momentous occasion he again asked the advice of Bhavani,
and passing into a trance spoke as if repeating her instructions. Balaji Abaji recorded the divine message. Its
tenour* was that Jai Sing was a Hindu Prince and that he
could not be overthrown like Afzul Khan or Shaistekhan. Shivaji should therefore make terms with him. Though danger
might await him, yet he should fear nothing, for through it
all Bhavani would protect him. Shivaji, after waking from the
trance and consulting with his councillors and his mother,
resolved to send an envoy to Jai Sing and sue for peace. Shivaji's conduct on this occasion has been discussed both by

* *Sabhasad Bakhar.*

Grant Duff and by Mr. Ranade. The former has surmised that
he was actuated by superstition. Mr. Ranade attributes it
to some deep-laid scheme still undiscovered. The real reason
was, I think, the following. Shivaji remembered that his
father Shahaji had separately fought with success both Moghuls
and Bijapur. Combined they had overthrown him. Shivaji
had for this reason avoided hostility with Delhi· until he had
made terms with Bijapur. Trusting in Ali Adil Shah's honour,
he had then attacked the Moghuls. But as the recent invasion
of the Konkan showed, the Bijapur king was not to be trusted.
He was now in league with Aurangzib and was endeavouring
to recover his lost possessions. Shivaji therefore resolved to
make peace with the Moghuls, and with their help so to reduce
the power of Bijapur that never again would its intervention
against him be of any consequence.

Shivaji sent messengers to Raja Jai Sing as a brother Hindu,
asking for terms. But the Rajput chief had no intention of
being tricked as Sidi Johar had been. He therefore answered
Shivaji's message with civility but never ceased to press the
siege of Purandar or to devastate the enemy's possessions. At
last Shivaji sent to Jai Sing his confidential minister, Raghunath
Pant, who swore by the most binding oaths that this time
his master really was in earnest (June 9, 1665). Jai Sing in
the end believed him and desired that Shivaji should visit him.
On his part he swore by the sacred *tulsi* plant that if Shivaji
did so, not a hair of his head would be harmed. Shivaji was
at this time at Raygad. On receiving Jai Sing's message he set
out with 1000 horse.* When he reached Jai Sing's tents,
the latter sent a clerk with a body of armed Rajputs to inform
him that if he was serious in his intention to surrender, he should
enter ; if not, he had better go back as he had come. Shivaji
assured the clerk that he was really in earnest and the clerk
conveyed his assurance to Jai Sing. Jai Sing accepted it and
sent a messenger of suitable rank to receive his visitor. When

---

* Grant Duff says that Shivaji was accompanied by a slender retinue.
But both the *Shedgavkar* and *Sabhasad Bakhars* say that he took 1000 men.
It would have been dangerous to have taken less.

Shivaji entered Jai Sing's tent, the Rajput chief rose and embraced him. He seated Shivaji on his right hand and repeatedly promised that he would not only guarantee his safety, but would win for him the emperor's pardon and favour. Shivaji on his part assured the Rajput that he had no other wish than to become an ally of the emperor. After some further conversation, it was agreed that Shivaji should at once visit Diler Khan, who was still trying hard to take Purandar. Indeed, he had lost all patience at the length and difficulties of the siege. He had torn off his turban and had sworn not to wear it again until the place fell.* Nevertheless, on hearing that Shivaji had opened with Jai Sing negotiations to which he had not been a party, Diler Khan, so the Marathi chroniclers maintain, flew into such a passion that he tore his own wrist with his teeth.† He, however, received Shivaji with courtesy and soon fell under the charm of his address. Diler Khan presented Shivaji with a sword,‡ which the latter with ready tact at once fastened round his waist. The interview closed with an exchange of compliments and an immediate truce. Purandar fort was surrendered to Diler Khan but the garrison and the refugees were permitted to depart. The terms of the peace had still to be considered. What Jai Sing demanded was the surrender of all Shivaji's recent conquests from the Moghuls, all the territory which had once belonged to the Ahmadnagar kingdom, and Shivaji's homage to the emperor for the rest of his estate. On the other hand Shivaji, although not ready to surrender all demanded of him, was yet willing to make great sacrifices, provided that he might have a free hand against Bijapur. Eventually it was agreed that Shivaji should evacuate his recent gains in Moghul territory and all the ancient Ahmadnagar forts and districts except twelve. Included in his cession were Purandar and Sinhgad. He was to retain all his other conquests from Bijapur.§ In return for a large sum in cash payable in three instalments, he was permitted to collect the *chauth* and *sardeshmukhi*, that

---

* *Subhasad Bakhar.*
† *Subhasad Bakhar, Shedgavkar Bakhar.*
‡ Khafi Khan.   § The sum of money amounted to 40,00,000 pagodas.

is to say, a fourth plus a tenth share of the government revenue of certain territories in Bijapur. Shivaji was in addition to assist Jai Sing in reducing Bijapur, and his son Sambhaji was to accept a command of 5000 horse in the imperial service. These terms were submitted to Aurangzib for approval. And the emperor, after some harsh reflections on Shivaji's past conduct, graciously condescended to confirm them.*

---

* Aurangzib's letter, Appendix, p. 214. There is great confusion about the number of forts surrendered. Grant Duff writes that Shivaji surrendered 20. Khafi Khan's number is 23. The *Sabhasad, Shedgarkar* and *Shivdigvijaya Bakhars* mention that he surrendered 27. All authorities agree that he retained 12 forts. But there is a slight difference as regards the names between Grant Duff and Aurangzib's letter. The *chauth* and *sardeshmukhi* are not mentioned by the emperor. He probably did not understand their meaning. The terms occur in the *Shivdigvijaya Bakhar.*

APPENDIX

AURANGZIB'S LETTER TO SHIVAJI, DATED AUGUST 26, 1665.

After compliments,

Your present letter, couched in very humble strain, stating that account of your interview with Raja Jai Sing had been received.

We are glad to note that you desire a general pardon for your conduct. Your wishes had already been communicated to us by your officers, *viz.*, that you repent for your past deeds and that you surrender thirty (30) forts to them and would retain twelve (12) forts only with the adjoining territory, yielding in revenue 1 lakh of pagodas. In addition to these twelve (12) forts which formerly belonged to the Nizam Shahi government, you wish to retain another tract in the Konkan with a revenue of four (4) lakhs of pagodas, that you have taken from the Bijapur government and another tract under Bale Ghat in Bijapur territory with a revenue of five (5) lakhs of pagodas. You want a Charter from us to this effect and you agree to pay to us forty (40) lakhs of pagodas in annual instalments of three (3) lakhs.

Our reply is that the policy pursued by you has been so unscrupulous that it does not deserve forgiveness. Nevertheless at Raja Jai Sing's recommendation we extend to you a general pardon and allow you to retain, as you wish, twelve (12) forts detailed below.

The adjoining territory has also been granted to you. But out of the nine (9) lakhs of territory, that part which is in the Konkan and yields four (4) lakhs and is at present in your possession has been annexed to our empire. As for the other, with a revenue of five (5) lakhs, it will be given you subject to two conditions.

(1) You must recover it from the Bijapur government before Bijapur falls into our hands.

(2) You must join Jai Sing with a well-equipped army and discharge the imperial work to his satisfaction and pay the stipulated ransom after the Bijapur conquest.

At present a *mansab* of 5000 horse has been offered to your son. Every horseman will have 2 or 3 horses. A dress also has been sent to you. This mandate bears our testimony and our seal.

Details about the forts according to Raja Jai Sing's letter.

1.	Rajgad.	7.	Alwari.
2.	Bhorap.	8.	Rayari.
3.	Ghosala.	9.	Lingangad.
4.	Udedurga.	10.	Mahadgad.
5.	Torna.	11.	Pal.
6.	Talegad.	12.	Kuwari.

CHAPTER XIX

THE folly of which the Bijapur king had been guilty in breaking his treaty with Shivaji now became apparent. Aurangzib regarded Shivaji as little better than a hill bandit, who was never likely to be formidable beyond the foothills of the Sahyadris. But the reduction of Bijapur and Golconda was the darling wish of his life. It had throughout been the policy of the Moghul emperors to destroy the Musulman kingdoms which had risen upon the ruin of the Afghan empire. They had previously been provinces of Delhi. They had revolted when the central power was weak. They should be recovered when the central power was once more strong. Akbar, with far smaller resources than Aurangzib, had overthrown the kingdoms of Guzarat, Khandesh and Bengal. Shah Jehan had conquered Ahmadnagar. The conquest of Bijapur and Golconda would enable Aurangzib to overrun all southern India, until his frontiers everywhere reached the sea. He would then be free to guard with the whole strength of the empire the north-western passes against the barbarians of Central Asia.

In spite, therefore, of the aid given by Ali Adil Shah to the Moghuls in their attack on Shivaji, Aurangzib ordered Jai Sing and Diler Khan at once to invade Bijapur territory and if possible to storm the capital. Shivaji, with 2000 horse and 8000 or 9000 infantry, joined the Moghul army (November, 1665). Considerable success at first attended the expedition. Shivaji attacked Phaltan, the fief of the Nimbalkars, his relatives, and soon reduced it as well as the fort of Tathwada about 10 miles to the south-east. He also made a successful night attack on the Bijapur forces in the Konkan. In the meantime, Jai Sing and Diler Khan moved on Bijapur itself. They met with no serious resistance until they came to Mangalveda, a strong place about 60 miles north of Bijapur.   It was gallantly defended but fell after a week's siege.*

Diler Khan and Jai Sing now begau to draw their troops round Bijapur and to hold high hopes that it would soon capitulate.   But Ali Adil Shah rose to the height of the danger.   His light horse spread out in every direction to invade the Moghul territories and to cut the communications of the besiegers. He had the wells for miles round Bijapur poisoned and all stores and food supplies likely to fall into Moghul hands destroyed. At the same time he appealed to the king of Golconda to send him reinforcements.

Shivaji, after the fall of Phaltan and Tathwada, moved south-wards and took a number of minor forts.   While so engaged, he received from the emperor a letter† in which he expressed his appreciation of Shivaji's gallantry and informed Shivaji that he had sent him a jewelleds word.   Encouraged by this praise and his own recent successes, Shivaji invested Panhala. But the investment proved a failure.   The garrison inflicted on the besiegers such a serious check that they raised the siege and fell back upon Vishalgad.   While there, Shivaji received a second letter from the emperor.   In it Aurangzib invited the Maratha prince to court, promising him leave to return home when he wished.   At the same time Aurangzib again expressed his appreciation of his recent services and informed Shivaji that he had sent him a dress of honour.‡

Shivaji sought the advice of Bhavani, and again the words spoken by her through Shivaji's mouth and recorded by Balaji Abaji were favourable.   Ramdas§ also advised Shivaji to go to court and thus to remove all suspicions from Aurangzib's mind. Shivaji, after some further consideration, decided that he would accept the emperor's invitation.   He left his state in the hands of his mother Jijabai, Moro Pingle the Peshwa, Nilopant Sondev and Annaji Datto. §   To Jijabai was also entrusted the care

---

* Khafi Khan.
† Original letter from Aurangzib ; see Appendix A, p. 225.
‡ See Appendix B, p. 225.
§ *Shivdigvijaya Bakhar.*

of Shivaji's wives and of his second son Rajaram. Sambhaji was to go with his father, and among Shivaji's attendants were Raghunathpant Korde, Kadtoji Guzar, Trimbakpant Dabir, Hiraji Pharzand, Balaji Abaji, Yesaji Kank and Tanaji Malusare. Shivaji took with him also 1000 infantry and 3000 horse. He first went to Jai Sing's camp near Bijapur.† The Rajput general received him cordially and when bidding him goodbye sent with him his own son Ramsing. Jai Sing told Ramsing that he had guaranteed Shivaji's safety and that as Ramsing valued his father's word, he was to help Shivaji to the utmost if he fell into any kind of danger. On the journey north, Shivaji was constantly thrown into the young prince's company, and long before it had ended, Ramsing was Shivaji's devoted friend.

Some weeks of travel brought the party to the neighbourhood of Agra. There Shivaji halted and despatched Ramsing to inform the emperor that Shivaji was awaiting his pleasure. When Ramsing returned, he conveyed to Shivaji Aurangzib's wish that his guest should at once proceed to court. Shivaji had been led by the Raja Jai Sing to expect that an officer of high rank would be sent to invite him to Agra. But the only officer who accompanied Ramsing on his return was one Mukhlis Khan, a court official of little or no standing. Nevertheless Shivaji said nothing but started with his escort. On reaching Agra he was given an audience (May 12, 1666).‡

---

† *Shedgavkar Bakhar.*

‡ Grant Duff and Ranade following the Marathi *bakhars* place the scene of Shivaji's detention at Delhi. With the utmost deference to these eminent writers, I think that they are wrong. Khafi Khan, who is fairly reliable as regards Moghul matters, places the scene at Agra. He is strongly supported by the original order of Shivaji in the Parasnis MSS by which he rewarded Kashi Trimal and the mother of Krishnaji Vishvanath. It runs as follows :

"On leaving *Agra*, we left behind young Sambhaji, under the protection of Krishnaji Visvanath.

The said gentleman had brought him safe to Raygad and his mother and Kashi Trimal have accompanied Sambhaji to this place. We have therefore been pleased to pass an order to offer fifty thousand rupees as reward for the service.

Rs. 25,000 to Kashi Trimal.
„ 25,000 to the mother of Krishnaji Vishvanath.

Rs. 50,000 "

He presented a nazar or offering of Rs. 30,000. The emperor then ordered him to take his place among commanders of 5000 horse. This was a deliberate insult. Shivaji had recently taken the field with 10,000 men and commands of 5000 horse had already been conferred on his son Sambhaji and on his subordinate Netoji Palkar. The Maratha prince saw that he was being maliciously flouted and, unable to control himself, turned to Ramsing and spoke frankly his resentment. The young Rajput did his best to pacify him but in vain. Aurangzib, who had no doubt hoped for some such incident, at once took advantage of it. He dismissed Shivaji without ceremony or return presents. He ordered him to be conducted to a house prepared for him near the Taj Mahal outside the city and to be informed that the emperor had reported Shivaji's conduct to Jai Sing. Until Jai Sing's reply arrived, he was not to present himself at court. Shivaji's son Sambhaji, however, should do so, but as a retainer of Ramsing. After Shivaji had reached his house, a strong guard under a Musulman officer named Polad Khan* was placed round it.

Shivaji was now in imminent peril. Any attempt to escape would give the emperor the desired excuse to behead him. On the other hand, if Shivaji made no such attempt, he would probably remain a state prisoner for the rest of his life. Shivaji first resolved to appeal to Aurangzib's honour. He sent Raghunathpant Korde with a petition to the emperor. Therein he reminded Aurangzib of the safe conduct promised him and of the assurances of Raja Jai Sing. In return for freedom Shivaji undertook to assist in the conquest either of Golconda or Bijapur. Raghunathpant Korde was given an audience and supported his master's letter with such eloquence as he could himself command. But a certain Jaffar Khan, whose wife was Shaistekhan's sister and who was therefore connected by marriage with the emperor's family, had in the interval made every endeavour to poison Aurangzib's mind against Shivaji by distorted stories of his encounters with Afzul Khan and Shaistekhan. Aurangzib dismissed Raghunathpant Korde with

---

* He was a kotwal of Agra.

the cold answer that the matter would receive consideration.
With a heavy heart Raghunathpant repeated the reply to his
imprisoned master. The latter then wrote to his friend Ramsing
and begged him to intervene on his behalf.* Ramsing gene-
rously undertook the dangerous duty but met with no better
success. The emperor told the Rajput that the matter was no
longer any concern of his†. Eventually Aurangzib sent a
messenger to Shivaji to say that he could return to the Deccan,
provided he left behind him his son Sambhaji as a hostage.

Had Shivaji accepted this condition, he would have had either
to sacrifice his eldest son, or to betray his countrymen. He
declined it and began at once to consider all possible methods
of escape. The same night he saw in a dream Bhavani, who, so
he fancied, told him that he need fear nothing.† She would
provide not only for his safety but for that of his son. Comforted
by this vision, Shivaji's resourceful mind soon evolved a plan
which for ingenuity and daring has rarely been equalled. In
pursuance of it, he sent a further petition to Aurangzib, in which
he begged that he might at least send his troops back to the
Deccan. The emperor was only too glad to consent to a proposal
which robbed Shivaji of his only protectors. And if he felt
any suspicions, they were skilfully soothed by Shivaji's conduct.
After his troops had departed, Shivaji repeatedly said to Polad
Khan that he now no longer wished to depart. The emperor
provided for his comfort on a liberal scale. His residence at
Agra enabled him to save money, and if he could obtain the
emperor's leave he would send for his wives and mother to Agra
also. These words were reported to Aurangzib by Polad Khan
and the emperor smiled indulgently at what he deemed the petty
avarice and mean spirit of the Deccan chief. Shivaji next
asked leave to send his friends in Agra sweetmeats and choice
dishes prepared in the Deccan manner.‡   The leave was given
and Shivaji's friends gladly received the presents and sent him
similar gifts in return. Shivaji sent further presents and received

* *Shivdigvijaya Bakhar.*
† *Sabhasad Bakhar.*
‡ *Khafi Khan.*

further return gifts. Thus hardly a day passed without a stream
of wicker-work baskets passing into or going out of the prisoner's
door. At first Polad Khan had them all carefully examined.
But gradually his vigilance relaxed and the guards daily let the
baskets pass without troubling to examine them. Suddenly
Shivaji announced himself ill. He complained of acute pain
in the liver and spleen. He sent for the best doctors in Agra
and they prescribed for him various remedies. At first they
seemed to do the patient but little good. But in a few days
Shivaji declared himself better and ordered that more baskets
of sweetmeats should be prepared and sent to his friends, that
they might rejoice with him at his recovery. He also bought
three horses,* which he sent with some of his attendants along
the Mathura road. They were, he gave out, to be given as presents to the Brahmans there, whose prayers to Krishna had
won his recovery. That evening Shivaji and his son got each
into a sweetmeat basket and their remaining followers, disguised as porters, carried them out. One only of his retinue,
the faithful Hiraji Pharzand stayed behind.† He entered
Shivaji's bed, and covered his head with muslin, but left exposed
one of his hands upon which Shivaji had placed his own signet
ring.*

Next morning Shivaji did not rise, and as there seemed
a strange stillness about the house the guards entered it. They
saw, so they thought, Shivaji lying on his bed ill with fever,
while a boy massaged his legs. They went away satisfied that
Shivaji had had a relapse. In the meantime Shivaji, Sambhaji
and their attendants had made their way to the spot where
the horses awaited them, and had ridden as fast as possible
to Mathura. There they changed their dresses and assumed the
garb of religious mendicants, with whom Mathura is at all times
crowded. They sought shelter of three brothers Annaji, Kashiji,
and Visaji Trimal, who were brothers by marriage of Moro
Pingle, Shivaji's Peshwa. They willingly agreed to take the
fugitives to their house until such time as it might be convenient
for them to continue their flight. By now, however, Shivaji's

---

* Khafi Khan.   † *Sabhasad Bakhar.*

escape had become known. About midday Hiraji Pharzand
had left Shivaji's bed, had dressed himself and, on the pretext
of going shopping, had left the house with the boy who had
massaged his legs. They went to Ramsing's dwelling, informed
him of what had happened and then started on foot to return to
the Deccan.* Shivaji's house was now completely deserted
and when the guards paid it another visit to satisfy themselves
that he still lay on the cot, they found it empty. Polad Khan
reported the escape to Aurangzib, who instantly sent orders to
local officers everywhere to search for the missing prince. Once
in Mathura he was all but caught. A Brahman priest overheard
Shivaji,† as he sat with his companions on the banks of the
Jamna, discuss with them the various roads that led to the
Deccan and give them instructions as regards present expen-
diture. The priest addressed the little group, observing that
their talk was strangely out of keeping with their ascetic dress.
Fortunately a friendly priest named Krishnaji Vishvanath,
whom the three brothers had won to Shivaji's service, silenced
the curious questioner with a handsome present. And he, too,
became a devoted adherent of the prince.

The emperor failing to find Shivaji elsewhere had given
orders that a close search should be made for him among the
mendicants of Mathura. For the garb of the mendicant has
always been, and still is, the favourite disguise of the fugitive,
whether criminal or political. It was, therefore, necessary for
Shivaji to leave Mathura. But Sambhaji was too young to
stand the fatigues of the journey. His presence, also, would
add to the risk of detection. Shivaji left him behind with
Krishnaji Vishvanath's mother.‡ He himself, with Krishnaji
as his guide, started on his homeward journey. It was
unsafe to take a direct route. So Shivaji and his guide
made for Benares and went through the usual routine of
worship followed by pilgrims to that famous shrine. From
Benares they went to Allahabad and Gaya and thence to

---

* *Sabhasad Bakhar.*
† *Shivdigvijaya Bakhar.*
‡ See Shivaji's letter *ante.*

Bengal.* Then they turned back and journeyed to Indore. From Indore they went southwards until at last they came to a village which Shivaji's troops, enraged at his detention, had recently raided and sacked. They asked shelter of a farmer. He had suffered with the other villagers and had lost his crops and live stock. Nevertheless he shared what he had with the travel-worn mendicants. Next morning they left him and a few days later they were in Poona. It was free from Moghul troops. So Shivaji threw off his disguise and publicly announced his return.

The welcome which he received resembled that which six years before had awaited Charles II when he landed at Dover. The guns in every fortress of the Sahyadris boomed greeting to the well-loved leader. The common soldiers went mad with delight. The officers hastened in thousands to pay their respects and to hear from Shivaji's own lips his romantic story. From Poona, Shivaji rode in state to Raygad (December, 1666). There his mother clasped him to her bosom and resigned back to him the power entrusted to her and the other regents when he left for Agra. One thing was wanting to the joy of Jijabai and her son. Sambhaji was still exposed to danger. But not many weeks passed before he too reached home safe and well. After securely guiding Shivaji to Poona, Krishnaji Vishvanath returned to Mathura. Then taking with him his mother, Kashiji Trimal and Sambhaji, he once again began the long journey to Poona. The party journeyed without incident until they reached Ujjain. There a Musulman officer suspected that the handsome, highbred lad might be Sambhaji and addressed him. He was baffled by Kashiji's coolness and devotion. "The boy," he said, "is my son. But a short time ago my mother, my wife, my son and I started together on a pilgrimage to Allahabad. My mother died on the way, my wife fell ill at Allahabad and died also. I am now taking my orphan son back to my own village." "In that case," retorted the Musulman, "you will have no objection to eat with your son of the same plate." Although for a Brahman to eat with a Maratha, no matter how highly born, was to break the caste law and to incur a costly penance, Kashiji did not hesitate. He and Sambhaji shared the same dish. And the

---

* *Shivdigvijaya Bakhar.*

Musulman officer, satisfied with the test, let the prisoner go.
The party continued on foot as far as Rakshasabhuvan, a village
on the banks of the Godavari. There they hired horses and
rode with all speed to Raygad. Shivaji, overjoyed at his son's
return, gave to each of the three brothers the title of Vishvasrao.
He gave in addition to Kashiji Trimal an order for Rs. 25,000
and a similar order to Krishnaji Vishvanath's mother. Nor
did he fail to reward the hospitable villager of Malwa, who, in
spite of his own misfortunes, had yet extended a welcome to
two wandering beggars.

Sambhaji safe, Shivaji was free to take revenge on the Moghuls.
Their affairs in the Deccan had lately been going none too well.
Ali Adil Shah's defence of Bijapur had roused the sympathy
of the king of Golconda. And in answer to his rival's appeal
for help, he had sent 6000 cavalry and 25,000 infantry. They,
with the Bijapur horse, so harassed the besiegers that they were
soon in a worse plight than the Bijapur garrison. At last Jai
Sing reported to the emperor that he could no longer continue
the investment. At the same time he fell back on Dharur and
awaited orders.* But Shivaji now entered the field. He recap-
tured the Konkan surrendered by him, and then began to overrun
the Desh. Jai Sing saw his retreat threatened. He abandoned
all the forts in the Desh except Lohgad, Sinhgad and Purandar
and retreated to Aurangabad. The failure of Jai Sing's expedition and Ramsing's suspected connivance with Shivaji's escape
led the emperor to recall him. But the war-worn Rajput did not
live to regain the capital. Death overtook him at Burhanpur
as he travelled back to Delhi (July 12, 1667). In place of the
dead officer Aurangzib re-appointed his son, Prince Muazzim,
as Governor of the Deccan, and Jaswant Sing, Maharaja of
Jodhpur, as his second in command. The new viceroy had but
little capacity and no liking for war. Jaswant Sing had made
Shivaji's acquaintance at Delhi, and like all those who passed
under the wand of the magician, became the prince's enthusiastic
admirer. Shivaji on his part was willing to make peace provided

* Khafi Khan.

that his old possessions were restored to him and that, as before, he was given a free hand against Bijapur. A treaty ensued very favourable to the Maratha leader (A.D. 1668). The emperor conferred on him the title of Raja, thus confirming the honour granted to Maloji by the Ahmadnagar king, and continued the *mansab* or command of 5000 horse to Sambhaji. He restored to Shivaji his father's old fief of Poona, Chakan and Supa,* and the neighbouring forts except Sinhgad and Purandar. In lieu of his other claims on the old Ahmadnagar kingdom, Shivaji received a fief in Berar and, so it would seem, was allowed to retain the Konkan which he had recently reconquered. Shivaji on the other hand undertook to aid the Moghuls in a fresh attack upon Bijapur. In pursuance of their agreement Shivaji sent a fine body of horse under Kadtoji Guzar, now ennobled by the title Prataprao Guzar,† to join Prince Muazzim's army at Aurangabad. It does not, however, appear to have seen service. The Bijapur king, although he had forced Jai Sing to raise the siege, was heartily sick of the war, and with Shivaji once more an ally of the emperor, could hardly hope to repeat his recent successes. He sued for peace and obtained it by giving up the fort of Sholapur and other territory yielding 180,000 pagodas. But he had also to satisfy the claims of Shivaji to *sardeshmukhi* and *chauth* which had been granted to him by Aurangzib in their first treaty. Ali Adil Shah commuted them for payment of 3½ lakhs of rupees. Shivaji was now more powerful than he had ever been. For a whole year he remained at peace with his neighbours and absorbed in the task of restoring order to his kingdom. Nor did he provoke the war that afterwards broke out. The cause was the fresh treachery of Aurangzib.

* Ranade, p. 108. See also Aurangzib's original letter, Appendix C, p. 225.

† Shivaji at this period reduced Netoji Palkar and appointed Kadtoji Guzar as the commander of his cavalry. The reason is obscure. The *Sabhasad Bakhar*, p. 57, says the king, finding fault with him (Netoji Palkar) for not having attended his call in time, removed him from his office as *Sarnobat* cavalry commander).

APPENDIX A

AURANGZIB'S LETTER TO SHIVAJI

August, 1665

After compliments,

You are at present with your forces in the imperial camp. You reduced the forts of Phaltan and Tathwada which had belonged to the Bijapur government and you led the forces in the night attack in the Konkan, where the enemy had pitched his camp.

This we learn from Raja Jai Sing's letter and it is the cause of our warm appreciation.

In recognition of your services a handsome dress and a pretty little jewelled sword are sent you. You will like it and the more hereafter you exert yourself in this campaign the greater will be our regard for you.

APPENDIX B

AURANGZIB'S LETTER TO SHIVAJI

March 5, 1666

After compliments,

Your letter sent to us together with Mirza Raja Jai Sing's opinion has been favourably considered by us.

We have a great regard for you and therefore desire you to come here quickly and without further loss of time.

When we grant you audience we shall receive you with great hospitality and soon grant you leave to return. A present of a dress has been sent you, which you will accept.

APPENDIX C

AURANGZIB'S LETTER TO SHIVAJI

February 24, 1668

After compliments,

We hold you in high esteem. On hearing the contents of your letter we have dignified you with the title of Raja. You will receive this distinction and show greater capacity for work. Your wishes will then be fulfilled.

You have spoken to us about your achievements. Everything will be set right. Be free from anxiety and understand that you are in favour.

15

CHAPTER XX

AURANGZIB, whose besetting sin was mistrust of his subordinates, refused them his confidence either in war or in peace. He had never given Diler Khan or Raja Jai Sing sufficient troops either to destroy Shivaji or to take Bijapur. And now that Prince Muazzim and Shivaji lived on amicable terms, the jealous emperor came to suspect that they were plotting his overthrow. The suspicion had no foundation. Prince Muazzim hated war and Shivaji had no wish to attack the Moghuls until he had secured his southern frontier from the assaults of Bijapur. Nevertheless Aurangzib sent Prince Muazzim an order directing him to seize at once the persons of Shivaji and Prataprao Guzar. Prince Muazzim, before the order arrived, heard of it from his confidential agent at Delhi. He sent for Niraji Ravji, Shivaji's legate at Aurangabad, and advised him to leave with Prataprao Guzar before the order came. Niraji Ravji at once conveyed the warning to Prataprao Guzar, and the same night the latter led his contingent out of Aurangabad and by forced marches reached Raygad in a few days. When the official letter of the emperor arrived, Prince Muazzim was with perfect truth able to answer that it was impossible to seize either Shivaji or Prataprao Guzar, as there was no longer a single Maratha at Aurangabad. Shivaji could hardly have been otherwise than angry at the news conveyed to him by Prataprao Guzar, but he concealed his anger under a show of satisfaction. "The Moghuls," he said laughing, "have maintained my cavalry for two years at their own expense. I shall now show them how much my horses have profited by their care."*

---

* *Bhedgavkar Bakhar.*

The Moghul garrisons at Sinhgad and Purandar had long been an eyesore to Shivaji and to his mother. The recent treachery of Aurangzib showed him that it was impossible to remain at peace with the Moghuls. He therefore resolved to reduce the two great forts without further delay. A lively ballad* has preserved a fantastic but most interesting account of the attack on Sinhgad. One Monday morning, according to the ballad writer, Shivaji was at Raygad.† His mother Jijabai was at Pratapgad. The latter was combing her hair with an ivory comb. As she looked eastwards, her eyes fell on Sinhgad. It was shining in the sun like a new-laid egg. The sight goaded her to fury. She told one of her servants to ride to Raygad and call Shivaji to her, even if he had to get up from his dinner without washing his hands. Shivaji at once obeyed his mother's summons, donned his armour, took his sword and shield and tiger claws, mounted his black mare Krishna and, riding as fast as he could to Pratapgad, announced his arrival to Jijabai. When they met he asked her the cause of her urgent message. She gave him no direct answer, but challenged him to a game of dice. Shivaji at first declined, saying that it was not right for a son to oppose his mother even in a game. But Jijabai overcame his scruples and then prayed to Bhavani for help. With the goddess' aid she won the match. Shivaji then begged his mother to take as a forfeit any one of the fortresses in his possession. She refused them all, but demanded Sinhgad.

The king protested that the renowned Ude Bhan defended it and that it was impregnable. But Jijabai insisted and threatened to burn up his kingdom with her curses unless he gave her Sinhgad. Shivaji perforce consented and told her to go with him to Rajgad. There he spent several hours thinking whom he should appoint to capture the fortress. At last the name of his old comrade Tanaji Malusare, *subhedar* of Umrathe, occurred to him. He sent a written message to Tanaji, ordering him to be present at Rajgad within three days and accompanied by

* Shalegram Collection, p. 21. The writer was Tulsidas Shahir.

† In the ballad he is declared to be at Rajgad. But, as the commentator rightly observes, the route followed by the messenger shows that he must have been at Raygad.

12,000 men.   The messenger found Tanaji engaged in preparing
for the marriage of his son Rayaba.   But the wedding was put
off and with 12,000 men carrying clubs and sickles Tanaji started
for Rajgad.   As he went, a coppersmith bird flew across his
path.   His uncle Shelar urged him to return as the sight of such
a bird was an evil omen.   But Tanaji laughed at the old man's
fears and continued his march.   As they neared Rajgad, Jijabai
thought that they were Moghuls and begged Shivaji to fire on
them.   But the king recognised his own banners and guessed
that the troops were Tanaji's .   Shivaji greeted Tanaji warmly.
But the *subhedar*, with the freedom of an old friend, scolded
the king for disturbing him in the middle of his son's marriage
festivities.   Shivaji excused himself, pleading that it was not
really he but Jijabai who had sent for Tanaji.   As her son spoke,
Jijabai rose.   She first thanked Bhavani for Tanaji's coming,
then waved a lamp round Tanaji's head and cracked her fingers
on her temple so as to take to herself all his cares.*   Tanaji,
completely won by the queen's acts, took off his turban, placed
it at her feet, and promised to give her anything she wanted.
She told him to give her Sinhgad and assured him that if he did
so, she would regard him as Shivaji's younger brother and her
own son.   Tanaji gladly agreed to go forth on the perilous
quest.   Jijabai gave a feast of which his whole force partook,
and as they ate, Bhavani herself came and helped to serve
them.   After the feast was over, Jijabai gave to Tanaji's soldiers
clothes and weapons, and they started for Sinhgad.   On reaching
a spot called Anandi Bari, Tanaji assumed the dress of a village
headman and stole through the jungle until he reached the
enemy's outposts.   They were Hindus of the Koli caste and
seized him.   He gave out that he was *patil*, or headman, of
Sakhara and that he had just met a tiger and had fled to them
for shelter.   This satisfied the Kolis, whose hearts Tanaji soon
won by presents of betelnut and opium.   Lastly he distributed
pieces of jewellery amongst them and confided to them that he
was one of Shivaji's nobles and sought information about the
fort. They readily told him all that they knew and a great deal

---

* *Ala bala.* This is a very common practice among Indian ladies.

more. Sinhgad, they said, had a perimeter of six miles.* It was
defended by Ude Bhan and 1800 Pathans and a number of
Arabs. Ude Bhan was a tremendous warrior. He had no less
than eighteen wives and ate at each meal one and a half cows, one
and a half sheep and one and a quarter maunds of rice. He had a
man-slaying elephant called Chandravali and a lieutenant called
Sidi Hillal. The latter had nine wives and ate at each meal one
sheep, half a cow and half a maund of rice. There were also Ude
Bhan's twelve sons, all stronger than he himself was. Lastly, the
Kolis gave Tanaji Malusare a really valuable piece of information, namely that the right side of a cliff known as the Dongri
Cliff could be escaladed. When Tanaji heard this, he rose, and
promising handsome gifts to the Kolis if the fort were taken,
he returned to his men. The same night Tanaji and the army
went to the gate known as the Kalyan Gate. There Tanaji
took out of a box Shivaji's famous *ghorpad* Yeshwant, which
had already scaled 27 forts. He smeared its head with red lead,
put a pearl ornament on its forehead and worshipped it as a god.
He then tied a cord to its waist and bade it run up the Dongri
Cliff. Half way the *ghorpad* turned back. Shelar thought
this an evil omen and urged Tanaji to abandon the enterprise.
But Tanaji threatened to kill and eat the *ghorpad* if it did not
do his bidding. Thereupon Yeshwant climbed to the top of
the cliff and fastened its claws in the ground. Tanaji then led
the escalade. With their swords in their teeth, he and fifty
men after him climbed up the rope. When these had reached
the summit, so great was the rush of their comrades to climb
up also, that the rope broke. The fifty men on the top of the
fort were now in a desperate position and would have tried to
jump down its sides. But Tanaji kept his head and bade them
follow him and surprise the guards. The party crawled to
the Kalyan gate and noiselessly killed the Arabs guarding it.
They then crawled to the second gate, where they killed 300
Pathans, and a third gate where they killed 400 Pathans. One,
however, escaped and told Ude Bhan. The latter had just
drunk eighteen cups of wine, had eaten several balls of opium

* The perimeter is really under two miles.

and was about to seek the embraces of his wives. In spite of the urgency of the occasion, he refused to go himself, but ordered that his elephant Chandravali should be sent against the enemy. Its mahout gave the monster an incredible quantity of *bhang* and opium and drove it against Tanaji. The latter, however, evaded its charge and springing on its back killed it by cutting off its trunk with a single sword stroke. Ude Bhan next sent Sidi Hillal to meet the enemy. Sidi Hillal donned his armour, and killing his nine wives,* marked his forehead with their blood and then sought out Tanaji. On meeting him Sidi Hillal bade him take grass in his mouth, put his sandals on his head, and beg for mercy. Tanaji refused, and after warding off eighteen successive sword cuts, clove the Sidi open from the turban to the navel. Ude Bhan, however, still refused to leave his wives. He ordered his twelve sons to go forth to battle. But they were no more fortunate than their forerunners. Twelve strokes of Tanaji's sword cut them into twenty-four pieces. His sons' death at last roused Ude Bhan. He cut down his wives just as Sidi Hillal had done and rallying the rest of the garrison he went towards the Kalyan Gate. Seeing that the storming party only numbered fifty Ude Bhan and his Pathans rushed at them. Ude Bhan cut down Tanaji. But Shelar avenged his death by instantly killing Ude Bhan. Nevertheless the small Maratha force would soon have been overpowered, had not Bhavani of Pratapgad flung open with her own hand the Kalyan Gate, thus enabling Suryaji, Tanaji's brother, and the rest of the 12,000 men to enter the fort. The fight was then soon over. The garrison was killed. The imperial standard was torn down. Shivaji's banner was hoisted in its place. Five cannons were fired and some buildings set alight to announce to Shivaji that Sinhgad was his. Shivaji hastened from Rajgad and mounted the steep path that leads up Sinhgad. He entered the fort through the Kalyan Gate and rode until he saw the corpse of his gallant comrade Tanaji Malusare. As the king stopped to gaze at it, his soldiers crowded round him to congratu-

---

* He killed his wives to safeguard his honour in case he did not return.

late him on the capture of the Lion's fort.* But he silenced
them with a bitter laconism such as Julius would have envied.
" I have got the Fort," he said, " but I have lost the lion "
(Feb uary 17, 1670).†

The fall of Sinhgad was followed by that of Purandar, escaladed
by Suryaji Malusare ; and between February and June, 1670,
the Peshwa, aided by Nilopant Sondev and Annaji Datto,
had removed every trace of the Moghul occupation from Shivaji's
territories. The king next tried to surprise Shivner, the great
fort near Junnar. He had been born there and he had long
desired to win it, that he might thereby secure his northern
frontier. In this enterprise his good fortune deserted him.
When the leader of the storming party reached the summit
of the fort, he was seen by one of the wives of the garrison.‡
She flung a stone at him which knocked him over backwards.
As he fell he overturned those who followed him. And the
noise of their fall roused the garrison, who cut the ropes to which
the storming party clung and thus repulsed the attack with
heavy loss.

After this failure Shivaji turned once more to Janjira. He
took all the bridge-heads which Fatih Khan had established
on the mainland and drove him and such forces as he still had
with him back into the island. These defeats weighed heavily
on Fatih Khan's mind. It was hopeless for him to expect aid
from Bijapur, separated as it and Janjira were by Shivaji's
possessions. Shivaji's fleet too was by now more than a match
for Fatih Khan's ships and, attacked by land and sea, he despaired
of a successful defence. He therefore opened negotiations with
Shivaji, offering to surrender Janjira, provided that he and his
garrison were allowed to go free. Shivaji wished at any cost to

---

* " Sinh " means lion and " gad " fort. The Marathi words of Shivaji
were, " Gad ala, pan Sinh gola."

† A less romantic but more probable story is to be found in the *Sabhasad
Bakhar*. According to the author of that chronicle, Tanaji and his brother
Suryaji surprised Sinhgad without divine assistance and with a force of only
a thousand Mawal infantry. The garrison consisted of seven hundred Rajputs,
who defended themselves gallantly until over five hundred had been killed
or wounded in the attack.

‡ Fryer, *Eastern Travels*.

secure this powerful naval base and he readily agreed to Fatih Khan's terms. But the latter's design was frustrated when on the very point of execution. As I have previously related, the governors of the island, when it was under the kings of Ahmadnagar, were Abyssinian kinsmen or friends of Malik Ambar. Upon its transfer to Bijapur they became Fatih Khan's subordinates. Hearing of his treason, they resolved both to save Janjira from the infidel and to rid themselves of their Afghan superior. Their three leaders were named Sidi Sambal, Sidi Yakut and Sidi Khairyat. They suddenly seized Fatih Khan and put him in chains. They sent a despatch explaining to the Bijapur king their conduct. At the same time they sent another despatch to Aurangabad offering in return for aid from the Moghul fleet to hold Janjira as a dependency of Delhi. The Moghuls gladly consented and the Surat fleet relieved Janjira by joining the Sidi's fleet, which thus recovered command of the sea.

It was characteristic of Shivaji that adversity seemed to stimulate his mind and that brilliant successes closely followed his gravest disasters. During the last six years the town of Surat had recovered its prosperity. Yet in spite of the Maratha raid of 1664, the Moghul government had taken no steps to prevent its repetition. Shivaji resolved to profit by their negligence and to make Surat pay for the aid given to Janjira by the Moghul fleet that had sailed from the Tapti. On October 1, 1670, news reached Surat that a Maratha army 15,000 strong had entered Guzarat, and two days later its vanguard was seen to approach the mud walls. The inhabitants fled, as before, to the surrounding villages and the governor and his garrison repeated their former cowardice by at once retiring to the castle. The English, Dutch and French merchants got ready to defend their factories, and the guards of two seraglios, one maintained by Persian and Turkish merchants and another by a fugitive prince from Kashgar,* resolutely prepared to protect their

---

* This account is taken from the English letter of November 20 preserved in Hedge's Diary, Vol. II, p. 226. The prince of Kashgar is said to have been connected with Aurangzib and to have been dethroned by his own son.

charges. The rest of the city was abandoned as before to
Maratha plunderers. Shivaji, however, thought that the
Kashgar prince's seraglio would be worth capture. As it stood
close to the French factory, the Marathas made a continued
attack on both. The French resisted gallantly for some time,
but learning that the Marathas chiefly desired a passage to the
prince's harem, they agreed to allow it in return for their own
safety. Shivaji now attacked the seraglio from all sides until
dark, but without carrying it. During the night the Kashgar
prince took fright and fled with his servants, women and
portable treasure to the castle. But he was forced to leave
behind a vast store of gold and silver plate and handsome
furniture, which next day was taken by the Marathas. A body
of troops had tried on the previous day to storm the English
factory, but had been repulsed by the gallantry of the factors
led by Mr. Streinsham Master. A fresh attempt was made
by the Marathas on October 1, but again without result. The
Marathas then proceeded to pillage the town, while the garrison
did nothing but fire into it from the castle, setting fire to a
number of houses. On October 5 a Maratha force for a third
time appeared before the English factory and warned Streinsham
Master that unless the garrison made their submission by sending
Shivaji a present, the king would consider it incumbent on his
honour to storm the place. The English, who had no wish
to drive the king to extremities, gladly agreed to send him a
peace offering. The two Englishmen entrusted with it were led to
Shivaji's tent outside the town. The king received them, according to their own account, with the greatest courtesy. He took
their hands in his and told them that he regarded the English as
his best friends and that he would never do them any harm.*
The same evening Shivaji withdrew his army laden with booty.
But before he left he sent a letter to the principal merchants,
in which he informed them that unless they paid him an annual
tribute of 12 lakhs he would return and burn Surat to the ground.
At the time of his first raid Shivaji had returned to the Konkan

---

* The Company were so pleased with Master's daring and prudence that
they struck a medal to commemorate the incident.

through Dharampur. This time, confident in the number of his troops, he followed the main road from Surat to Aurangabad, which passed by Salher fort and Chandwad town. At Chandwad he proposed to leave the main road and return* through the Nasik pass to the Konkan. But the news of his raid on Surat and of his line of retreat had reached Aurangabad. A body of Moghul cavalry under Daud Khan set out to harass his rearguard, while a large Moghul army marched to the Sahyadris and blocked the Nasik pass. The plan, both well-conceived and well-executed, failed through the excellence of Shivaji's information. He sent his plunder through other passes in the mountains, and then turning with a body of horse on Daud Khan's cavalry overwhelmed it at Khadase. Returning swiftly, he charged with his whole army the Moghuls who held the Nasik pass and completely routed them. He then led his troops and treasure safely to Raygad.

With the spoil of Surat Shivaji equipped 30,000 fresh troops and a powerful fleet. With the latter he made a demonstration along the Guzarat coast as far as Broach. The Moghuls, anticipating a raid on Broach similar to that twice made on Surat, sent all their available reinforcements into Guzarat. This was what Shivaji had desired and he now led an army into Khandesh. The garrisons of the Khandesh towns fought with great courage but they were separately defeated. The forts of Aundha, Patta, Trimbak and Salher fell and Shivaji laid waste the whole of the fertile province as far as Burhanpur on its north-eastern frontier. While Shivaji overran Khandesh, Moro Pingle descended through the Nasik pass, reduced the Jawhar State and exacted contributions from the Kolwan, now the northern part of the Thana district (January, 1671). Shivaji then fell back upon the Sahyadri Mountains. But as he did so, he made the headman of every village undertake to pay him a fourth of the revenue as a safeguard against further attack. Thus was the *chauth* imposed for the first time on a Moghul province. These disasters to the Moghul arms led to a change in the Aurangabad government. The emperor recalled Jaswant Sing and in his place he sent Mahabat Khan, the veteran officer who had

---

* See *Sabhasad* and *Shedgavkar Bakhars* and Scott, *Deccan*, Vol. II, p. 25.

conquered Daulatabad for the Emperor Shah Jehan, together
with a new army of 40,000 men. The Moghuls now re-assumed
the offensive. They at first met with some successes. They
re-captured Aundha and Patta before the monsoon broke, and
early in the next year (1672) they invested Salher and cut to
pieces a body of horse* sent by Moropant Pingle to reinforce
the garrison. Shivaji ordered Moropant Pingle and Prataprao
Guzar to proceed in person with all their available troops
to relieve Salher. Mahabat Khan sent the greater part of his
army under one Iklas Khan to attack the relieving force as it
approached the fort. The Marathas were advancing in two
columns, Prataprao Guzar on the west, and Moropant Pingle
on the east, of Salher. Iklas Khan tried to prevent their junction
by throwing himself between them and destroying them one
after the other. The plan failed. But the Moghuls with the
utmost courage fought a confused running battle of which the
result was long doubtful. After twelve hours the superior
mobility and numbers of the Maratha horse prevailed. They
joined in the centre, and there holding Iklas Khan, turned both
his flanks. A last vigorous charge completed the Moghul defeat.
Only 2000 men, with Iklas Khan and his lieutenant Bahlol
Khan, escaped from the rout. The rest of the Moghul army,
about 20,000 strong, either fell on the field or surrendered.
6000 horses, 125 elephants and a vast spoil of jewels and treasure
became the prize of the conquerors.† But the gain in prestige
was greater still. For the first time the Marathas had won a
pitched battle against a disciplined Moghul army, led by a soldier
trained in the school of Akbar and Shah Jehan. Deserters from
Bijapur and Delhi and recruits from all parts of the country
flocked in thousands to the standard of the king. To continue
the siege of Salher was now hopeless and Mahabat Khan retired
with his shattered army behind the bastions of Aurangabad.

---

* *Sabhasad Bakhar.* The *Bakhar* gives the number as 1000. Grant
Duff estimates it at 2000.

† I have based my account of the battle of Salher on the *Sabhasad Bakhar.*
Grant Duff's account is somewhat different. On Shivaji's side Suryajirao
Kakde, a distinguished soldier, fell. To the wounded prisoners Shivaji behaved
with great humanity. He tended their wounds and, when well, dismissed
them with presents.

AFTER sixty years of miserable servitude to Castile, the Portuguese nation rallied round the Duke of Braganza and with French aid and their own courage achieved their independence. To secure it they entered into a marriage connexion with the royal house of Stuart. In 1661, Charles II, who had just won back the throne of England, married Princess Catherine of Portugal. As a dowry to his daughter, the Portuguese king gave Tangier on the north-west coast of Africa and the fort and island of Bombay on the west coast of India. To the Lisbon government the dowry seemed a small one. Tangier proved a death trap to the English soldiers who guarded it. The island of Bombay was a low-lying group of rocks off the Konkan coast. Only eleven Portuguese families resided there* and seventy "Mosquiteers" or armed Indian Police were deemed a sufficient garrison. But it formed a magnificent refuge for ships, by affording them a shelter from the fury of the south-west monsoon. And the Portuguese viceroy, De la Costa, with prophetic truth wrote to his king that the Indian empire would be lost to his nation from the day that the English landed on the island. At first, it is true, the cession did England but little good and the quarrels between the English governor and the Portuguese viceroy as to the interpretation of the grant caused Charles II in a fit of vexation to transfer on March 27, 1668, Bombay to the East India Company.

Although it was not until 1674 that the wise and chivalrous Gerald Aungier transferred the head-quarters of the Company from Surat to Bombay, the acquisition of the island drew the

---

* See Malabari, *Bombay in the Making*, p. 93.

English, almost at once, into the sphere of Indian politics. At
Surat they had wasted little thought on matters other than
bills of lading or books of accounts. Even the seizure of their
factors at Rajapur and Shivaji's two attacks on Surat disturbed
but for the moment the even tenour of their lives. Now the
possession of the Bombay harbour with its great advantages
as a naval base made their alliance desirable both to
the Moghuls and to Shivaji. Shivaji passed the monsoon
of 1672 in improving his conquests in the Kolwan and
in forcing the Koli chiefs to pass treaties and to promise
contingents when needed. He also demanded tribute from
the Portuguese settlements at Daman and Salsette. The
Portuguese refused, and a body of Marathas tried to surprise
the fort of Ghodbunder on Salsette Island, still a Portuguese
possession. The Portuguese repulsed them. But the attack
alarmed the English factors, who began to fortify their new
acquisition and to beg Shivaji to enter into a treaty with them.
Shivaji in reply pressed them to join him against Janjira and
with their ships to help him destroy the Sidi's fleet. The English
explained that the presence of their factory at Surat forced them
to keep neutral. Shivaji then bade them return to Rajapur
and re-establish their settlement there. But the English insisted
that, before they did so, he should indemnify them for their
previous losses there. This Shivaji refused to do, and for the
time the negotiations fell through.

The disaster of Salher had caused intense irritation to Aurang-
zib. He at once recalled Mahabat Khan and Prince Muazzim
and appointed Bahadur Khan Koka, afterwards known as Khan
Jahan Bahadur, and then governor of Guzarat, to be viceroy
of the Deccan with Diler Khan as his second in command.
The new governor soon proved himself quite unfit for the post.
In spite of Diler Khan's advice, he gave up all offensive opera-
tions against the Marathas and tried to bar their entrance into
Khandesh by a chain of blockhouses along the Western Ghats.*
The Marathas, however, turned aside from Khandesh and overran

---

* Scott, *Deccan*, Vol. II, p. 33. The Persian author gives the names of the
places where Bahadur Khan built blockhouses.

the country between Ahmadnagar and Aurangabad. The viceroy pursued them from place to place, but was always too late to catch them. In fact so imbecile was his conduct that Shivaji was led to disregard him entirely. And while part of his army plundered the Moghul territories, he engaged with the rest in a distant and profitable expedition.

While the English and the Dutch merchants at Surat had worked up their trade on business lines and had thereby made considerable profits, the French had not been so successful. Their factory, founded in 1642, was equipped on too lavish a scale to yield any return. At last M. de la Haye thought that an establishment on the Coromandel Coast might bring him more profit. Close to the site of modern Madras was the little town of St. Thomé. It had once been a Portuguese settlement, but in 1669 the king of Golconda had taken it by storm. De la Haye raided it from the sea and drove out the Golconda garrison. The Golconda king equipped an army and sent it to recover the little fort. When his forces were well on the way to the Coromandel Coast, Shivaji appeared with a large Maratha force at the gates of Hyderabad. Resistance was useless and the Golconda king was obliged to ransom his chief town by the immediate payment of two million pagodas. Shivaji then returned with his usual expedition to Raygad. In his absence, however, another mishap had befallen him at Janjira.

Sidi Sambal had died shortly after the overthrow of Fatih Khan* and been succeeded as governor by Sidi Yakut (A.D. 1672). The new governor was a man of enterprise and ability and his ships constantly captured Maratha vessels and sent the heads of their sailors to Aurangabad. Hearing of Shivaji's absence, he again asked Bahadur Khan for the aid of the Moghul fleet. The latter consented and begged leave of the English† to let his fleet drop anchor in Bombay so that the Moghul troops might land and attack Shivaji's neighbouring possessions. The king's agent warned the English that if they consented, it would mean war with his master and the certain loss of Bombay.

---

* Khafi Khan.

† Orme, *Historical Fragments*, pp. 30-31.

The English placed their difficulties before Bahadur Khan and informed him that they were but merchants and could not take sides with either of the contending governments. The Moghuls then pretended to give up their project in disgust. But a little time after returning to Surat, they set out for a cruise. Suddenly altering their course they entered the port of Danda Rajpuri. There they destroyed a number of Shivaji's ships and took 200 Maratha sailors. These Sidi Yakut tied to stones and flung overboard. He then attacked Danda Rajpuri itself. This fortress, which Shivaji had conquered from Fatih Khan, was of the utmost value to the garrison of Janjira. Without it the garrison ran a great risk of being starved out. With it as a bridge-head, they commanded a large stretch of fertile country. One night Sidi Yakut sent Sidi Khairyat, his second in command, to attack Danda Rajpuri from the land side, while he himself led a force in boats to attack it from the sea. The commandant was the Ragho Ballal Atre who had killed Chandra Rao More at Jaoli. Usually an efficient soldier, he allowed his vigilance to relax in the celebration of the Holi.* Surprised by Sidi Khairyat's party, he summoned the whole garrison to repel it. Sidi Yakut in the meantime swiftly climbed the unprotected western wall of the fortress. The garrison, taken between two fires, were overpowered and mercilessly massacred. Following up this success Sidi Yakut attacked six or seven minor forts in the neighbourhood. All but one succumbed to the first assault. One held out for a few days in hope of succour. At last, greatly distressed and tempted by Sidi Yakut's oath that he would spare the garrison, the commandant surrendered. Sidi Yakut then did what Shivaji would never have done. He broke his word and inhumanly put to death every male in the place, whether armed or not. Forcibly converting the young women and the children to Islam he reduced them to slavery. Only the old women were permitted to return to their homes.

On December 15, 1672, Ali Adil Shah, the king of Bijapur, died. The state had suffered greatly during his reign. The

---

* *Khafi Khan*, Elliot and Dowson, Vol. VII, p. 290.

Moghuls had taken all its territories north of the Bhima River. Shivaji had conquered the Konkan as far south as Phonda and the western *desh* or plateau to the east of the Sahyadris. Ali Adil Shah had, it is true, reduced a number of petty chiefs, who had made themselves independent upon the fall of Vijaya-nagar, and had pushed his frontier far to the south. But these conquests, in the decaying condition of the central government, weakened rather than strengthened its power. Latterly Shivaji in return for an annual payment of three lakhs had abstain-ed from invasion. But now that Ali Adil Shah, with whom he had made the treaty, was dead, the Maratha king held himself absolved from his engagements. In this view he was no doubt confirmed by his agents' reports of the state of Bijapur, where reigned faction and discord. In March, 1673, he collected a large force at Vishalgad and retook Panhala, which had been in the power of the Bijapur king ever since its capture by Sidi Johar. But the main object of the expedition was the plunder of the rich town of Hubli to the south-east of Dharwar. During the prosperous days of the Bijapur kingdom, Hubli had been a great mercantile emporium, and renowned for the manufacture of cloth. The English company had stationed a broker there in order to buy cloth specially intended for sale in England. The Maratha vanguard under Annaji Datto surprised and routed the Bijapur garrison and the plunder exceeded even that of Surat. From the English depot alone cloth worth nearly £3000 was taken, and when the Maratha army had left, the Bijapur garrison returning completed the ruin of the town. The English demanded compensation, but Shivaji maintained that his troops had spared their storehouse and assessed their losses at £70 only. The English at Bombay were naturally indignant and they soon had an opportunity of putting pressure on the king. In May, 1673, the Moghul fleet appeared off Bombay and again asked leave of the English to spend the monsoon in the harbour. Had the English consented, the Moghul fleet would have been in a position to raid any point it pleased on Shivaji's coast. Gerald Aungier brought this to Shivaji's notice and pressed for compensation for the raids on

Rajapur and Hubli. But the damage done to the English at Hubli seems not to have been communicated by Annaji Datto, the Maratha commander, to his master; for Shivaji maintained to the last that it did not exceed 200 pagodas. He declined, therefore, to settle the Hubli claim but promised to pay the Rajapur claim, provided that the English again settled at Rajapur. To this they agreed; but they evaded the Maratha king's demand to furnish him with cannon. While thus negotiating with Shivaji, Gerald Aungier managed with great dexterity not to offend the Moghuls. He allowed four of their frigates to take shelter in Bombay harbour, and the rest of the Moghul fleet returned to Surat.

During the monsoon of 1673,* the Bijapur governor of Karwar, the capital of the modern collectorate of Canara, revolted and plundered both the Portuguese and the English. This enabled the Maratha king to increase the confusion of the wretched Bijapur kingdom. He wished, however, to remain for the time being at peace with the Moghuls. He, therefore, sent large sums of money to Bahadur Khan to ensure his neutrality. He then attacked Bijapur by land and sea. His navy anchored off Karwar and landed a strong detachment of Maratha troops. They drove out the rebel governor, plundered Ankola and Karwar, and compelled the Raja of Bednur to bind himself to pay an annual tribute to Shivaji. At the same time a land force operating from the Jaoli district surprised Parali, a fort six miles south-west of Satara, and afterwards took Satara, Chandan, Wandan, Pandavgad, Nandgiri, Tathwada, the line of forts between Satara and Phaltan captured by Shivaji for Aurangzib and restored by him to Bijapur in the treaty of A.D. 1668. When the rains had ceased, Shivaji went in person to attack Phonda, which blocked his communications with Karwar and Ankola. Phonda had been the last refuge of the Savants and had again fallen into the hands of Bijapur. It was now stoutly defended by a Musulman garrison. While Shivaji was vainly trying to overcome their resistance, the Moghul fleet ventured out from the Surat harbour. On October 10,* the Sidi entered

---

* Orme, *Historical Fragments.*

16

Bombay harbour, and disregarding the protests of Gerald
Aungier, who drew his supplies from that part of the mainland,
landed at the mouth of the River Pen and laid waste the adjoining
country. The Marathas, after expostulating with Aungier
for allowing the Moghuls to land, first surprised and cut to pieces
a detachment of Moghuls and afterwards defeated the main
body in a pitched battle. The Abyssinian then withdrew his
men and returned to Surat, where he gave so flowery an account
of his feat of arms that he received a handsome money reward.

The long defence of Phonda encouraged the Bijapur government to try by a counter-attack to regain Panhala, a most
valuable bridge-head from which to make raids on Shivaji's
territory. They ordered Abdul Karim, the viceroy of the
western province of Bijapur, to advance on Panhala. Shivaji
at once detached Prataprao Guzar to plunder the country on
his line of communications. This Prataprao Guzar did so
successfully that Abdul Karim fell back towards the capital.
The two armies met at Umbrani between Miraj and Bijapur.
Prataprao's cavalry soon turned both of Abdul Karim's flanks.
By sunset the latter was in so critical a position that he sent an
envoy to Prataprao Guzar, undertaking to abstain absolutely
from any hostilities against the Marathas and to permit them
to plunder his viceroyalty at will, provided they allowed him
now to retire unmolested. Prataprao Guzar, a gallant and enterprising soldier, but not a diplomat, was fooled by the humble
promises of his enemy. He should have guessed that it was
not in Abdul Karim's power to keep them. If ordered to attack
the Marathas, he would be bound to do so or resign his post.
Nevertheless Prataprao allowed Abdul Karim and his army to
escape. Shivaji, on hearing the news, grew extremely angry.
He censured Prataprao Guzar severely. The latter, in a fit of
insubordination,* led his cavalry on a raiding expedition through
the heart of the Aurangabad provinces as far as the frontiers of
Berar, thus breaking Shivaji's truce with the Moghul viceroy,
Bahadur Khan. Nor did Abdul Karim keep his compact with
Prataprao. He had no sooner reached Bijapur, than he recruited

* *Shedgavkar Bakhar.*

another army and again advanced on Panhala. So serious was
the danger that Shivaji compounded with the commandant of
Phonda, and raising the siege returned northwards through the
Portuguese territories near Goa, plundering them as he went.*
When Abdul Karim had almost reached Panhala, Prataprao
Guzar returned from his raid.* The king sent him word that
he should not show his face at court until he had destroyed
Abdul Karim's army.† The message reached the Maratha
general as the battle opened. Once again his temper got the
mastery of his judgment. He made a headlong charge on Abdul
Karim's army. The Bijapur troops were more heavily armed
than the Marathas, whom they repulsed with great slaughter.
Among those who fell was Prataprao Guzar himself. Abdul
Karim pushed his advantage vigorously and the main Maratha
army was soon fleeing wildly towards Panhala. At the most
critical moment of the battle Hasaji Mohite, the commander of
5000 horse kept as a reserve, fell on the flank of the Bijapur
troops as they pressed on in the disorder of victory. Instantly the fate of the battle changed. The Marathas rallied, and
inflicting a severe defeat upon Abdul Karim forced him to fall
back once more on Bijapur. The king heard the news of the
battle with sorrow. All satisfaction at the success was lost in
grief at the death of Prataprao. He reviewed the victorious
army at Chiplun and in its presence referred feelingly to its
dead commander. He bestowed handsome estates on his
relatives and chose Prataprao's daughter to be the bride of his
second son Rajaram. To Mohite, whose skill and daring had
won the losing battle, the king gave the title of Hambirrao and
the vacant post of commander-in-chief of the royal cavalry.

The anomalous position occupied by Shivaji had long exercised
his mind. He enjoyed the hereditary title of Raja conferred
on his family by the Ahmadnagar government. But the Nizam
Shahi dynasty had long ceased to exist. He had been confirmed
in the title and created a noble of the Delhi empire. But since
Aurangzib's last treachery, Shivaji had renounced his fealty

---

* Orme, *Historical Fragments.*
† *Sabhasad Bakhar.*

to the Moghul throne. It was, therefore, impossible to say
whence he derived his authority. Nor was this difficulty merely
academic. For although the high-spirited Deccan nobles gladly
followed Shivaji in the field, they were unwilling in private life
to concede to him any precedence. And at state dinners they
resented that a Bhosle should sit on a seat raised above those
assigned to Mohites, and Nimbalkars, Savants and Ghorpades.
He spoke of the matter to his secretary, Balaji Abaji Chitnis, and
the latter urged him to take the royal crown from the hands,
not of a Moghul emperor, but of a Benares priest. The king
consulted his mother Jijabai, the saintly Ramdas and his
favourite goddess Bhavani and found them all favourable
to his secretary's suggestion. The next difficulty was to induce
a Brahman priest of sufficient standing to leave the banks of the
Ganges, and undertake the long journey southward. It was
soon overcome. It so happened that one of the leading Brahmans of Benares, Gaga Bhat by name, was on a visit to Paithan
on the Godavari, and Balaji Chitnis urged that he should be
approached on the subject. The king agreed and sent his
secretary on a confidential mission to Gaga Bhat. The secretary,
on reaching Paithan, invited the holy stranger to come to Raygad
and there crown the king after the manner of the ancient Hindu
Emperors. Gaga Bhat objected that Shivaji was a Maratha
and that the ceremonies observed at Ayodhya and Hastinapura
were reserved for Kshatriya or Rajput kings. Chitnis met the
objection by obtaining from Raygad a genealogical tree which
showed the unbroken descent of Shivaji from Udesing, Maharana
of Udaipur. Gaga Bhat asked for time to consult his brethren
on the banks of the Ganges. From them he received a favourable answer and agreed to comply with Shivaji's request. He
however attached to his consent an important condition. The
king was no doubt of Rajput origin. But of late years the
Bhosle family had allowed the Rajput observances to lapse.
Shivaji must therefore be invested with the sacred thread
before he was anointed after the manner of the ancient Kshatriya
kings. To this condition Shivaji consented. He sent a cavalcade
headed by two saintly men, Bhalchandra Bhat Purohit and

Somnath Bhat Katre, to lead the high priest from Paithan. In the meantime he made every preparation to erect at Raygad buildings suitable to the tremendous ceremony. No less than seven new public rooms and a number of state reception rooms were built.* On completion they were consecrated by the singing of Vedic hymns, by sacrificial fires and holy oblations. Thereafter a new throne was erected in the audience hall. Round it were placed wooden figures of lions, tigers and elephants and on its base were carved the 32 points of the compass that the spectators might learn that the whole earth was the destined prey of the Maratha king's irresistible armies.

As Gaga Bhat drew nearer, Shivaji and his ministers rode to Satara, where they met the sage in state and accompanied him by slow stages to Raygad. On May 21, 1674, the ceremonial began. Shivaji passed the day in worshipping the various Hindu gods and separately invoked their help to bring it to a successful conclusion. Three days later he was invested with the sacred thread. He first anointed himself with perfumed oil and prostrated himself before his mother. Gaga Bhat then flung over his head the silken thread that marks the three higher castes and whispered to him the *Gayatri mantra*—the awful invocation to the Sun-god, which is reserved for their ears alone. This rite concluded, it had been intended to amuse the spectators by letting water into a little lake recently excavated and honoured by the name of Ganga Sagar. A magician struck the ground; the sluice gate in the walls was drawn back and the water, as if obedient to the wizard's wand, poured into the artificial lake. A rough Mawali soldier, completely deceived by the pantomime, fancied that the magician had plotted to drown the king. He drew his sword and cut down the unhappy mummer. His widow and children rushed to Shivaji for justice and he soothed their grief by a grant of land close to Raygad valued at Rs. 200 annually. On May 31, 1674, Shivaji, now a Rajput beyond all dispute, worshipped Ganpati and implored

* The account of the coronation is taken from the *Shivdigvijaya Bakhar* nd other manuscripts in the Parasnis collection.

that kindly god to bless his coronation. Between May 31 and
June 6 the priests burnt sacrificial fires and purified themselves
by fast and vigil. The king paid a visit to Pratapgad* and
bestowed on the temple of his favourite goddess a massive
gold lamp and other precious gifts.

On June 6, the day found propitious by the wisest astrologers
in all India, the coronation was held.† In one of the open court-
yards was erected a mighty *shamiana* or state tent. Inside
it was a temporary throne raised upon a square dais. At the
prescribed moment, the ministers appeared in procession leading
Shivaji, clad in white, to the throne. Behind the king followed
Jijabai, and behind her came the queens and the wives of the
high officers of the kingdom. After Shivaji had seated himself,
Moropant Pingle, the Peshwa, took his stand to the east of the
throne holding in his hand a gold pot filled with *ghee*. To
the south stood Hambirrao Mohite holding a silver vessel filled
with milk. To the west stood Ramchandra Nilkant with a
copper vessel filled with curds. To the north stood Raghunath
Pant with a golden pot of honey in one hand and in the other
an earthen pot of Ganges water. To the south-east stood
Annaji Datto, who carried the state umbrella. To the south-
west was Janardan Pandit, who held a fan. To the north-west
and north-east Dattaji Pandit and Balaji Pandit plied fly-whisks.
In front of Shivaji, and facing him, stood Balaji Abaji Chitnis,
the private secretary, and to his left Chimnaji Avaji. the chief
accountant. One after the other, those ministers who had
vessels in their hands, sprinkled the contents over the king
to the accompaniment of sacred hymns. After they had
resumed their places, a married woman performed the *arti*
by flashing a lamp in front of the king's eyes. He then gazed
at his own reflection in a bronze pot filled with *ghee* and afterwards in a mirror. After a short pause he made some gifts to
Brahmans, worshipped a small golden image of Vishnu and
fastened it to his right hand. Lastly, he worshipped his sword
and shield, his bow and his arrows.

---

* Fryer, *Travels*, Vol. I, p. 202.
† Shivaji's Rajshaka era commences from this day, June 6 (Jeshta Shudha
13, Shake 1596).

SPOT AT RAYGAD WHERE SHIVAJI WAS BURNT

LAKE AND TEMPLE AT RAYGAD

[To face page 263]

The preliminary ceremonies were now over. The king took off the white dress in which he had entered the *shamiana*. Sixteen Brahman women and sixteen Brahman girls were placed in front of him. They anointed him with perfumed oil, poured warm water over his back and shoulders and waved tiny lamps around his head. Shivaji was now pure enough to mount the permanent throne in the audience hall. He put on his royal robes and covered himself with jewelry. Gaga Bhat then stepped forward, and taking him by the hand, led him out of the *shamiana* to the foot of the throne. Over it had been placed a tiger skin, a velvet bag stuffed with cotton and over it again a piece of transparent muslin. Shivaji knelt for a moment in front of the kingly chair and then took his seat upon it. Instantly every gun in the fortress boomed a royal salute. As the sound reached the neighbouring forts, they one after the other fired their homage, until, from Kalyan in the north to Savantvadi in the south, every stronghold in the Sahyadris had proclaimed the accession of the new Rama-chandra.

After Shivaji had been duly installed, he had himself weighed against gold coins.* These he distributed among the Brahmans who had flocked to see the great king's coronation. Dresses of honour and new titles were conferred on the eight chief ministers and the rites ended with an elephant procession round Raygad. On the following day Shivaji received an embassy from Bombay. The English had never ceased to press their claims for losses suffered at Rajapur and Hubli and to ask that their rights should be defined by a regular treaty. The king had after some delay announced that he would receive the embassy at Raygad after his coronation Durbar. Mr. Oxenden together with two English factors started from Bombay and travelled through Chaul, Ashtami, Nizampur and Gangavli, and after an uneventful journey reached Pachad at the foot of Raygad. They stayed at Pachad as the king's guests until he could receive them, which he did on the day after he was

---

* He weighed 16,000 hons or pagodas. His total weight was 140 lbs., *i.e.*, 10 stone.

crowned. Some twenty requests had been made by the East India Company. Of these the most important were :—

(1) The English should be permitted freely to trade in the king's dominions on paying an import duty of $2\frac{1}{2}$ per cent.

(2) The English should be permitted to build permanent factories at Rajapur, Dabhol, Chaul and Kalyan.

(3) English coins should be allowed to circulate freely throughout the king's territories.

(4) All English ships wrecked on the king's shores should be restored to them.

(5) The king should compensate the English for their losses at Hubli and Rajapur.

The king received the embassy in state. The Englishmen were permitted to advance to the foot of the throne. There Oxenden presented a diamond ring and received in return a robe of honour. Some days later, the king approved a treaty with the English. He refused to grant any compensation for the losses at Hubli but allowed them 10,000 pagodas for their losses at Rajapur. All the other requests presented by Oxenden were granted. Taking advantage of the king's urbanity, Oxenden ventured to suggest that the Marathas should make peace with Janjira.* But his unsought mediation was politely rejected. As the English ambassadors were returning homewards, an amusing incident occurred.† The butcher who had under Shivaji's orders supplied them with meat begged for an audience with them. To obtain it he followed them up Raygad Hill. After gazing at the little party for some time he explained that he had wished to gratify his eyes by the sight of men who had in one month eaten more of his meat than the rest of his customers had eaten during years together.

---

* Orme, *Historical Fragments.*

† Fryer, *Travels.*

CHAPTER XXII

THE GREAT SOUTHERN CAMPAIGN

A.D. 1674 TO 1678

SHORTLY after Shivaji's coronation, his mother Jijabai died. Throughout his life she had been the counsellor to whom he had always turned in cases of doubt or difficulty. To his prayers alone she had renounced her resolve to follow, like a high-born Maratha lady, her husband through the flames. Possibly overfatigued by the excitement of the great ceremonial which she had witnessed and in which she had played a part, she was suddenly attacked by fever. In two or three days the violence of her fever was such that the doctors gave up hope. On the fourth day she resigned herself to her approaching fate and distributed much of her wealth among the Brahman community, especially the Brahman priests of Pratapgad. On the fifth day of her illness she died. Her body was burnt at Raygad. After the period of mourning* had elapsed her ashes were at Shivaji's command conveyed to Allahabad and there cast into the confluence of the Ganges and the Jamna.

The king found solace for his grief in organizing a raid on the Portuguese districts round Bassein (1674). He sent Moro Pingle with 10,000 men to Kalyan.† Thence Pingle sent to the Portuguese a demand for *chauth*, giving as his reason the recent forcible conversion of Hindus to Christianity. The Portuguese, unwilling to bring on themselves the wrath of the king, seem, without admitting their liability to *chauth*, to have paid a sum of money and averted the danger.* In 1675 a large body of Kolis and other irregulars from the Dharampur state invaded the Kalyan district. They were no doubt insti-

---

* *Shivdigvijaya Bakhar.*
† Orme, *Historical Fragments.*

gated by the Moghuls. Moro Pingle therefore retaliated by retaking the forts of Aundha and Patta in Khandesh. And Shivaji made a second attempt to surprise Shivner. It was more nearly successful than the first one had been. Three hundred Marathas had actually scaled the fort walls. But the governor, Abdul Aziz Khan, was a gallant and experienced officer. Although he had sent a part of his garrison to defend the town of Junnar, he yet managed to save the situation. With the remainder of his troops he attacked the storming party, captured their rope ladders and drove them into the interior of the fort. The next day the few survivors surrendered after a gallant resistance. With admirable bravado, Abdul Aziz Khan sent them back to Shivaji and invited him with their aid to retrieve his fortunes by another assault. The king, however, had other aims. He was determined to overcome the resistance of the Phonda fort. Raising the siege of Shivner, he marched south and invaded the open country round Phaltan, which Abdul Karim had recovered, during his advance on Panhala two years before, for its chief the Naik Nimbalkar. He then marched into the Konkan to besiege Phonda. But as he marched westwards Nimbalkar re-entered Phaltan and drove out his garrisons. Shivaji, however, did not turn back. He once again sat down before Phonda. The commandant had gone to Bijapur during the rainy season. But hearing of Shivaji's return he hastened back to defend the fort. This he did most gallantly until the following April, when owing to the explosion of a mine under his walls he was forced to capitulate (1676). Shivaji had now an open road southwards. He marched along the coast and levied large contributions from the Raja of Sonda, established several forts to overawe the district and again plundered the town of Karwar. During his absence Hambirrao Mohite, the new cavalry commander-in-chief, had raided the Moghul territories in Guzarat, as far as Broach and had after hard fighting brought his booty safe to Raygad. On the other hand the Sidi of Janjira had made a naval descent upon Shivaji's coast line.

The rainy season of 1676 Shivaji spent at Raygad. But directly the monsoon had abated he turned his attention to the Phaltan country. He again drove out the Naik Nimbalkar and built four forts between Tathwada and Panhala, named Wardhangad, Bhushangad, Sadashivagad, and Machendragad. By this means he made himself permanent master of Nimbalkar's country. The fatigue, however, of the recent Konkan campaign had been too much even for Shivaji's iron frame. For some months he was confined to bed at Satara by intermittent fever and so grave was his illness that a baseless rumour spread that his son Sambhaji had poisoned him. Yet never had the great king's intellect been clearer than during this enforced idleness. As he lay in bed he planned an expedition, which by its boldness in design and skill in execution sufficed by itself to place Shivaji in the front rank of the world's greatest generals.

Fully to understand the grandiose character of the king's new campaign, we must return to events at Bijapur.* Upon the death of Ali Adil Shah, two leading Bijapur nobles struggled for power. They were Khavas Khan and Abdul Karim, the general who had twice fought battles with Prataprao Guzar. Khavas Khan was an Abyssinian and headed the combined African and Deccan party. Abdul Karim was an Afghan adventurer, who had followed the fortunes of Khan Jehan Lodi and had after his death entered the Bijapur service. During the reign of Ali Adil Shah, Abdul Karim had been appointed viceroy of Miraj, the southern Maratha country and the Konkan. Khavas Khan had been appointed regent by the dying king. To secure himself in favour he made overtures to Bahadur Khan the Moghul viceroy of the Deccan. The viceroy gladly accepted them and betrothed his second son to Khavas Khan's daughter. In return Khavas Khan agreed to hold Bijapur as a Moghul fief and to marry the late king's daughter Padshah Bibi to one of the emperor's sons. The alliance between the Abyssinian regent and the Moghul viceroy spelt ruin for Abdul Karim and the Afghan party of which he was the leader. He therefore had recourse to treachery. He affected to desire a reconciliation

* The following account I have taken from Scott's *Deccan*, Vol. II.

for the good of the common weal and thus induced the slow-
witted African to visit him at his house at Bijapur. There
at a private interview Khavas Khan was seized and shortly
afterwards murdered. The Moghul viceroy, who had reported
to the emperor his negotiations with Khavas Khan, received
immediate orders to attack Bijapur and punish Abdul Karim's
perfidy. Bahadur Khan collected his troops near Sholapur.
An indecisive battle took place between him and Abdul Karim
on the banks of the Bhima and both armies entrenched themselves. But during the night some Bijapur troops rushed the
imperial camp and inflicted such loss that Bahadur Khan retreated to the north of the Bhima. There he received reinforcements and began to resume the offensive. In the meantime,
however, Diler Khan had joined Bahadur Khan's army and,
as an Afghan, was favourably disposed towards Abdul Karim.
The two leaders called a truce and entered into a formal offensive
and defensive alliance for the subjugation of the Golconda
state.

       That kingdom had also been torn by internal strife.
The last king, Abdul Kutb Shah, had been completely sub-
servient to Moghul policy. In 1672 he died and his son-in-law
Abu Hussein succeeded him. The idleness of Abu Hussein's
youth had led him into dissipation, and his succession was
approved by Aurangzib, who looked forward eagerly to the
disruption of Golconda and its easy conquest by Moghul arms.
But work and responsibility reclaimed Abu Hussein and, to
the surprise of Aurangzib, a wise and vigorous king began to
direct the affairs of Golconda. He soon showed himself hostile
to the Moghuls and raised two Brahman brothers, Madannapant
and Akannapant, to the highest posts in the state. His policy
brought on him the combined hostility of Diler Khan and Abdul
Karim. But Abu Hussein's ruin would have exposed Shivaji
to a similar fate. He, therefore, resolved to ally himself to
Golconda. At the same time his fertile brain conceived another
and a far more imposing design. He knew the history of the
Vijayanagar state and the gallant resistance which it had for
centuries offered to the Musulman invaders. He also had no

illusions as to the precarious tenure by which he held his own kingdom. Fortunately Aurangzib still regarded him as little more than a rebellious zamindar. But the day that the emperor considered him a real danger, he would mobilize against the king the entire military resources of Hindustan. Nothing then would save Shivaji unless he could with his army fall back to some refuge in Southern India. Shivaji's design, therefore, was to win a new kingdom which would stretch right across Southern India from Bednur to Tanjore. Having won it he would guard its northern frontier from Moghul attack by a line of forts and extend his conquests as far south as possible. He might then defy the armies of Delhi by retreating before them, until they were so weakened by their endless line of communications that he might attack them in the field with some prospect of success.*

It was necessary that this plan should be concealed from the Moghuls. So Shivaji announced that he wished to go to Tanjore and recover from his brother Vyankoji his half share in Shahaji's jahgir. This fief included Bangalore, Kolar, Uscotta and a number of places in Mysore. By taking advantage of quarrels between the rulers of Tanjore and Madura, Shahaji had forced them to pay tribute. And Vyankoji had, on succeeding to his father's inheritance, made himself master of all Tanjore. In 1675 he moved his capital there from Bangalore. Shivaji now gave out that he was entitled to half of Shahaji's inheritance and that if necessary he meant by arms to enforce his claims. He could not, however, leave his kingdom while the Moghuls were actively hostile. He therefore induced the Moghul viceroy Bahadur Khan, whose besetting sin was avarice, to accept tribute on behalf of the emperor and a large bribe on his own account. He entrusted the general care of the kingdom to Moro Pingle and the defence of the southern frontier to Annaji Datto. Then, with a force of 70,000 men, he boldly marched through Bijapur territory until he reached the borders of the Golconda state. The assurances of Bahadur Khan to

---

* Ranade, p. 89. This eminent writer was the first to discover the profound policy which underlay Shivaji's Carnatic expedition.

Abdul Karim that Shivaji wished merely to secure his share in his father's inheritance were supported by recent events in Tanjore. Shahaji's old minister Raghunathpant Hanmante had recently quarrelled with Vyankoji. With the familiarity of an old servant he had openly lectured him on his failings and had laid stress on the inferiority of his character compared with that of his famous brother. Vyankoji resented the lecture and rebuked the minister. Hanmante, losing his temper, in his turn resigned his office and, threatening that Vyankoji would soon regret his conduct, left Tanjore for Hyderabad. These circumstances, together with the severe discipline in Shivaji's army and the regularity with which he paid for all supplies, induced Abdul Karim to allow it to pass through Bijapur territory unmolested. When Shivaji reached the Golconda frontier, he sent word to Hanmante, begging him to convince the king that he meant no harm and to urge on him the advantages of an alliance between Abu Hussein and the Marathas. Both Hanmante and Madannapant happened to be eminent students of Sanskrit metaphysics and their common studies enabled Hanmante to secure the ear of Madannapant. Through him he obtained an interview with Abu Hussein, whom he completely won by the fluency with which he spoke Persian.*
The Golconda king sent to Shivaji a formal invitation to Hyderabad. Shivaji accepted it gladly and continued his march until twelve miles from Hyderabad. There Madannapant and the leading nobles awaited him. After the usual state visits, negotiations were begun and after a month the two kings contracted an offensive and defensive alliance. Shivaji was to guarantee the safety of Golconda in case of aggression from Bijapur or Delhi. In return Shivaji was to receive a sum of money and a park of artillery and to have a free hand against Bijapur and the Hindu chiefs of the south. After the treaty had been signed, Shivaji struck his camp and headed due south. He crossed the Krishna at its junction with the Tungabhadra. There he directed his army to march southwards towards Cuddapah, while he visited the

---

* *Shivdigvijaya Bakhar.*

shrine of Shri Mallikarjun at Parvatam, about 50 miles lower
down the Krishna.

The temple is a famous one and stands on a hill overlooking
the Krishna. There Shivaji fasted for nine days and at last,
influenced by his penance and devotion, conceived the idea of
offering his life as a sacrifice to the deity.* From this purpose
he was dissuaded by a vision of Bhavani, who told him that
she still had work which he alone could accomplish. Bhavani's
commands were supported by the advice of Hanmante, who
urged the king to display his piety in a more practical manner.
Instead of offering to the shrine a life of priceless value to the
Maratha nation, let him honour the shrine by building ac-
commodation for the pilgrims. who at recurring seasons flocked
there to worship. Shivaji consented. Before leaving Parvatam, he gave a large sum to the priests. Some of it was
to be distributed among the poor. The rest was to be spent
in building bathing places and rest houses along the banks of
the Krishna. Shivaji then visited several other sacred
spots in the neighbourhood and eventually rejoined his army
at Cuddapah. His first objective was Jinji.† a fortress to the
north-west of Pondicherry and destined afterwards to become
doubly famous from Aurangzib's siege and De Bussy's escalade.
The country through which Shivaji now marched belonged
nominally to Bijapur. But owing to the decay of the government, it had passed into the hands of local chiefs, who were
in no condition to oppose the Maratha army. The only resistance with which Shivaji met came from a Bijapur officer named
Sher Khan, who held the important town of Trimali Mahal,
corrupted by the English into Trinomali (May, 1677).

With 5000 horse, Sher Khan made a gallant effort to stem
the invasion. He attacked Shivaji's vanguard. But he was
routed, enveloped and captured with his entire force. Shivaji
occupied Trinomali and prepared to besiege Jinji. The fall
however of Trinomali so dispirited the Bijapur commandant
Ambar Khan, that he went in person to Shivaji's camp and

---

* *Sabhasad Bakhar.*
† The Maratha name is Chandi.

handed him the keys of the fortress. Ambar Khan's eight sons, whom he had left at Jinji, showed a higher sense of duty. They did their best to defend their father's charge ; but after a vigorous attack their courage gave way. In return for a grant of land they capitulated and the king entered Jinji in triumph.

While Shivaji was advancing southwards, he left a part of his force to attack Vellore, a large town on the Palar River, some fifty miles due north of Jinji. The commandant, being summoned to surrender, returned an insulting answer and defended the town with resolution and success. The fall of Jinji, however, enabled Shivaji to return to Vellore. His experienced eyes noticed that two hills in the neighbourhood commanded the defence of the town.* Posting batteries on the hills, which he named Sajara and Gojara, he overcame the commandant's resistance, and in September, 1676, Vellore surrendered. Shivaji did not await its fall but after erecting his batteries he went with his mounted troops to Trivadi, a town some forty miles south of Jinji and on the road to Tanjore. Thence he sent a letter to his brother Vyankoji. It recited that ever since their father Shahaji's death, his estate had been in the hands of Vyankoji to the exclusion of his own rights. He now called upon Vyankoji to submit his accounts and hand over half the hereditary estate together with mesne profits from the date on which it came into his possession. The close however of his letter showed that he was unwilling to exact his claims to the uttermost. He begged Vyankoji to send to his camp a certain Govind Bhat with four other men, whom he named,† to settle the dispute amicably.

It must be admitted that Vyankoji's case was not without its strong points. The estate to which Shivaji laid claims was not an ordinary inheritance. It was a fief granted to Shahaji by the Bijapur government and upon Shahaji's death had been regranted in its entirety to Vyankoji. Shivaji, however, met this argument by pointing out that, although Shahaji's possessions

---

* *Shivdigvajaya Bakhar.*

† The names of the four other men were Kakajipant, Nilo Naik, Raghunath Naik, and Tomaji Naik.

were nominally held in fief, he was really an independent ruler. Bijapur had in its turn regranted them to Vyankoji. But the grant had been made *ex parte* and Shivaji's case had received no hearing. After discussing the matter through his agents, Vyankoji decided to visit Shivaji himself, and to try to induce him to see the dispute with his eyes. He wrote to his brother of his intention and in reply received a cordial invitation to the royal camp. Vyankoji thereupon set out for Trivadi, where Shivaji received him with every honour. He stayed at the king's camp for over two months and the two brothers repeatedly discussed Shivaji's claims on his father's inheritance. Shivaji was willing to compromise the dispute. But Vyankoji, whose understanding was narrow, refused to recede from his position that it was not undivided property governed by Hindu laws of inheritance, but a fief granted to him alone. The king bore his brother's obstinacy with exemplary patience. And when the fall of Vellore required his presence there, he dismissed Vyankoji with the same honours that had greeted his arrival. But that Vyankoji should not fancy that the king had abandoned his claims, Shivaji a few days later sent him a letter in which he restated them and warned his brother that he meant to enforce them, unless he made a reasonable compromise with the three agents, Shamaji Naik, Konherpant and Shivajipant. whom he was sending to Tanjore. Their arguments fell on deaf ears. Shivaji's army had returned to Vellore, and Vyankoji may have hoped that the move was the beginning of a retreat to Maharashtra. He therefore referred the matter to the Bijapur government. It gave an unexpected reply. Far too frightened of Shivaji to give him a pretext for a direct attack on the capital, it begged Vyankoji to give his elder brother all he asked for and let him depart in peace. Vyankoji, disgusted with the answer, resolved to defend by force what he believed to be his by right. In this resolve he was supported by the Musulman soldiers who had served Shahaji and had continued in Vyankoji's service. Hastily gathering a considerable force, he sought to surprise a Maratha detachment which Hambirrao Mohite commanded not far from the Tanjore frontier. The attack was badly executed and easily repelled. In the pursuit a large number of Vyankoji's soldiers were slain and the remainder fell back upon Tanjore. In the meantime Shivaji, despairing of an amicable settlement to the dispute, had taken the most effective means of ending it. He invaded all the fiefs which Vyankoji had inherited outside Tanjore. Arni, Kolar, Bangalore, Balapur and Sira all fell in 1677.

The defeated Vyankoji could do nothing to help the garrisons and after their surrender Shivaji, his communications secure, was free to carry out his design and conquer a kingdom that stretched from sea to sea (1678). He marched northwards from Sira along the banks of the Velavati River, until he reached the town of Bellari, a corruption of Belvadi, or the orchard of the sacred *bel* tree. The commandant had attacked one of his patrols and had carried off their carts and horses to Bellari. The king first attempted to blockade it. But Bellari was so well supplied with food that the king resolved to take it by assault. He set fire to some houses not far from the fort walls, which caused considerable confusion among the outposts. Taking advantage of it, he drove them back on the fort with great loss. The commandant, trying to rally his men, fell. But his widow Savitribai* acted with admirable courage. She mounted one of her husband's chargers, checked the fleeing garrison and repulsed the Marathas. For twenty-six days of hard fighting she kept the great king and his troops at bay. On the twenty-seventh day, the Marathas carried by assault the main defences and forced the garrison back into the citadel. Then only the gallant lady surrendered. Shivaji received her with chivalrous courtesy. All the districts south of the Tungabhadra now submitted, and Shivaji crossing that river near Vijayanagar entered the Doab, the strip of land for which the chivalry of Islam and of Vijayanagar had so often fought and died. Before advancing further he decided to settle if possible his dispute with Vyankoji.

---

* *Shivdigvijaya Bakhar.* The *Shedgavkar Bakhar* gives her name as Malwai.

That unhappy prince had been deeply depressed by the defeat of his entire army by Hambirrao Mohite's single detachment. His Hindu officers became mutinous and openly expressed their wish to fight under Shivaji's banner. While in this melancholy condition, he received a sharp letter from his brother. In it, Shivaji reproached him both with his treachery and with his stupidity in taking the advice of his Musulman courtiers. The king then restated his case and warned him that unless he at once submitted his accounts and peacefully resigned his rights to half Shivaji's inheritance, Shivaji would remove him from Tanjore by force and give him for his support some lands near Panhala, thus reducing him to the state of an ordinary Maratha noble in his train. In despair, Vyankoji sought the advice of his wife Dipabai. She, with the ability and prudence often possessed by Maratha ladies, urged him to abase himself before Raghunath Hanmante and to obtain his intercession. Vyankoji had no alternative but to follow this unpleasant advice. He sent a humble letter to Hanmante. At first the latter could not resist humiliating his former master. He wrote back that he was Shivaji's servant and could not comply with Vyankoji's request. The unhappy prince wrote again in even more slavish terms, begging Hanmante to return to Tanjore. After the latter's vanity had been sufficiently gratified, he consented to visit Vyankoji. The prince received him in state, placed him on the throne by his side and did all that humility could effect to win his former minister's good graces. Hanmante, touched by his master's abasement, wrote to Shivaji. He described eloquently the pitiable state of Vyankoji and begged Shivaji to show him the consideration due from an elder to a younger brother. Now that Vyankoji was anxious to be reconciled, it befitted the great king to treat him with generosity equal to his power. Shivaji received the letter gladly. He replied to Hanmante that with all his heart he forgave his brother. Provided Vyankoji entered into an alliance with Shivaji, the latter would permit him to retain Tanjore and would give him in addition adjacent lands valued at seven lakhs a year. The hereditary fiefs in Bangalore and elsewhere he would bestow as gifts on his sister-in-law Dipabai, whose admirable advice had influenced her husband. At the same time Shivaji wrote to Vyankoji. His words were few and to the point. The terms which he had granted to his brother would continue only so long as Vyankoji remained a true ally. To ensure that he did so, Shivaji imposed on his brother Hanmante as his first minister. The alliance offered by Shivaji to Vyankoji was worthy both of a brother and of a king. And Vyankoji gladly accepted it. The king's line of communications was now perfectly safe and he could turn again to the conquest of the Doab.

The Bijapur government did its utmost to save this last fragment torn by it from the Vijayanagar kingdom. The governor Yusuf Khan Mayna received strong reinforcements and strict orders to hold the Doab at all costs. Agreeably to these orders, Yusuf Khan decided to attack Shivaji's troops near Torgal, while Nimbalkar, chief of Phaltan, supported the governor by a raid into the territory round Panhala. But the great king was more than a match for any armies which Bijapur, shorn of its strength, could raise. A body of horse* under Niloji Katkar attacked and defeated Nimbalkar. Hambirrao Mohite, no longer needed at Tanjore, joined the king with his detachment. The combined forces won a signal victory over Yusuf Khan. Repelling his attack with great slaughter, they continued their pursuit until he retired northwards across the Krishna, leaving the entire Doab in the king's hands. Shivaji had now successfully concluded his campaign. With two enemies, one on either flank, and a doubtful ally on his line of communications, he had crossed India from west to east and back again from east to west. In the course of eighteen months, at a distance of 700 miles from his base, he had conquered a territory as large as his former kingdom. While a single reverse would have been fatal, he had not suffered even a single check. Victory had succeeded victory ; town had fallen after town. As he went, he organized his conquests ; and when he returned to Raygad, as he now did, his new possessions were securely bound together from sea to sea, by a line of fortified strongholds held by garrisons brave to the death and devoted to his cause.

* Grant Duff, Vol. I, p. 285.

CHAPTER XXIII

IN spite of Shivaji's presents to Bahadur Khan, the Moghuls had not remained idle during the great king's southern campaign. Diler Khan and Abdul Karim disapproved of the truce with the Marathas. The latter had allied themselves to the Golconda king, whose destruction Diler Khan and Abdul Karim had planned. Indeed Shivaji was actually plundering Bijapur territory. The two Afghan chiefs pressed their views on the emperor and urged him to sanction an attack by them upon Golconda as Shivaji's ally. The fall of Golconda would cut the communications of Shivaji and stop his supplies. He might then be overtaken and defeated. The emperor, convinced of Bahadur Khan's treachery and incapacity, recalled him to Delhi. In his place the emperor appointed Diler Khan as Moghul viceroy. He and Abdul Karim now united their forces at Gulbarga and attacked Malkhed, the frontier fortress of Golconda (A.D. 1677). After a defence long enough to enable the Golconda troops to march towards their relief, the garrison evacuated Malkhed and joined the main army. The Golconda forces, reorganized by Abu Hussein and his two Brahman ministers Madannapant and Akannapant, soon proved their metal. They successfully resisted Diler Khan's attack until the monsoon of 1677 burst. The rains fell with unusual force. The supplies in the Moghul camp rotted and the activity of the Golconda cavalry prevented their renewal. The Moghul troops maintained their discipline. But the troops of Bijapur, long unpaid, lost heart. They deserted in such large numbers that the Bijapur army soon ceased to exist. Abdul Karim fell ill and Diler Khan, unable single-handed to cope with Abu

Hussein's army, decided to retreat to Gulbarga. He first asked for and obtained an armistice from Abu Hussein, promising him to grant peace. He really intended to obtain reinforcements from Gulbarga and renew the attack. Abu Hussein first allowed him to retire unmolested but, learning his treachery from deserters, he overtook Diler Khan and with continued fury attacked his rearguard. After a most arduous retreat of twelve days, in which the Moghul army suffered immense losses, Diler Khan reached the shelter of Gulbarga. There the valour of the Rajput contingent enabled the army to rally and Abu Hussein fell back within his own frontiers. Abdul Karim never recovered from his illness. An empty treasury and a phantom army made it impossible for him either to avenge his recent defeat or to remain regent. Diler Khan visited the dying man and induced him to resign the regency in favour of an Abyssinian leader named Sidi Musaud, who undertook to pay the Bijapur army their arrears. Once, however, Sidi Musaud had obtained power, he refused the troops their dues. They mutinied and besieged the house of Abdul Karim. Death released him from his troubles. But the mutineers forced their way into his house and plundered his women and his son of every thing they possessed. They then entered the service either of Diler Khan, who had fallen back on Aurangabad, or of Shivaji's Peshwa, Moropant Pingle.

The emperor was incensed at the result of the last campaign and again reduced Diler Khan to the post of second in command, reinstating Prince Muazzim as viceroy of the Deccan. It was now useless to attack Golconda. But some compensation for the late disasters might be extorted from the unhappy state of Bijapur. To effect this, Diler Khan received orders to press all Afghans still in the service of Bijapur to enrol in the imperial service. All who did so were to receive their arrears of pay and regular salary. His army thus reinforced, Diler Khan was at once to march against his unfortunate ally and his capital. Diler Khan obeyed Aurangzib's order and detached the Afghans who still remained in the service of the minor king, Sikandar Adil Shah. He then marched against Bijapur, advancing as a pretext that he wished to take away the king's sister Padshah Bibi, whom the former regent Khavas Khan had betrothed to one of Aurangzib's sons. Sidi Musaud Khan, the regent to whom Abdul Karim had resigned his office, refused to surrender her and in this refusal he was supported by the populace of the capital. Diler Khan declared war and marched upon Bijapur. In despair Padshah Bibi* resolved, by sacrificing herself, to save her country. Accompanied by the court physician Shamsuddin and an ample escort, she rode out to meet the Moghul general.† He received her with all consideration and sent her with a body of Moghul horse to the emperor at Delhi. Then with shameless inconsistency he continued his advance against Bijapur. The spirit of the populace burnt to a white heat of fury. So valiant was the defence that Diler Khan never succeeded in establishing a blockade. In revenge he began to destroy the canals and gardens that stretched for some miles outside the city. But the villagers fought like veterans and after a fearful slaughter drove Diler Khan back for some distance from the city. Large reinforcements, however, came from Delhi and Musaud Khan, the regent, turned in his despair to Shivaji. In a touching letter he referred to the many services which Shahaji had rendered to the late king and now implored his son to forget recent animosities and remember only ancient friendship. With Shivaji's help, he wrote, Bijapur could be saved. Without it Bijapur must capitulate and its fall would shortly be followed by that of Shivaji.

The king had already wished to send help to the tottering kingdom. He had so shaken its foundations that it could no longer harm him. And he had no desire that its treasure should go to strengthen the Delhi government. Issuing from the neighbourhood of Panhala, he advanced close to Bijapur. There he left a large body of horse to cut the Moghul communications. Then with the rest of the troops he crossed the Bhima and made his way due north into Khandesh. There

---

* Grant Duff, Vol. I, p. 189.

† Scott, *Deccan*, Vol. II, p. 52.

he plundered Dharangaon and Chopra, two towns to the north
of Aurangabad and between it and Burhanpur. He hoped by
severing the connection between Aurangabad and Delhi to induce Prince Muazzim to recall Diler Khan's army from Bijapur.
He then turned south-east and attacked Jalna, a prosperous
town to the east of Aurangabad. Jalna was barely more than
50 miles from the Moghul capital of the Deccan. There Shivaji
remained for three days. Every act that might rouse the
prince to fury he committed. But no act could sting the heavy,
thick-skinned prince to action. He waited until Shivaji loaded
his booty in carts and began his return journey. Then he sent
10,000 men under one Ranmast Khan to harass Shivaji's retirement. The Musulman officer did his duty with skill and courage.
He overtook Shivaji near Sangamner and fought with him a
drawn battle until darkness fell. Next morning Shivaji made
a counter-attack. Although outnumbered, the Musulmans
fought with great bravery. On the Maratha side Hambirrao
Mohite fell wounded. On the Moghul side Ranmast Khan
was unhorsed and taken prisoner. At last the desperate valour
of the king himself turned the drawn fight into a brilliant victory.
But the battle was hardly over when another Moghul force
tried to cut him off from the passes. He received information
of the Moghul intention from a Maratha officer in the Delhi
force.* Happily the king's spy Bahirji Naik chanced to be
with him and he offered to save the royal troops by leading
them through a passage in the hills known to him alone. The
king accepted the offer and after a long and difficult march
brought his army and his booty in safety to Patta in
Khandesh.

This fortress had recently been strengthened by Moro Pingle.
It was impossible for the Moghuls to take it defended, as it
now was, not only by a garrison but by Shivaji's whole army.
They therefore fell back on Aurangabad. Shivaji did not pursue
them but reduced all the forts near Patta which Bahadur Khan
had built to guard the passes into Khandesh. He had hardly
made himself master of these valuable bridge-heads, when he

---

* *Shedgavkar Bakhar.*

received a despairing letter from Musaud Khan.* In it he
thanked Shivaji for his efforts to cut the Moghul communications.
In spite however of those efforts, he added, Diler Khan was
vigorously conducting the siege and had reached the main
fortifications of the capital. Nothing could save it except
direct aid from Shivaji. The great king, who in his life never
betrayed either a woman or a friend, resolved at once to send
an army to attack the Moghuls outside Bijapur. He placed
Moro Pingle in command of the infantry and entrusted the
cavalry to Hambirrao Mohite who had speedily recovered from
his wound. Shivaji himself returned to Panhala. Before he
reached it, he learnt that his eldest son Sambhaji had deserted
to Diler Khan's camp.

The young prince had all his father's bravery and a large
share of his ability. But he had been born in the purple
and had in idleness acquired vices from which his
father's strenuous life had kept him free. Sambhaji had
been attracted by the courtly Afghan,† whom he seems to
have met at Aurangabad. He had recently quarrelled with
his father and had been confined in Panhala. He now broke
loose and sought a refuge with his Aurangabad acquaintance.
Directly Shivaji heard of his son's flight he sent Maratha horse
in pursuit. But Sambhaji managed to get a message through
to Diler Khan, who sent his own nephew Aklas Khan with a
strong force to meet him. Sambhaji with their help eluded the
Maratha horse and was received by Diler Khan with every
honour. His coming was reported to the emperor, who bestowed
on him the command of 7000 horse and a riding elephant.
Diler Khan also bestowed on the prince dresses of honour and
similar gifts. He then directed him to storm Bhupalgad,
a fort which Shivaji had taken from the Bijapur king and which
was situated about half way between the latter's capital and
Satara. The commandant of Bhupalgad was that Phirangoji
Narsala who had so gallantly defended Chakan. Phirangoji now
found himself in a somewhat delicate position. Nevertheless his

---

* *Shivdigvijaya Bakhar.*
† *Shedgavkar Bakhar.*

duty was clear. The king was his master. Sambhaji, although Shivaji's son, was a rebel and should have been treated according-ly. Phirangoji tried a middle course. He sent to Sambhaji a Brahman agent, who implored the prince not to attack the fort. Sambhaji lost his temper, drew his sword and cut down the unfortunate agent. The same night the prince drove in the outposts of the garrison and appeared at dawn before the main defences of Bhupalgad. At this point Phirangoji Narsala completely lost his head. He handed over his command to one of his subordinates and fled to Panhala to lay his difficulties before the king. Deserted by their commandant, the garrison still made a gallant defence. But Sambhaji's impetuous attack carried everything before it. And long before Shivaji could send succour to Bhupalgad the place had fallen. Not unnaturally the king was incensed against Phirangoji Narsala, to whose indecision and cowardice he ascribed the loss of the fortress. He ordered his execution and had him blown to pieces from a cannon's mouth.

In the meantime, however, Aurangzib had changed his mind about Sambhaji.* Diler Khan had in a letter recommended that the emperor should recognize Sambhaji as king of the Marathas. This, he hoped, would create two factions among that nation, who would then destroy each other to the emperor's profit. Aurangzib at first approved of, but afterwards rejected, Diler Khan's recommendation. He conceived the fear that Sambhaji, instead of helping the Moghuls, might seduce the Hindu officers in the Moghul army to Shivaji's cause. He therefore bade Diler Khan arrest Sambhaji and bring him to Delhi. Diler Khan, Afghan though he was, would not stoop to such treachery. He informed Sambhaji of the emperor's orders and advised him to return to his father. To avert suspicion Diler Khan openly insulted Sambhaji, reduced his troops and left his allowance unpaid.† Sambhaji pretended to be much displeased at his treatment and after communicating with Shivaji, was helped by Maratha agents to escape from Diler Khan's camp and return to Panhala. There his father

---

* *Sabhasad Bakhar.*   † *Shivdigvijaya Bakhar.*

received him cordially, but refused him a command and confined
him in the fortress.*

In the meantime, Hambirrao Mohite and Moro Pingle had
made their way to the neighbourhood of Bijapur. As they
went they met some 10,000 Moghul horse, sent under Ranmast
Khan to reinforce Diler Khan. A long running fight took
place (1679). In the course of it, Ranmast Khan strove to
retire to Aurangabad. Before he could reach that city he
was brought to bay and completely defeated.† This victory
encouraged Hambirrao Mohite and Moro Pingle to change
their plans. Moro Pingle with half the army blockaded Aurangabad. Hambirrao Mohite and his cavalry established themselves firmly on Diler Khan's lines of communication. Diler
Khan was now completely cut off from all help from Aurangabad.
It was useless to continue the siege of Bijapur. But he would
not raise it without one last desperate assault. It was repulsed
with enormous losses. Next day Diler Khan struck his camp
and retreated northwards. Even so he did not escape from
his difficulties. Near the Bhima, Hambirrao Mohite furiously
attacked the rearguard commanded by Diler Khan in person.
After cutting in pieces several bodies of Afghan horse, Hambirrao
drove the rest in confusion back upon the main army, which
after great hardships succeeded in reaching Aurangabad.

Bijapur had, for the time being, been saved from Delhi.
The regent and the nobles celebrated Diler Khan's defeat by a
series of brilliant festivities. They invited Shivaji to be present.
The king's practical mind cared little or nothing for their merry-
making. He knew that without his aid Bijapur must have
fallen. And he was determined to obtain a full cession of all his
recent conquests. He therefore demanded as a condition of
his acceptance that the regent should cede to him the whole
line of conquered territory from the Krishna River to Tanjore
and that Vyankoji should no longer be recognized as a feoffee
of the Bijapur king, but of Shivaji. Musaud Khan‡ had no

---

* *Sabhasad Bakhar.*
† *Shivdigvijaya Bakhar.* This was not the same Ranmast Khan as the
one taken prisoner at Sangamner.
‡ *Shivdigvijaya Bakhar.*

alternative but to comply. He informed Shivaji that on his arrival at Bijapur, a *sanad* granting all his demands would be handed to him by the minor king, Sikandar Adil Shah. Upon the receipt of this reply Shivaji went in state to Bijapur. His arrival became a triumphal progress. The populace forgot the provinces which he had torn from the ancient kingdom. They only saw in him the soldier who had saved their beloved city from the clutches of the Moghuls. The young king, the regent and the courtiers vied with each other in the magnificence with which they entertained their Maratha guests. But Shivaji soon wearied of what he deemed a childish waste of time. He longed to return to his own country and to strive once again to reduce Janjira (A.D. 1680).

Although Shivaji had everywhere triumphed on land, he had not had similar success at sea. Anxious as he was to remain friends with the English, he had for some years looked askance at their compliance with the demands of the Moghul fleet. In July, 1676, Sidi Kasim, who had succeeded Sidi Sambal as admiral of the imperial navy, had entered Bombay harbour and had received permission to anchor off Mazagaon.* It cannot be denied that such a concession amounted to a breach of neutrality. Indeed the English, with their factory at Surat, hardly could be really neutral. Shivaji therefore resolved to attack and burn the English fleet in Bombay. He ordered his admirals Daulat Khan and Darya Sarang to sail thither (A.D. 1678). But the monsoon burst earlier than usual and the Maratha fleet was forced to take shelter in the Panvel creek almost exactly opposite Bombay island. Thence they made occasional raids on Portuguese territory. In 1679 Shivaji largely increased his fleet and seized two islands, Khanderi and Underi, known to the English as Kenery and Henery, about 16 miles due south of the island of Bombay. The English resented this and on October 15 an action took place between the English fleet and Daulat Khan's vessels. The Marathas attacked with great vigour. In a short time an English ship named the *Dove* hauled down its colours and five other English

---

* Orme, *Historical Fragments*.

ships fell out of the line.   But a powerful 16 gun frigate named
the *Revenge* changed the fortunes of the day.   Its guns were
heavier than any of the Maratha artillery, and, well-handled
by its commander, Captain Minchin, it sank five Maratha
ships in succession.   Daulat Khan then withdrew to Khanderi.

On November 10 the Sidi's fleet appeared.   It numbered
two large battle-ships, three three-masted frigates and fifteen
stout gallivats.   On board were 700 excellent soldiers.   But
although the Sidi came ostensibly as an ally of the English,
he was, if possible, more unwelcome than Daulat Khan.   For
he gave out that he intended to take Khanderi and convert
it into a Moghul naval base.   The English at once tried to open
negotiations with Shivaji.   But the latter was too concerned
at Sambhaji's defection to answer their message and shortly
afterwards Sidi Kasim, professing to act on behalf of the English,
landed on Shivaji's coast and carried off a number of slaves.
This made all negotiations impossible.   The Sidi, emboldened
by his success, attacked Underi and drove out the Maratha
garrison.   A naval engagement ensued between the Moghul and
the Maratha fleets.   The Maratha sailors fought their ships
bravely ; but the superior build of the Moghul ships enabled
Sidi Kasim to win a decisive victory.   The Marathas lost several
vessels and some 500 killed and wounded besides prisoners.
At last they fled in great disorder back to Rajapur creek.
Early in March, 1680, the English again opened negotiations
with Shivaji.   He was now free from anxiety as regards
Sambhaji.   Bijapur had been saved.   His recent ill success at
sea had shown him the value of an English alliance.   He made
peace with the English and he agreed that they might, if
thereto compelled, shelter the Moghul fleet during the monsoon.
The English on their part undertook to prevent the Sidi from
using Bombay as a naval base against the Marathas.

Shivaji at this time had reached the zenith of his power.
He had freed the bulk of the Marathi-speaking people.   By his
new alliance with Bijapur and Golconda and still more by the
chain of fortresses which he had built from Bednur to Tanjore,
he had secured his conquests.   Nevertheless he was not without

grave anxieties. His eldest wife Saibai was dead and her son Sambhaji had shown himself unfit for the throne. His third wife Soyarabai, the mother of his second son Rajaram, pressed the latter's claims as superior to those of Sambhaji. The king, distracted by her importunity, conceived the idea of dividing his kingdom between his two sons.* At the same time he was grieved by the attitude of Vyankoji, his brother. In his first feelings of gratitude, the latter had acted with courtesy towards Hanmante.† But the declaration by the Bijapur government that Vyankoji was Shivaji's vassel preyed on his mind. He refused to see Hanmante or to dispose of any administrative work. And gradually he adopted the habits of a religious recluse. Hanmante reported Vyankoji's conduct to Shivaji, who sent to him an admirable letter.‡ In it he encouraged his brother, urged him to accept his present situation and bade him use his army to conquer fresh lands for himself.

Shortly after writing this letter, Shivaji seems to have had a premonition that his end was approaching. He visited Ramdas at Parali and spoke to him sadly of the rivalry of Rajaram and Sambhaji. The saint bade him do his utmost to reconcile them and to pray to the god Rama for guidance. Shivaji then asked Ramdas to pardon him for any faults that he might unwittingly have committed. Ramdas noticed the gravity with which Shivaji spoke and asked him what ailed him. Shivaji embraced Ramdas and told him that this was their last meeting. Ramdas tried to cheer the king and asked him gently whether such thoughts were the fruits of his teaching. Shivaji did not reply, but bidding the saint farewell made his way to Raygad.§ On March 28, 1680, after his return from a raiding expedition, ‖ a painful swelling appeared on his knee-joint. In spite of medical aid it grew worse. Fever intervened and after a seven days' illness the great king, on April 3, 1680, died at Raygad. His son Sambhaji, deeply affected by the news of his father's

---

* *Shedgavkar* and *Sabhasad Bakhars.*
† *Shedgavkar Bakhar.*
‡ Grant Duff, Vol. I, p. 294.
§ *Ramdas Charitra.*
‖ *Maasuri L'alamgiri,* Elliott and Dowson, Vol. VII., p. 305.

RAJA SAMBHAJI

(SHIVAJI'S ELDEST SON)

[*To face page* 279]

illness, made a desperate effort to see him before his death. Setting out from Panhala on a camel he rode night and day, but he came too late. His father's spirit left his war-worn frame as Sambhaji reached the foot of the hill. Furious with grief and disappointment, the prince drew his sword and with a single stroke decapitated the camel. Not satisfied with this, he ordered the image of a headless camel to be erected at the outer gate of the fort, as a warning to other beasts of the same species. It stands to this day, a monument of the prince's childish folly.*

Shivaji has by a curious fate suffered more at the hands of historians than any other character in history. They have one and all† accepted as final the opinion of Grant Duff, which again was based on that of Khafi Khan. They have at the same time rejected Orme's far more accurate conclusions. And while judging Shivaji with the utmost harshness, they have been singularly indulgent to his enemies. The thousand basenesses of Aurangzib, the appalling villainies of the Bijapur and the Ahmadnagar nobles, have been passed over with a tolerant smile. The cruel trick by which Ghorpade betrayed Shahaji has provoked no comment. Shivaji, however, is depicted as the incarnation of successful perfidy, a Cæsar Borgia to whom there came no ill fortune, a more faithless and more daring Francesco Sforza. Nor can it be denied that the authors of the Hindu *Bakhars* are in some way responsible for this absurd and inaccurate legend. Hating the Musulmans with the fiercest of passions, they deemed no trap too inhuman provided that it brought about their enemies' downfall. It was reserved for an Indian of modern times, Mr. Justice Ranade, a man truly great, judged by no matter what standard, to see correctly the deep religious feeling, the many virtues, the chivalrous temper and the vast ability of the great Maratha king.

If Shivaji had been a treacherous assassin, such as he has been commonly portrayed, he would never have achieved

---

* I have seen the image and been told the story at Raygad.

† From this statement I gladly except Mr. Rawlinson's admirable monograph on Shivaji. For Orme's character, see Appendix, p. 278.

what he did. The high-born, high-spirited Deccan nobles would
never have accepted his leadership ; or if they had, they would
have copied their leader and become as treacherous as he.
The fact that no one ever betrayed Shivaji is strong evidence
that he himself was not a betrayer.   Starting with this premise,
Mr. Ranade next examined the evidence and pointed out that
with one exception the instances of treachery mentioned by
Grant Duff were all capable of innocent interpretation.   The
capture of Purandar was effected by the consent of the garrison
and the subsequent acquiescence of the commandants.   The
killing of Afzul Khan was an act of self-defence.   The one
exception was the attack on Chandra Rao More.   Later in-
vestigation, however, has shown that even this instance had
not the sinister character usually attributed to it.   From the
recently discovered Mahableshwar account, it is clear that
Shivaji repeatedly strove to win More to his side, that More
as often tried treacherously to take Shivaji prisoner and that
he eventually fell in a quarrel between him and Ragho
Ballal Atre, while the latter was delivering him an ultimatum.
Shivaji was thus clearly innocent of More's death. The most that
can be said against him is that he did not punish Ragho
Ballal as he should have done.   But the same charge can be
brought against William III. His most ardent admirers have
been forced to admit that he punished neither the murderers
of the De Witts nor those guilty of the slaughter ˙of the
Macdonalds of Glencoe.

It is difficult, without writing in a strain that may seem
exaggerated to English readers, to give to Shivaji the place
in history to which he is rightly entitled. He has been compared
not unhappily with Bruce. Nevertheless the comparison does
the Eastern prince less than justice. Bruce had, it is true,
to cheer the spirit of the Scottish nation, depressed by the defeat
of Falkirk and the capture and death of Wallace. But the
Scottish people had been free for centuries. Naturally high-
spirited and brave, they were eager to gather round anyone
who would help them drive out the hated English. Shivaji
had to create his victorious army from the half savage hillmen

of the Western Ghats, wholly ignorant of war, and from the Marathas of the plains, broken by three hundred years of servitude. To Shivaji's warlike genius were joined civil talents of the highest order. While training troops, devising strategy, inventing tactics, scouring the Deccan in every direction, he yet found time to think out a system of administration which, as Mr. Ranade has pointed out, is the basis of British success. The curse of Indian governments had always been the power of the feudal nobility, which grew dangerous directly the central authority weakened. Shivaji was wise enough not only to see the disease but to invent a remedy. He refused to make grants of land to his nobles. He governed his territories by means of paid agents, Kamavisdars, Mahalkaris and Subhedars. They could be dismissed at will and were so dismissed on proof of incapacity or insubordination. They collected the assessment due from the peasants and paid it into the royal treasury. From the treasury Shivaji paid his soldiers and officers regular salaries. It was not, however, possible for a single man, however able, to check all the accounts which such payments and receipts involved. Shivaji therefore created two ministers. The first was the Pant Amatya or Finance Minister. The second was the Pant Sachiv or, as we should call him, the Accountant General.

Besides these two ministers Shivaji nominated six others, who helped him in his general administration. They also, curiously enough, had duties similar to modern members of the Indian government. The Peshwa was the President of the Council. The Mantri was th Home Member. The Senapati was the Commander-in-Chief. The Sumant* was the Foreign Minister. Besides the above, there were the Pandit Rao, who was in charge of ecclesiastical matters, and the Sir Nyaya-dhish or Chief Justice. To-day no merit, however great, enables a man to bequeath his charge to his son. In the same way Shivaji would not permit sons to succeed their fathers in office, unless themselves fully qualified. Nor would he allow men to

---

* To-day the Viceroy combines the offices of President of the Council and Foreign Minister.

18

retain posts which they were incompetent to fill. So wise indeed were these provisions, that they were beyond the grasp of Shivaji's successors. They once more let office become hereditary. They granted great landed fiefs to which incompetent men succeeded because they were their father's sons. Their folly had its reward and in the end Shivaji's kingdom went the way of other Eastern empires.

Shivaji was also shrewd enough to see that light assessments were the secret of large revenues. While in the neighbouring states the peasant was lucky if he escaped with an assessment of 50 per cent., Shivaji never demanded more than two-fifths of the gross yield. *Tagai*, or advances by the government to the cultivators, often wrongly believed to be a modern institution, were freely granted, and their repayment was extended over several years. While taxing the peasantry, Shivaji, unlike his neighbours, realized that in return for taxes they were entitled to protection. He divided his kingdom into 15 districts, all amply provided with great fortresses. They were close enough together for their garrisons to assist each other and drive away marauding bands. They also afforded shelter to which the cultivators could take their cattle or their crops upon the first appearance of the enemy.

The government of these forts was admirably conceived. The commandant was a Maratha. Under him was a Brahman Subhedar or Sabnis, who kept the accounts and had civil and revenue charge of the villages assigned to the upkeep of the fort, and a Prabhu Karkhanis, who was responsible that the garrison had ample military supplies and food stores. Thus, although the garrison was under the orders of the commandant, any treachery on his part would at once have become known to his chief subordinates. The soldiers of the garrison were paid regular salaries and every tenth man was a Naik or corporal, who received a slightly higher emolument. Where villages were not assigned to the upkeep of any fort, Shivaji for administrative purposes arranged them much as the British since have done. The unit was the Mahal or Taluka, of which the revenue varied from Rs. 75,000 to Rs. 1,25,000. Three Mahals

made a Subha or District.   Each District was in charge of a
Subhedar, whose pay was 400 hons a year, or about Rs. 100
a month.

Shivaji's military establishment was organized with the
same care and skill as the garrisons of his fortresses. A battalion of 1000 men under a Hazari was the infantry unit.*
This was divided into ten companies, called Jumalas, each
under a Jumaledar. Each company was divided into half
companies of fifty men, each under a Havildar or sergeant.
Each half company was divided into five bodies of ten sepoys, of
which the chief was the Naik or corporal.   Seven such battalions
formed a brigade, under a Sarnobat or brigadier.   The cavalry
system was slightly different.   The unit was a cavalry regiment
1250 strong. Its commander was, like the infantry commander,
called a Hazari.   The regiment was divided into ten Jumalas,
or squadrons of 125 troopers. Each Jumala was subdivided
into five sections or Havalas consisting of 25 bargirs or troopers.
Each such section had its own farrier and water carrier.   Five
Hazaris formed a cavalry brigade, under a brigadier known as
the Panch Hazari.   The pay of these officers was carefully
regulated.   The brigadiers received 2000 hons a year, or
Rs. 500 a month.   In the cavalry the regimental commander's
pay was 1000 hons a year, or Rs. 250 a month.   In the infantry
the battalion commander received 500 hons, or Rs. 125 a month.
The pay of the company commander and his subordinates
varied from Rs. 9 to Rs. 3 a month.   The pay of the squadron
commanders and their subordinates varied from Rs. 20 to Rs. 6.
During the rainy season the troops and horses were fed at the
king's expense in large barracks.   In the fair season they were
expected to live on the enemy's country.   But no private
looting was allowed. All prize money or other plunder had,
under pain of the forfeiture of his surety bonds, to be paid by its
captor into the regimental treasury.   From it the commanders
fed and furnished their troops.

But, great organizer and military genius that Shivaji was,
it is in far-seeing statesmanship that he stands supreme.   In

* Ranade.

all history there is no such example of modesty in the face of continued success. The insolent, overweening vanity which has proved the ruin of so many commanders, both in ancient and modern times, found no place in Shivaji's admirably balanced mind. He won victory after victory against Bijapur and the Moghuls, yet his head was never turned. He realized always that he had yet to meet the full power of the Moghul empire. His one aim was to secure the freedom of his country-men. That he might do so, he sought to win the friendship of Aurangzib. When that proved impossible, he resolved to secure a place of shelter against the coming peril, which he so clearly foresaw. At last there came a time when his genius bore fruit. Four years after Shivaji's death, the emperor realised that the Marathas were a serious danger. He ceased to send a succession of small armies to Aurangabad. He mobilized the whole military resources of northern India and an army several hundred thousand strong, led by the emperor in person, poured through the Vindhya passes to the conquest of the South. Within three years both Golconda and Bijapur had fallen. Within five years all Maharashtra was overrun. Sambhaji had been taken and executed. Shahu and his mother were prisoners in Aurangzib's camp. But the Maratha generals, headed by Rajaram, adhered to the strategy laid down by the great king. Falling behind the southern line of fortresses, built by Shivaji from Bednur to Tanjore, they held the South against the might of all Hindustan. At length the great offensive weakened. The Maratha captains in their turn began to attack. Slowly but surely they drove the Delhi forces back again across the frontier of the old imperial possessions. At last Aurangzib, his treasury empty, his grand army destroyed, died a broken man in his camp at Ahmadnagar. Maharashtra was free. Southern India was safe. The single wisdom of the great king, dead twenty-seven years before, had supplied the place of two hundred battalions.

But there was yet another side to the character of this versatile prince. In an earlier chapter I have sketched his relations with Ramdas and Tukaram. But they were not the only wise and pious men to whom Shivaji was drawn. The poet Mahipati has in the *Bhaktivijaya* told the story how the great king went from Pandharpur into the woods to visit an Ujjain mendicant called Ganeshnath. Shivaji made Ganeshnath return with him to his camp and gave him a soft bed with rich coverlets to sleep upon. But the mendicant shamed the king . strewing pebbles over the downy mattress. Shivaji took the lesson so to heart that he sold the couch and gave its price in charity, sleeping ever afterwards on a village cot. Other friends of Shivaji were Keval Bharati of Kenjal, Taponidhi Devbharati of Khandesh and Siddheshwarbhat of Chakan. He even extended his favour to a Musulman fakir named Bava Yakub. Such was the liberator of the Maratha nation, a man of talents so varied, of life so regular, of disposition so tolerant, that it is little wonder that his countrymen came to regard him not as one of themselves but as the incarnation of a god. His kingdom has long passed away; but the Maratha people still worship his image at Raygad and Malwan, just as the Athenians, long after their empire had ceased to exist, continued to worship with pathetic devotion the memory of Theseus.

Shivaji was in all married seven times. His first wife, Saibai, was the daughter of Vithoji Mohite Newaskar. An affectionate and charming lady, she became by a curious freak of fortune, the mother of the headstrong and wayward Sambhaji. Happily for her, she died too soon to see her baby grow into a vicious and headstrong man. She bore also to Shivaji a daughter named Ambikabai, who was given in marriage to Harji Raje Mahadik of Tarale, appointed by the king to be governor of Jinji. Shivaji's second wife was Putalibai. She bore him no children and, faithful unto death, committed *sati* upon her husband's funeral pyre. Shivaji's third wife was Soyarabai, a girl of the Shirke family. Beautiful, talented and politic, she was the mother of the brave and chivalrous Rajaram, the second founder of the Maratha empire. She had a daughter named Dipabai, who married a Maratha noble named Visajirao. Shivaji's fourth wife was Sakwarbai, whose only daughter Kamaljabai became the wife of Janoji Palkar. Shivaji's fifth wife, Lakshmibai, had no issue.　Shivaji's sixth wife, Sagunabai, bore him a single daughter Nanibai, whom he gave in marriage to Ganoji Raje Shirke Malekar.　His seventh wife Gunvantabai was childless.*

The great king's body was cremated at Raygad, which, looking down on a hundred lesser peaks, formed a fitting resting place for that commanding spirit.　His death is a convenient point at which to end this first volume.　In the succeeding volumes it will be my task to narrate how the great edifice founded by his genius prospered or decayed with the various fortunes of his successors.

---

* This passage is based upon the genealogical tree of the *Shedgavkar* Bhosles.　The Phaltan State records refer to yet another daughter, Sakhubai, married to Mahadji Naik Nimbalkar (*Itihas Sangraha*, Vol. VIII).

APPENDIX

Orme, in his *Historical Fragments*, p. 94, thus sums up Shivaji :—

" In personal activity he exceeded all generals of whom there is record. For no partizan appropriated to service of detachment alone ever traversed as much ground as he at the head of armies.　He met every emergency of peril, however sudden or extreme, with instant discernment and unshaken fortitude ; the ablest of his officers acquiesced to the imminent superiority of his genius, and the boast of the soldier was to have seen Shivaji charging sword in hand."

INDEX

A